Fraud Points!

The Small Business Owner's Guide to Outwitting Embezzlers, Thieves, and Scallywags

Cheryl Obermiller

With sincere thanks and much love, I offer my appreciation to the friends and family who supported me through both the embezzlement, and the process of writing this book.

I make special mention of my former CPA, Leslie Szutenbach, who restored my faith in accountants, and helped educate me about financial processes. Although she did not live to see the publication of this book, her sweet influence is felt throughout its pages. You are sorely missed, dear friend.

And finally, I dedicate this book to my beloved husband and eternal companion, Roy Obermiller. I am who I am today because of your love, support, and influence. You are my rock, my friend, and the love of my life.

FraudPoints!
The Small Business Owner's Guide to
Outwitting Embezzlers, Thieves, and Scallywags
by Cheryl Obermiller

PotHole Press
1805 Waters Road
Harrisonville, MO 64701

For special sales, contact: www.FraudPoints.com

Cover, Interior design, and eBook conversion: Rebecca Finkel, F + P Graphic Design
Book Consultant and Editor: Judith Briles, TheBookShepherd.com

Library of Congress Catalog Number: data on file

hardback: 978-0-9994951-0-0
paperback: 978-0-9994951-1-7
eBook: 978-0-9994951-2-4
audiobook : 978-0-9994951-3-1

Business | Accounting | Financial Management

Printed in the USA

Contents

Why This Book, and Why Now? Because, It Can Happen to You!

Since accounting is NOT at the top of most people's "list of favorite things to read about," why would someone like me, a married woman with eight children and sixteen grandchildren (and growing), who already runs a multi-million dollar construction company and who hates accounting, be crazy enough to spend more than five years writing a book on accounting fraud? Simply this:

- I went through one that cost me in excess of $1,000,000 in losses, and was barely able to keep my company together.

- I spent three brutal years battling the IRS and negotiating payment arrangements with unpaid creditors.

- I nearly buckled under the emotional tsunami that hit me from the completely unexpected betrayal by a close friend and trusted employee.

When I started my business in 1993, it was intended to be a small supplement to our family income. Within just a few years, it completely surprised me—and exceeded all expectations for success—by becoming a major source of income for our household. I expanded into heavy construction, took on major commercial clients, and bought a yard full of trucks and construction equipment. But the biggest surprise of all came on January 7, 2010, when I discovered that my wonderful business, which by this point also provided income for a number of employees and their families, had been the victim of an embezzlement which had spanned more than eight years and cost many hundreds of thousands of dollars.

Little could I have envisioned I would spend years unraveling a devastating financial and legal mess, dealing with unbelievable demands and accusations from state and federal tax collectors, working closely with a special agent from the FBI to investigate and prosecute a federal crime, reaching out to Kit Bond, my U.S. Senator, for protection against the IRS, and at the same time face incredible challenges required to rebuild my business. Ultimately, my business survived, the taxes were all paid, my accountant spent 33 months in the federal penitentiary, and I started being able to sleep through the night, at least most of the time. It was a road I never want to travel again.

FraudPoints! will assume you are a normal, non-accountant business owner like I was. It is not a typical, boring accounting book. What business owner has the time or desire to learn all the nuances of accounting and tax law? We don't. It's why we have business accountants to handle the details—so we can run and grow our businesses.

FraudPoints! is your new best friend—a survival how-to book that will show what every small business owner needs to do to safeguard their business. It will show you how to prevent and detect financial fraud in your company. I had to learn it the hard way—hopefully, you don't.

Over two-thirds of all fraud crimes are committed by employees working in the financial segment of a company. Why—because that's where the money is!

Most accountants and bookkeepers are NOT inherently dishonest, but if financial fraud occurs, they are the people most likely to commit it. Why? Because they have easy, probably unmonitored, access to your money and accounts!

When an accountant is given multiple responsibilities like:

- Getting and sorting your mail

- Handling your payables and receivables

- Producing job cost reports

- Reconciling bank statements

- Setting up and maintaining vendor files

- Managing payroll

- Making tax payments and filing returns

And so on …

They not only have almost *unlimited access to your money*, they also have *nearly total control over what you know about your money*. The idea that an orderly, professional-looking report generated from your own office computer, and which was compiled by a person you trust personally and professionally, could be a complete work of fiction does not even occur to most business owners. It certainly never crossed my mind.

But consider this—by using only an inexpensive scanner and printer, the average high school student can edit and reproduce a bank statement that is nearly indecipherable from the original—one that can easily be substituted to keep you from discovering unauthorized transactions. Now imagine what damage a trained accountant with full access to your accounting systems can do, especially if you trust him or her too much to even think to check the work!

In *FraudPoints!* you will learn:

- The tremendous risk embezzlement poses to small business owners *just like you*;

- How to recognize potential fraud risks and eliminate them *before* you see any actual warning signs;

- How to recognize "red flags" for potentially business-killing financial crimes that may be occurring *right under your nose*; and

- Quickly gain the expertise to *manage* the financial workings of your business better than many people with advanced degrees.

If you now understand the need to protect your business but don't know where to start, don't worry.

FraudPoints! will change that forever.

I am proud to say that now, even though I remain a typical small business owner, I have also become an expert in recognizing and preventing many of the most common and destructive forms of financial fraud. I am excited to show you some of the key areas in which a *little* knowledge would have saved me a *lot* of money, time, and anguish!

My ignorance of financial controls cost me at least a million dollars, and nearly cost me my business and my home. However, by applying the principles outlined in *FraudPoints!* you can learn to protect your own business for a fraction of what it cost me to learn these same lessons.

I want to be clear that most people who work in accounting and bookkeeping are honest, hardworking people and do not steal from their employers. And yet, did you know that over two-thirds of all fraud crimes are committed by employees working in the financial segment of a company? Why? Because that's where the money is! And if you want your money to stay put, you had better learn how to watch over it.

*To be conscious that you are ignorant
is a great step to knowledge.*
~ Benjamin Disraeli

CHAPTER 1

How Could I Make $1,000,000 and Go Broke?

**No one ever sees it coming, and for many,
the first real clue is also the death knell—either overdraft notices
on a mysteriously empty bank account or a certified letter
of demand from the IRS for tax delinquencies.**

On November 15, 1993, I founded my company, Obermiller Construction Services, Inc., with $500 and some used office equipment. I started out doing soil tests for septic systems—which means drilling holes in the ground and measuring how fast water ran out of them, fascinating stuff, as well as construction inspections for subdivision developers. For the next seven years, I gradually expanded into doing asphalt and concrete pavement, averaging about $100,000 gross per year.

My *big break* came in January of 1999 when I hit a pothole. Shopping for my large family, I drove my new Lincoln right into a huge crater in the parking lot of our local big box store—a hole so big that I thought it had ripped my muffler off and caused major damage. Miffed, I called the store manager the following Monday morning and chewed him out—letting him know that that my husband and I had two businesses and eight kids and we spent thousands in his store every month. And I wouldn't be coming back if shopping there would ruin my car and if the parking lot continued to be unsafe to drive through. But what was really frustrating was that I owned a construction company a few blocks up the street and could have fixed his potholes within 48 hours.

The next day, the national pavement manager for the company called me and gave me a contract to do temporary repairs to the parking lot and remain on "oversight" duty so any new holes could be immediately filled. Apparently, the idea that I might go shopping somewhere else was so horrifying they felt they had no choice but to fix the potholes. It was the start of a relationship that has lasted over eighteen years, and provided my company with tens of millions of dollars in revenue. That call changed my life.

I was elated to land one of the country's largest retailers as a client, and I did over $1.5 million in work for them over the next year. No longer could I handle the company bookkeeping on my own. In August 2001, I hired Tammie, my first *real* accountant.

She seemed like a godsend. Bringing just the kind of professionalism and order the company badly needed, she organized the finances, record-keeping, and general office management. Tammie upgraded and improved everything she touched and became my *right-hand man*. I depended on her assistance daily and trusted her completely.

Tammie wasn't the godsend I thought she was.

Over the next eight and a half years, we discussed our marriages, our children, our religions, and our politics. We supported each other through the deaths of family members. I kept up with her daughter's cheerleading and dancing accomplishments. We ate lunch together, exchanged birthday and holiday gifts, and loaned each other interesting books to read.

Unbeknownst to me, in December 2001, just a few months after being hired, she also did one of the most significant things that would ever happen to my business—*she forged her first check*. This went on, right under my nose, for the next eight years. Finally, on January 7, 2010, her crime was discovered—as many fraud schemes are—totally by accident. Oops, Tammie wasn't the godsend I thought she was. My trusted employee and friend Tammie was a crook.

I discovered not only that she had perpetrated an elaborate fraud scheme that nearly destroyed my company, but I was also on the verge of having my business seized by the IRS for nonpayment of payroll taxes—and was in equally hot water with the state of Kansas over unpaid state sales taxes.

Fast forward to November of 2011. My former friend and trusted employee reported to the federal penitentiary in Florida to begin serving a 33-month prison sentence. Upon release, she would be required to start paying back nearly half a million dollars she was convicted of stealing from my company, although not for the entire amount which was likely stolen. Why not? In reality, due to statutory limitations and other legal reasons, the FBI chose to go back only four years, even though the crime appears to have spanned eight-plus years, and is conservatively estimated to have done at least a million dollars in damage to my company.

This is my story. Sadly, it is one of thousands, maybe millions, just like it. In fact, I am one of the lucky ones—my business survived. My family survived. And I survived. About 20 percent of small business owners who experience large-scale financial fraud are personally bankrupted by the crime. No one ever sees it coming, and for many, the first real clue is also the death knell—either overdraft notices on a mysteriously empty bank account or a certified letter of demand from the IRS for tax delinquencies.

Although I learned the hard way that being in business can be more difficult than I would ever have imagined, it is still the only way of life I know—and I love it! Seeing your own business grow and thrive, working with your family every day, and knowing that your success is often limited only by your own willingness to achieve it outweighs nearly any of the negatives. The hours I have been able to spend with my husband and grown children, the freedom to leave work and go have lunch with my grandchildren and visit their classrooms, and the ability to plan vacations and time off based on *my* desires and not someone else's schedule, are just a few of the things that make entrepreneurship such a wonderful way of life, despite the potential risks.

Fortunately, you can do a great deal to manage those risks, if you just know how!

Growing Up in a Small Business

I grew up in the 1960s, the daughter of a schoolteacher and a butcher. My mother taught third grade, and later became the school librarian—in family circles, she is affectionately known as the Grammar Nazi. My father was a butcher in the grocery store his mother and father started in the early 1930s. People familiar with Grandview, Missouri, probably remember the great steaks they could get at Wilson's Meat Market on Main Street.

My childhood taught me a lot about working in a small, family-owned business. For one thing, it was darned hard work. For another, working with family was not always easy or profitable, and you didn't let *anything* go to waste. I am living proof that growing up on a steady diet of brown meat and expired canned biscuits will *not* kill you! One of the best and most long-lasting lessons was that working for yourself beat working for someone else hands-down, pretty much every time! Given my history, it should not be surprising that as an adult, I chose to follow family tradition and open my own business.

I spent several years in my early twenties working as a model, and eventually started my own small agency, Models by Cj, doing promotional and tearoom modeling, as well as a little runway work at bridal shows. It wasn't terribly profitable, but it was a lot of fun. You may have been surprised when I revealed I had eight children. Two of the eight came with my remarriage—we were raising a blended family with six children, all under age seven—so I decided to "retire" for a few years. Although I don't really think that raising the six children we already had, as well as delivering child number seven, can be considered leaving the workforce, I nevertheless stopped earning a paycheck for my work. My husband is an engineer, and I worked part-time with him in his engineering business, doing basic secretarial and accounting tasks, along with running our household for the next several years. At that point, we did some evaluating of our personal finances, as well as assessing our financial security should he become unable to provide for us. Things didn't look too reassuring.

Like many couples who own and operate a small business, my husband Roy was the only person drawing a paycheck. This kept our employment taxes minimal, but also left me without Social Security benefits or any credit of my own. I didn't have the ability to run his business if he should die, as he is a licensed professional engineer and I'm not. We decided that rather than going to work for someone else, I would set up and run my own business again. And so, Obermiller Construction Services, Inc., was born in November 1993, in Harrisonville, Missouri. While working with Roy, I saw the need for construction support services and with my office and management skills, it was a fit.

I had no idea what I was getting myself into …

The business grew fairly well, and made a small, but steady income. It was not too demanding on my time, which was good. Just like giving away all of your maternity clothes—apparently starting a business is also a very effective fertility treatment; baby number eight was born the following year. Our little family wound up being comprised of two businesses, four sons, four daughters, two dogs, several cats, and an assortment of small animals that at one time or another included half a dozen parakeets, a parrot, a python, a rose-hair tarantula, numerous tropical fish, and a variety of domestic rodents. Life was good!

And it was good for both our businesses—they grew. I no longer had the time to help with Roy's finances because my business did something unexpected and amazing—*it exploded!*

After seven years of steady but slow growth, I drove our Lincoln into the "pothole of fate" and made the phone call that landed my first major client—and a call that changed my life forever.

That was the good news. Do you want to hear the bad news?

I was completely unprepared to succeed on that level!

Up to that point, I had only managed myself and a couple of employees. My bookkeeping was simple and quick. No one else had access to my money. Since I had no high-level business training, I did what many of you reading this book do—I hired people who knew how to do what I did not and trustingly turned those tasks over to them. I realized that in order for my rapidly growing company to succeed, I needed people with the expertise to handle certain critical functions, like accounting, more professionally than I could. What I did not realize was that without proper supervision, accounting can be even riskier than construction!

Financial Apocalypse
at Obermiller Construction Services ... the Day the IRS Hit the Fan!

January 7, 2010, started out like a normal business day, with one exception: Tammie had been snowed in and couldn't get to the office. Her husband had gone to work quite early and shortly after he left, a windstorm came up that drifted several feet of snow into her driveway and buried her car. Since she rarely took any of her available sick or vacation days, I was not at all concerned about her absence. Additionally, January is a very slow month for construction, and we normally spent a lot of time doing busy-work like cleaning up the office, organizing files, and closing out the previous year's records.

I spent the day doing low-key tasks such as tidying up my office and answering emails. I heard the mailman come into the building around two o'clock, but my husband took care of him. A couple of hours later I walked through Tammie's office and noticed that the stack of mail on the corner of her desk had a certified letter from the IRS on the top. I almost didn't open it since she handled all the taxes and I knew she would bring anything important to my attention. But since it was certified, I felt it must be important so I opened it.

To my surprise, I found a final notice of demand for payment of over $35,000 in delinquent payroll taxes. Not only did the IRS want the money within 10 days, they made it quite clear that failure to pay would result in having my assets seized. Additionally, since I had ignored all of their letters for the past six months, they were prepared to move forward aggressively.

Of course, this letter was absurd. In fact, it was so outrageous that it didn't even occur to me that I had anything to worry about. I knew full well that all of my taxes were paid and was really upset that the IRS would bully me like this over something that was clearly their own mistake. Obviously, they had mixed my account up with someone else's. Now I was going to have to waste my time to clear it up—*how annoying!*

I couldn't ignore a letter that was threatening to seize my assets.

Immediately, I called Tammie to see if she knew anything about the IRS letter. She said that everything was fine; there were no overdue taxes, and promised to get on it first thing in the morning. She told me not to waste my time on something she could quickly straighten out herself. The letter was definitely a mistake.

Somewhat relieved, I told her I was going to go ahead and call the number on the notice. After all, I couldn't ignore a letter that was threatening to seize my assets, even if we both knew it was in error. She attempted to dissuade me from calling, promising again she would take care of it first thing in the morning, and encouraging me to leave it all up to her. Again, I told her that I simply couldn't wait even a day to respond to this kind of a threat. Hanging up, I paused. Toward the end of our conversation, I had sensed there was something different about Tammie—her voice, the way she responded. I couldn't put my finger on it, but something seemed off. She was different.

Irritated with the letter and the interruption of my day, I shook off the feeling as being silly and called the IRS hotline number on the letter, hoping to resolve the issue quickly. After holding for quite some time, a pleasant woman answered. Giving her the account information on the letter, I added that I had no idea what this was about and that I was pretty unhappy at having to waste my time on what was clearly a huge mistake.

She looked over my account and responded, "Your third and fourth quarter tax payments and filings for 2009 are all in order and paid. But the first and second quarters are not. In fact, the first quarter has seven deposits missing and no quarterly return was filed. The second quarter return has been filed, but no payments were made for the entire period." Then she added, "Oddly enough, starting in July, all required payments and filings resumed as though nothing was wrong."

By the time she added that six previous certified letters of demand had been sent to my company, but they had no record of any response, my head and stomach were spinning.

I said to my IRS contact, "My accountant is snowed in. I called her prior to calling you and she assured me that there were no overdue filings or payments, and that we have not received any letters prior to this current one."

Then the woman said, "Since previous to the first quarter of 2009, all of your taxes were in perfect order, I'll put your case on hold for 30 days to allow your accountant to return to the office and gather information on the payments. It is possible your payments were credited to the wrong account and as soon as you can provide proof of payment, the IRS will close the matter."

I thanked her and called Tammie back to update her on the situation. Her response was not what I expected.

When she answered the phone, I told her about the call and all of the missing payment information. I complained about wasting our time going through records. I don't remember exactly what she said at first, but then she started talking kind of fast saying, "Possibly, there could, maybe, be one, or maybe two late payments—I'm not quite sure, but there might have been one, I can't quite remember …"

My intuition started telling me something was wrong, but I didn't know what.

She rattled on like this for several minutes—she couldn't remember exactly how much might be due, or past due, if any returns were missing, and so on. As I listened, I became more and more uncomfortable about her ramblings. My intuition had already started telling me something was wrong, and our current conversation made that even clearer, but I still didn't know what.

I asked her several more questions about the taxes, she continued to give me answers that were vague, confusing, and evasive. This was not like her at all, and I started becoming concerned that there was much more here than met the eye. For years I had joked that I could sit in my office and yell, "Hey, Tammie, how much did we pay per cubic yard of concrete in northern Nebraska last year?" and she could answer me to the penny without looking up any records. For her to be anxious and confused about perfectly routine tax payments was very strange, and more than a little bit unsettling.

It felt odd. I got off the phone and decided to start checking into things myself. I headed to her desk.

First, I got onto her computer, which I virtually never did as we used a complex accounting system written for accounting professionals. It wasn't user-friendly, and my experience with it was limited. Finally, I was able to locate the section detailing tax payments, and found that our record of payments matched to the penny what the woman at the IRS call center had told me. All payments they had a record of receiving were shown there. The payments they said were missing, were missing from my system, as well.

The Ticking Time Bomb

I didn't know what to think. Without having any idea exactly what I was looking for, I started going through Tammie's desk drawers and what I found rocked me to the core.

It is worth noting that I actually felt like I was snooping into her personal things as I did this; I was very uncomfortable. I felt like I was "checking up" on her, and I didn't like it one bit. If you have ever had to go through someone's personal things because you suspected wrongdoing—even if, as a parent or boss, you had a perfect right to do it—you will know what I am talking about. Looking in someone else's drawer for scissors or a pencil feels very different from going through their personal space to see if they are hiding something.

Most things seemed pretty much in order. I continued to look, without any clear idea of what I was actually looking for. Finally, in the very back of one of her desk drawers, I found a green folder hidden under a stack of papers. The folder contained every notice that the IRS claimed they had sent, but Tammie told me we had never received. Each of them had been neatly affixed to their original envelope, date stamped on the day we received them, and then been carefully secreted away. They were all there; every letter, in order, each one more threatening than the last. All of them. Deliberately hidden from me. *But why?*

By this time, it was close to 6 p.m. and I called my husband to come and go over what I had found. Roy had no idea what to think either. Tammie was the most honest, trustworthy person in the company and we were completely at a loss to explain why she had clearly lied about the taxes. The IRS notice suddenly went from being an annoying mistake to a real crisis. I had a double-whammy on my hands.

The next step came out of the blue. For no reason that I can explain but somehow knew was urgent, I called the bank and instructed them to put a hold on my checking account. I felt a little strange as I hung up the phone. I had no evidence there had been any problems with my bank account, but I strongly felt it was the right thing to do. I simply told the bank manager I had an issue in my office I was uncomfortable with, and not to clear any checks without talking to me first. Thank goodness I did!

My husband and I left the office and went home in total shock; we had no idea what was going on. In fact, I told him I was afraid I was going to be very embarrassed when there turned out to be a perfectly reasonable explanation for everything and I wound up looking like a paranoid idiot. I also called our sons that worked for me and told them not to let Tammie into her office if she came in early the next morning. I didn't know what was going on, but I didn't want anything being tampered with before I figured it out. Thank goodness, again!

The next morning, one of our sons called at 7:30 a.m. and said that Tammie had gotten there half an hour early. He'd told her to wait in the foyer. We were already on our way to work and told him to have her wait there for us. Just as I hung up, another call came in. It was my banker. She said that two checks had come in overnight and she wanted my permission to process them. The first was a routine check for utility payments, and I instructed her to pay it. The second check was one she said I had written to Tammie on Tuesday. When I told her that I couldn't have written a check on Tuesday—I had been out of the office with a sick child, she assured me that I had signed it and it was dated on Tuesday. I pushed back, again saying that I had not written any checks that day. Then I said, "What was the amount of the check?"

She replied, "It was written to Tammie for $3,760."

With her words, I froze; I felt speechless.

After what felt like an eternity, I found my voice and said, "I absolutely did not write that check. You need to pull my signature card for comparison." She put me on hold, and I told my husband what had been said. We were both stunned. Clearly, something very serious was going on. Thirty seconds later, the branch manager was on the line.

"The signature is clearly not yours. I'm going to immediately start pulling the past few months' records that are housed here at the branch, as well as call the main bank for copies of your archived storage. I will meet you at your office in a few hours."

By this time, we had arrived at our office, and agreed to say nothing to Tammie about the check until we had additional information. I couldn't believe that I actually suspected her of doing something wrong, and I didn't want her to know what the bank had said until I had proof. It was just too surreal. Now, before you judge my reaction too harshly, keep in mind the level of trust I had for this woman. She'd been my close friend and daily companion for over eight and a half years. Also note, this is one of the primary reasons that embezzlements often go on for so long without being detected. We let the relationship trump our business sense.

When I walked in the office, I pulled Tammie aside to talk with her privately. I asked her about the tax payments, and told her I had found all of the past due tax notices and demand letters. She was very upset. She kept apologizing and saying that she had made a mistake and it would never happen again. I persisted. "Why were the taxes unpaid? I had the money to pay them. Why did you hide this from me?"

She really didn't have an explanation, but kept saying "I love my job. I will help you clear everything up, and I'm terribly, terribly sorry for my mistake."

I said nothing about the call from the bank. I told her that until I was able to investigate the extent and cause of the tax problems, she would not be able to return to work. She kept repeating apologies and asking to be allowed to keep her job, until I finally just sent her home and told her that I would call with any questions. This was one of the hardest things I had ever done; I was simply at a loss for how to proceed. It was also the last time I ever spoke to Tammie.

Less than two hours later, the local bank manager was in my office with more than twenty-seven thousand dollars in forged checks spread out on my conference table. These checks represented only the ones that had been forged on a single account over the past few months. Little did I know at the time that there were many, many more to come. Roy called the police. Neither the detective nor the bank manager had any trouble seeing what I still couldn't grasp, even though it was right in front of my eyes. I had been seriously and systematically embezzled by someone I had trusted like a member of my own family.

The rest of that day, and many others after, I **Tammie was a thief.** operated in kind of a fog. I was so stunned that I could barely breathe. I remember listening to the banker and the detective discussing what they saw, what else to look for and how to proceed, but I just sat there in a complete daze. I would try to stand up and help review evidence, but I kept having to sit down because I was too disoriented to stand up. I was so dizzy and nauseous I was afraid to eat anything, because I thought I might throw up.

I felt like I was in a dream … it couldn't possibly be real. I wanted to go home and pull the covers up over my head until the whole thing went away. It was the sort of thing you saw on television—*NOT* something that happened in real life, and definitely *NOT* to me.

The idea that Tammie had been stealing from me was unimaginable. I kept racking my brains to come up with a reasonable explanation for all of this. There had to be something that we were missing. *This simply couldn't be true!*

Although many things about that day are lost in the density of the fog I was immersed in, I will never forget the sickening realization that there was simply no other explanation for what was going on. Tammie was a thief and an embezzler!

How Prepared Are You for Financial Success?

- **Do you understand** basic accounting functions and terms?
- **Do you know** how to navigate your accounting system?
- **Do you have special administrative passwords** set up in your accounting system to give employees "as needed" access only to the areas they are authorized to use?
- **Do you understand** what Prevention and Detection controls are?
- **Do you have systems in place** to track all your checks from the moment you order them from the printer, through the time they clear your bank and are reconciled?
- **Do you know** which sensitive financial and office duties should be segregated? And if they can't be segregated, how to safeguard them?
- **Are you competent** to MANAGE and OVERSEE all of your accounting functions? (This is very different from being able to DO all of them.)
- **Do you know** when all of your tax filings are due?
- **Do you routinely confirm** that your taxes have been paid on time and in the correct amount? This is particularly important if you are using a service to handle your tax filings and payments.
- **Do you understand** how to recognize areas where your company may be vulnerable to fraud? Can you think like a thief?
- **If you have a partner,** do you have procedures in place to keep your dealings with one another honest and transparent? Friendship is not a fraud control.

Why a Business EXPLOSION Is the Last Thing You Want!

I cannot tell you how many times I've heard excited business people tell me that their business is "about to explode!" They think it would be a wonderful thing, but consider this: The dictionary defines an explosion as "a violent, cataclysmic disruption." Explosions bring chaos, destruction, confusion, and sometimes, even death. *Is that really what you want in your business?* Since we all want our businesses to grow and prosper, it is probably natural to assume that faster is better. Maybe it is. But you must have systems in place to make sure that sudden, massive growth doesn't destroy you.

Very few stop and consider the reality of managing a large business with high-dollar cash flow, especially if they have no business training. Many have the idea that they can just hire people to "do all that accounting stuff" without having a terribly accurate idea of what "stuff" actually needs to be done, and how it can be managed. Additionally, very few understand the incredible damage an unscrupulous employee can do—at least until it is discovered. Now, couple that with a lack of knowledge on how to prevent and detect fraud. In reality, it is probably a wonder MORE of us aren't embezzled!

The above represent just a few of the things you need to consider BEFORE your small business grows into a larger one. Can you answer YES to all of the above questions? Most likely, it's NO. Very few business owners have any type of protection strategies in place. The simple reason is they never contemplated it could happen to them.

If you already have a thriving business, don't think these things are not a problem for you just because you haven't discovered any fraud yet. The faster your company grows, the more unavoidable disorganization will be part of the mix as you adapt to your new circumstances, and the greater the likelihood that a dishonest person will be able to take advantage of it *right under your nose.*

If your business "explodes" before you have these critical areas under control, how will you ever find the time to take charge of them AND manage all the additional demands of a rapidly growing company?

Your answer starts with *systems.* You must know how to set up systems *and* procedures—the right systems and procedures—in your company that are used whether you have only one employee—you—or one hundred! Your systems will become everyday habits, habits that will protect you from internal events that could easily destroy you and your business.

Keep in mind that no business owner in the history of the world ever landed their first high-dollar client, and then decided to sit down and read an accounting book. First, they celebrate, next they hire office help, and then they go happily off looking for more big clients. If you want your business to turn into a profitable, secure, million dollar business, then start treating it like one today!

When you make these habits second nature, you will be ready to change the very nature of a growth EXPLOSION from a dangerous liability to a tremendous success!

CHAPTER 2

Why I Was an Easy Target, and You Probably Are, Too!

**The trust that small business owners
put in their employees is the main thing
that makes them—us—vulnerable to fraud.**

A t a meeting for women business owners, I gave a presentation on the risk of financial fraud. Half of the women there admitted to having experienced some form of internal fraud. After the meeting, I was told that several other members had also suffered fraud losses, but they had chosen not to disclose it publicly. Later, the president of the organization confided that she believed everyone there had experienced some form of fraud; some of them just hadn't discovered it yet. I agreed with her.

One of the primary reasons these women, like many business owners, are at risk for fraud is that they are busy managing other things. They let "the hired help" take over handling the lifeblood of the business—*the cash flow!*

In reality, most hire financial help so they can devote their time to business matters that are perceived to be critical to the overall success of the business. Tasks that involve client relationships, expanding their companies, marketing, networking, and so forth, are usually thought of as high priority items that are worthy of the owners' attention. Tasks that seem more routine, such as bookwork, inventory, and processing mail are delegated to people who then report back to the owners.

Rarely is there any oversight, and that's where the trouble begins. It is so convenient and easy to fall into the dangerous habit of relying primarily on second-hand information to monitor the financial workings of a business, that without a clear understanding of the risks involved, for most business owners careless delegation simply becomes the norm.

It is a tremendous relief to have a competent person, one who carries a high level of trust, handling the paperwork burden that is a huge part of even a very small business. Let's be real ... mundane tasks like sorting mail, answering phones, entering financial data into the computer, processing checks, balancing the bank accounts, etc., are tedious for energetic entrepreneurs who are anxious to grow their companies.

Having financial processes, junk mail, and nuisance calls screened can be a tremendous timesaver, but beware—*it also means that you will only see what the person doing the screening wants you to see!*

And to add to the reality check, most owners feel overwhelmed by more immediately pressing things and may neglect routine, but critical, recordkeeping and reporting. Having a good office staff getting the bookwork done efficiently and accurately can make or break a business. But unless business owners understand the need for basic fraud controls and how to monitor what employees are doing, they can quickly lose touch with what is happening right under their noses.

Let's face it, it is easy for "the Big Boss" to feel a little egotistical about only doing what he feels is important enough to be worth his time. If not careful, he may find himself in an ivory tower of his own making, and be easily misled by relying only on information that has passed through someone else's hands first. Having financial processes, junk mail, and nuisance calls screened can be a tremendous timesaver, but beware—

it also means that you will only see what the person doing the screening wants you to see!

The women I spoke to that afternoon in my business group were all smart, saavy, successful business owners. Like most business people in general, they had varying degrees of knowledge about the importance of managing risk, but virtually all of them signifigantly underestimated the risk fraud posed to their businesses. Without a simple, concise system to guide them, they were so busy running other aspects of their businesses that they didn't think they had time to manage their accounting: *They were wrong!*

A million here, a million there
~ it adds up to real money!

If you own a business and don't think you have ever had a fraud loss, you either haven't been in business very long, or you aren't watching your business very closely. The sad truth is that if you have something worth stealing, sooner or later someone is going to try to figure out how to do just that. Some losses seem minor—such as people helping themselves to your office supplies. Others are far more expensive—like forging checks or buying home improvement materials on your company accounts.

What may seem like minor thefts can over time become huge losses, and perhaps even more importantly, they establish a culture of entitlement with regard to company resources which can spread to other employees. You can unconsciously become a money pit for their pleasures.

In my opinion, we employers should all be as generous to our employees as possible. They need to know that we value and care about them, that we want to pay them fairly, and that extra effort on their part will receive additional rewards. Employees also need to know that dishonesty in any form will be dealt with swiftly, with zero tolerance for violations—any violation.

There is a tremendous responsibility that comes with running a business. Those who work for us believe we will manage our businesses well enough to provide adequate income, reasonable job security, and benefit packages that make life easier. Being sincerely generous and compassionate on one hand, and a little bit of a control freak about money and security on the other, may seem to be counterintuitive, but they are not.

Countless numbers of honest, hardworking employees have lost their jobs, had their benefits cut, or even had their paychecks bounce, due to the dishonesty of a single person in an organization. After the embezzlement in my company, we kept our personnel to a minimum and

I was duped and betrayed.

cut expenses to the bone—we had to in order to survive. Although my family was the hardest hit since my husband and I were personally responsible for the company debts, my employees and their families were also impacted by the company's lack of money, since we were unable to give raises on schedule or keep people working on maintenance tasks during the off season.

I made fewer purchases and my suppliers suffered from our financial woes. They were eventually paid in full, but often 60 to 90 days late, something I had never done before... Because I kept in good touch with them, and made small payments as often as possible, most were willing to work with me. Additionally, I had a great relationship with my bank, which was fortunate, because they would have been well within their rights to call in all of my loans and put me out of business within days.

Instead of being free to go out and pursue new clients and projects, or to repair and replace equipment to increase profits, I had to focus at least half of my working time every week for over a year assisting the FBI in building their case, and in fighting off the IRS. I also had to hire expensive accounting and legal services to help me deal with the mess. These things ate up money at an astonishing rate, and did so right at the time I desperately needed to save money and focus on saving my business.

The Sleight-of-Hand

One of the most difficult things I had to deal with was the sickening realization that Tammie's methods were so simple that I would have caught them easily *if I had just known what to look for!* None of the things she did were complex or highly technical. In fact, most were so obvious and simple I couldn't believe I hadn't figured it out years earlier.

How can something like this go on right in front of you—sometimes quite obviously—without having you realize what is happening? There are many possible explanations, but one is a fascinating phenomenon called selective attention. In other words, you can become so focused on what you are looking for and expect to see, that you are oblivious to unexpected things going on right in front of your eyes—a sleight-of-hand. Do a search on YouTube for *The Monkey Business Illusion* video and watch it to experience an incredible example of how this works. So I don't ruin the fun, a discussion of this video is included at the end of this chapter. Be sure to watch the video before reading the comments!

When fraud happens, it's not petty cash. In 2014, the Association of Certified Fraud Examiners' Global Fraud Study revealed that the typical organization loses a median of five percent of revenues each year due to fraud. Collectively, that percent translates to $3.7 trillion in losses. In my business, the two methods my trusted internal accountant used most often were check forgery and abuse of a company debit card. Far from being unusual, these simple, easy to detect schemes are the basis for the majority of small business fraud cases. In my own research, I have read about thousands of embezzlements, and these two methods show up repeatedly. The good news is that they are also among the easiest to catch!

Electronic Banking Increases Your Risk

Like me, your first thought about check forgery may be, "But what about my signature card?" Yes, what about it? I hate to break this to you, but these days the primary use for a signature card is to prove that the signatures on the stack of forged checks the bank already paid are not yours! This was totally amazing to me, but there has been a dramatic shift over the years in how banks verify transactions.

There was no big announcement, just a gradual change over time that took many of us by surprise. With the advent of ATMs and online banking, most banks will now honor electronic or automated transactions that would never pass scrutiny in person, and which would have been impossible to pull off just a few years ago. In fact, few banks even look at checks unless they meet a numerical threshold, such as being over $5,000.

When I started my business in 1993, I was the only person signatory to my checking account. I banked at a small, local bank where I knew everyone by name, and they all knew me, as well. On two separate occasions, I was out of the office and my husband needed to issue a check on my behalf. He made out the checks and signed my name, with my permission, and sent them off. As soon as those checks hit the bank for payment, I got a call from one of the friendly ladies who worked there, informing me that she was processing a check from my business and the signature didn't look like mine. A real person looked at every check and was familiar enough with the authorized signatures that such things were routinely caught.

That was then … this is now.

The Anatomy of the Paper Check Scheme

Now, fast forward to today. Someone can take one of your blank checks, write it for thousands of dollars, use a signature that bears no resemblance whatsoever to yours, and deposit it into their account via an ATM or phone app with no questions asked. No human eye may ever see this transaction unless **you** find a problem and file a dispute. If you are not routinely confirming the checks that clear your account, a forgery scheme could easily go on for years—*just as mine did!* Looking at the bank reconciliation reports prepared by your accountant is no substitute for looking at the actual statements straight out of the envelope which you have opened yourself!

According to a family member of mine who worked in bank management, unless someone who is not an account holder at your bank comes to the teller window trying to get cash money for a check drawn on your account, it is unlikely anyone will verify whether or not the signature is yours. Although electronic banking can be convenient and safe, it has its own unique risks in terms of exposure to fraud and we must learn to handle it accordingly.

In my situation, Tammie routinely took checks from my check stock. Pre her embezzlement, I did not have a system in place to track them—*I do now*. She made them out to herself for thousands of dollars, and then entered them into the accounting system showing they were made out to an authorized payee. If you had looked at my check register you would have seen a check entry that looked totally legitimate—such as a transfer to another company account or an insurance payment. In reality, the actual check was made out to her and then deposited in her account via the ATM.

"But," you may say, "that can't be done!"

And I'm here to say, "Oh yes, it can."

Your system does not know if it printed the payment on a bank check or a sheet of plain copy paper.

Here's how: The accounting check register only shows a record of checks that were printed by the system and many will not let you alter that information (this is true of most standard accounting programs). You can enter a hand-written check, but many systems flag those, or require administrative approval to enter them. If your register shows a check made out for $200 to pay an insurance premium, then a $200 check to the insurance company was probably printed.

But, consider this: If I go into my accounts payable system and process an invoice for payment, but then *insert a blank sheet of paper* into the printer instead of a check, the system will show that a legitimate invoice was paid and a check was printed. Your system does not know if it printed the payment on a bank check or a sheet of plain copy paper. It only knows that it processed a payment, and it updates the check register to reflect that activity.

A dishonest accountant can now throw away the sheet of paper with the check information printed on it, and take the blank check to use as he or she pleases. Unless you are confirming every single check from the time you remove it from a secure location until it has cleared the bank in the correct amount and to the proper entity, getting and using a check improperly is as easy as pie. Just make the stolen check out for the same amount of money as the pretended payment (so the account will balance without any journal adjustments) and then put in the desired name as payee on the actual check.

If you are not monitoring your checks carefully, as well as the source documents that back them up, you will probably only catch this scheme by accident. A quick glance at your account is nearly worthless. Even a professional auditor has only a small chance of catching many fraudulent activities unless he or she is confirming every single transaction. In fact, a professional audit is estimated to have only between a three to eight percent chance of discovering fraud.

That is only one of a multitude of simple ways an embezzler can use checks to drain your bank account. Once you open your mind to seeing how simple fraud is to commit, you will find the most amazing thing is that it isn't more common. I have described to hundreds of people how this particular check/paper substitution scheme works, and the looks of surprise and horror on their faces as they realize how brilliantly simple it is, are priceless. It does kind of make you want to put down *FraudPoints!* and go look at your checking statements, doesn't it?

On the next page, I reveal 11 common ways that money can be stolen from an average business. If you run your company as many owners do, your bookkeeper or accountant could easily be duplicating any number of them.

11 Easy Ways Employees Get Checks and Steal Money

1. **Tells the boss that the printer ate a check and another one is needed to finish paying bills.** This is like when you told your mom that your chores were all done so you could go swimming, and you made sure to tell her when she was running out the door for work or a meeting and was probably in too much of a hurry to check under your bed. *It works best if the boss is really busy.*

2. **Takes a check from the bottom of the check stock when no one is looking; it will never be missed.** After all, who looks to see if checks are missing from the bottom of the stack or from the back of the checkbook?

3. **Pretends that a paycheck was in a shirt or pocket that ran through the wash, and replacement is urgently needed.** This is a variation of "the dog ate my homework." *Don't fall for it!*

4. **Steals a signed check designated to pay the electric bill, then uses one of many simple ways to change who it is made out to, and deposits the check using an ATM or remote deposit app.** Then when a shut-off notice for nonpayment arrives, tells the boss the check must have been lost in the mail and another needs to be sent ASAP. Employee will most likely promise to void the "lost" check—*wink, wink!*

5. **Steals one of the blank checks provided to pay bills, and then doesn't pay one.** An easy and safe way to do this is to just leave the last check in the printer tray. If the boss notices when signing them that one is missing, the employee can blame the computer for not printing the last check. *Darn these computers, anyway ….*

6. **Gets the boss to hand over a signed blank check to use for an authorized purchase.** The check is then used however the fraudster desires. *Ideally, when the boss is busy and will likely forget about the check.*

7. **Charges what looks like a business purchase to a personal credit card, then turns in the receipt for reimbursement,** even though the purchase never made it to the office. Most likely, the charge is coded to routine supplies and equipment the business uses. *Those paper clips and ink cartridges can fly off the supply shelf!*

8. **Takes a stolen check and uses it to set up an automatic monthly payment for a personal installment purchase.** The payment is then entered in the business register using a name of an individual or vendor

that the boss won't recognize as not being legitimate. *After all, he will never guess that the payments to DBI, coded as a maintenance plan on company vehicles, are really going to Dream Boat Industries for an automatic monthly payment on a new bass boat!*

9. **Uses a stolen check to secretly order additional company checks.** This can give the culprit hundreds of checks to use instead of having to steal them one at a time. If caught, the employee may pretend that it was time to reorder and the new supplier had a better price than the one normally used.

10. **Makes out paychecks to "ghost" employees, like a husband or sister.** The boss will probably not pay attention to the names on individual paychecks, just the gross amount of payroll.

11. **Gets a friend to send the company fake invoices that are passed off as real bills.** The company pays them ... and then the employee and friend split the money!

There is one opinion that I have very little patience for, and have had some fairly harsh discussions about: The popular idea that businesses, particularly corporations, are evil. To me, that is simply ignorant.

After doing a poll among colleagues who are entrepreneurs and small business owners, I feel I can at least offer some personal thoughts on the subject of small businesses and their owners. They include:

- Most do not have formal business training.

- Even the most successful ones have had to guarantee company debts with personal assets, including their homes.

- They work hard, often putting in far more hours than when they worked for others.

- They pay their employees first—when times are hard, bosses are the last people in line for a paycheck.

- They take personal pride in their business, to the point that it is almost an extension of themselves.

- They are frustrated with the complexity and expense of tax compliance as well as with other government requirements that place heavy burdens on their businesses, even when they are struggling.

- They value and trust their employees and go to a lot of trouble to treat them well.

Far from being overindulged, undertaxed, oppressive one-percenters, most business owners are decent people doing their best to run their businesses well, and are not getting rich from them. In fact, the trust that they put in their employees is the main thing that makes them—*us*—vulnerable to fraud.

Not only do most small business owners lack the training to set up really effective financial controls, most don't feel the need to do it in the first place since they trust their employees. That is wonderful! I trust my employees, too. However, *now hear this:*

Trust is an emotion,
NOT an accounting control!

When Special Agent Jackson of the FBI first came to my office (I actually have my own "man in black" on my speed dial—how creepy is that?), he asked me a lot of routine questions about Tammie and her duties in my business. Questions like:

- *Did she get the mail?*

- *Did she answer the phones?*

- *Did she have access to checks?*

- *Did she pay the bills?*

- *Did she balance the checkbook?*

All of these questions could be answered with a single word: YES. As we visited, I came to the painful realization that *trust without verification* had cost me an extraordinary amount of money, and was going to cost my accountant her freedom. She would spend years behind bars.

Never allow yourself to trust anyone so much that you do not routinely verify the work.

The most shocking thing to me about my embezzlement was that someone I trusted so highly could do this to me. I felt as though I was the only person in the world dumb enough to not see what was going on. But I was wrong. As I continued my research into financial fraud, in case after case, I read about the experiences of other completely shocked business owners—many echoed mine:

- *She was the most trusted person in the company.*
- *He was my father's best friend; I have known him since I was born.*
- *She was my best friend all through high school.*
- *He saved my life when we were teenagers; we have been like brothers our entire lives.*
- *I loaned him money when his wife was dying.*
- *She used to babysit my kids … they call her Grandma.*
- *We spend every Christmas together.*
- *I co-signed for a car loan when her husband left her.*
- *He was like a member of the family.*
- *Or even sadder, she IS a member of the family.*

For me, the complete betrayal of trust was harder to deal with emotionally than the loss of money. It would be like discovering that my husband was having a long-term affair with my closest friend, or that my father wasn't actually my father. There are no words to describe how deeply painful this complete betrayal was.

Does this mean you should refuse to trust your employees? No… far from it! But, this is essential for the livelihood of your business: *never allow yourself to trust anyone so much that you do not routinely verify their work.* The accounting controls you put in place are not established because you don't trust people; they are established because they

> I came to the painful realization that *trust without verification* had cost me an extraordinary amount of money.

are simply part of running a business professionally. Accounting controls are tools for managing your company. And contrary to what some may believe, they are *not* an insult to your staff.

Think of it this way: If you go to a store and make a large purchase with lots of items, do you expect to get a receipt? How would you feel if the checker told you the store wasn't giving receipts anymore—it was all being done on the honor system? If you would insist on having the ability to look at the cost of items included in a small grocery bill, shouldn't it be even more important that you have a way to see what your accountant is doing—not what you *think* she is doing, but what she is *really* doing—with the thousands of dollars entrusted to her care?

More Dirty Laundry from My Accountant's Drawers

When I discovered my embezzlement, a good friend and CPA from my church community offered to come help me start sorting things out and compiling evidence for the police. For Curtis, this was fascinating stuff. He loved every minute of going over the books for anomalies. I could always tell if he had hit "pay dirt" because he would yell, "Oh my gosh—look at what she did here!" I finally I told him—in jest—that if he didn't quit having such a good time I was going to slap him. He saw another piece of an intriguing puzzle fitting together, and I saw another ten thousand dollar lie. Uncovering these layers of lies was like discovering I had been working with a complete sociopath.

Some of the things we discovered were:

- She neglected to close a debit card account from a past employee, and then made a confusing trail of internal transfers to fund it and use it for purchases.

- She charged airline tickets for weekend trips, amusement park entry fees, and hotel rooms in local vacation spots.

- She took her family out to dinner and a movie—complete with concessions—two or three times a week.

- She made daily trips to a local fast food restaurant for ice cream.

- When all the popcorn and ice cream made her gain weight, she charged prepackaged diet meals delivered to her home.

- She filled up the family cars one to two times per week.

- Even though she added family members to my company health insurance policy without paying the premiums for them, she then turned around and paid the co-pay charges with a company debit card.

- She bought expensive craft supplies and gifts for the cheerleading team she coached.

- She made donations to her local school foundation.

- She charged expensive Christmas gifts for my husband and me one year, and when I told her she shouldn't spend so much money on us, she said that none of the other employees helped, but she didn't mind. When I discovered the gifts had been charged to a company debit card during the investigation and told my son about it, he had a fit. He had collected cash donations from the other employees and given them to Tammie to purchase our gifts. Apparently, she pocketed their cash, charged the gifts to the company card, and then had the nerve to take full credit for being so generous.

It was a few dollars here, and a few dollars there. Her greed became an insatiable need, so multi-thousands more. When combined with the other costs of the embezzlement and its aftermath, all totaled the sum likely exceeded $1,000,000. Take a minute and let that amount of money sink in. I lost over a million dollars!

Shortly after discovering the embezzlement, I tearfully confided to a close friend that I couldn't believe I had been so stupid about what was going on. She quickly consoled me by pointing out, "You are *not* stupid—you are honest! Because you would never do this to someone else, you never thought someone would do it to you and so you weren't looking for it."

Although that made me feel a little better personally, it didn't change the situation. The sad fact is, no matter how honest and kind you are to others, not everyone will treat you the same way. I was duped and betrayed. While this realization doesn't need to make you cynical, it should teach you to be very, very careful!

The Monkey Business Illusion

If you are reading this, I will assume you have watched the video *The Monkey Business Illusion*, which directs viewers to watch a group of basketball players and count how many times they passed the ball as they played. At the end of the video, the viewer was asked a question. Interestingly, it was not about the number of passes generated between the team members. Instead, the question was: Did you see the gorilla? While viewers were focused on counting the number of passes, a man in a gorilla suit slowly walked into the middle of the game, stood in the middle of the players, beat his chest, and then walked off. Less than 50 percent of viewers saw the gorilla, even though they had meticulously counted the passes between team members. Once told to watch for the gorilla, they couldn't believe they hadn't seen it before.

Disclaimer: I was in the percentage that didn't see it. I actually closed my browser and reopened the video in a new link. I was sure it was some sort of trick and that the gorilla was inserted into the replay.

In other words, video viewers were so focused on what they expected to see that they were oblivious to the "monkey-business" happening right before their eyes.

When you like and trust your accountant, you are not looking for ways they might be stealing from you. Why would you? The result is that you may overlook even the most obvious signs of fraud. Suspicion and distrust are not the answer; education is. Unless you learn how fraud happens and what to watch for, you may find that your accountant was the one in the gorilla suit, and that you never saw what was going on right in front of you. Every business owner needs to ask the question: Is there a gorilla in my business?

Summing Up

If you have anything in your business that is worth stealing, sooner or later, someone will probably give it a try. Identify likely FraudPoints in your business, limit and monitor access to those areas, and verify their security through source documents and physical confirmation. Your business assets will become highly secured, good employees will be much less likely to fall into temptation, and the embezzler pros will probably be inclined to move on to an easier target.

CHAPTER 3

Embezzling for Beginners

**It is a sad fact that not everyone
is worthy of trust, and you need to protect
your business assets accordingly.**

The number of articles and studies about financial fraud I've read since my embezzlement is sadly endless. Not a day goes by without hearing reports of new occurrences of fraud perpetrated on individuals, businesses, or organizations. The areas they focus on generally fall into three basic categories:

1. *Information that is interesting to academics,* which has no real value outside of intellectual or theoretical circles.

2. *Data about the personal characteristics of fraudsters,* which can cause you a lot of trouble if you try to make use of it when hiring or firing.

3. *Actual statistics on how common and devastating fraud is and how it occurred,* which are likely to scare your pants off.

Let's explore each of them.

First, information that is only useful to academics would include such fascinating tidbits as:

- Studies proving that most embezzlers want to live a more lavish lifestyle than they can afford. (Duh…)

- State-by-state comparisons on the frequency of fraud incidents. (If you want to start a business you should move to a safe state?)
- The educational credentials of convicted fraudsters. (As if a college degree could make you immune to greed and dishonesty.)
- And the list of useless trivia goes on ...

Second, personal information about fraudsters is listed in great detail and analyzed. This is worse than useless. It is dangerous for you to hire or fire based on information such as age, gender, ethnicity, or income bracket. This sort of analysis includes observations such as:

- 58% of embezzlers are female.
- Male embezzlers commit a smaller number of crimes, but when they do steal, they take nearly three times as much money as females.
- People between the ages of 40–49 are the most frequent culprits.
- The District of Columbia and California often have the highest number of fraud and identify theft crimes.
- Vermont has the highest number of frauds per capita.

Not only are these facts of little use to a business owner, if you base hiring decisions on them you may be in real trouble! Just try establishing a policy that you only allow men under 40 in your accounting positions because they are less likely to steal, or that you refuse to hire anyone from Vermont, and then let me know how your meetings with the Equal Employment Opportunity Commission and their attorneys work out for you!

Since employers are strictly forbidden to use this type of personal information as the basis for nearly all hiring and firing decisions, the only people who should care about statistics based on these facts are people who *study* embezzlement, not those who actually try to *prevent* it, like you and me.

Third, are the real facts and statistics about how common financial fraud is, how easy it is to commit, and how badly it can hurt you. Are they important to you? Of course they are! *Those* are the ones that should really matter to you. It is the information which—I hope—will impress you enough to take real action to protect yourself from dishonest employees, and help you to understand and address the unique types of risk your business may face.

According to the U.S. Census Bureau and the Small Business Administration in 2014, American business overwhelmingly consists of small businesses—businesses with less than 100 employees. There are more than 5.83 *million* small business firms employing over 120 million individuals. These numbers do not include the self-employed who have no other employees. Small businesses aren't in the minority—they make up *89.4* percent of all businesses, employing more individuals than all Fortune 500 companies combined.

> Fraud is not the victimless crime many in law enforcement consider it to be.

As a small business owner, when fraud happens, your business creates a domino effect, harming vendors who serve your business, and who are most likely also small business owners. According to Joseph T. Wells, founder of the Association of Certified Fraud Examiners, small businesses are 100 times more likely to be embezzled than a large company.

Fraud is not the victimless crime many consider it to be. It is ironic that someone could enter a store with a banana in their pocket, attempt to rob the cashier for $20, and get up to 15 years of jail time and probation because there is a perceived threat to the victim. Yet an embezzler can steal thousands, even millions, and get little to no jail time. The fact is that in many ways our society still holds the perception that embezzlement is not a serious threat, and the penalties for it reflect that attitude.

Really?

Companies, no matter how big or small, are owned by individuals. Individuals who have financial obligations, vendors, employees, and personal creditors. If monies aren't available to pay them, isn't there a threat?

I recently saw an advertisement for a training session intended for fraud examiners that discussed how to get inside the minds of embezzlers and understand what may be motivating them. The only thing I could think was—*whatever for?* This may sound harsh, but there is only one thing I care about, in terms of psychoanalyzing my accounting staff: Is there something going on in my company that is so horribly unfair or abusive that a reasonable person might actually be able to justify *"making things fair"* by hurting the company in some way?

- Have I bought a new sports car or other luxury item while cutting company insurance in order to save money?

- Have I reduced working hours to part-time to keep from paying full-time benefits, even though there is plenty of profitable work to do?

- Do I or my management treat my employees in a way that is insulting, rude, or generally demeaning?

- Could my actions be viewed as taking unfair advantage of people in some way?

- In short, am I doing anything that could make people feel they would be justified in evening the score, or doing something to hurt me in return?

Not everything you do will be liked or understood by your employees. Sometimes hard decisions must be made. But be aware, you *can* unintentionally foster an environment which is conducive to fraud. A bad attitude or unfair policy on your part doesn't excuse fraud, but it may encourage it.

A business must be profitable to survive, and those profits benefit everyone.

Outside of eliminating policies and practices that are clearly unfair, there really isn't anything you can do about how your employees feel about life, or why they feel that way.

People steal for reasons that you and I will never be aware of, and couldn't have any influence over if we did. I can't do anything about the fact that when employee "A" was a child, her family was poor and the other kids made fun of how she dressed, so now she steals my money to buy her kids clothes at a trendy store.

As an employer, I must be mindful that I am treating my employees as well as I can, while still watching my bottom line to make sure the company is profitable. Most people understand that there has to be a balance between profits and benefits. Once I have those issues in order, there are three critical things I want my employees to know if, for whatever reason, they are tempted to commit fraud:

1. **Fraud will be hard to commit.** I have established procedures to protect company assets that everyone will follow. Compliance with these procedures is non-negotiable for anyone who wants to work at my company.

2. **Fraud will be easy to catch.** I have accounting controls—some known and some secret—which allow me to clearly see what people are doing with my money. This is not only my right; it is my responsibility as owner. A lot of families are depending on the paychecks provided by my company to pay their bills, and it is up to me to be sure those checks will clear the bank.

3. **Fraud will be very, very risky.** I have clearly defined which behaviors I consider honest, and which I consider dishonest. There are no "gray areas" about what constitutes stealing from this company. Excuses like "I didn't know I shouldn't use the company gas card to fill up my wife's car; I was going to pay it back later, and besides, everyone else does it" are grounds for immediate termination. Furthermore, I will not just fire you and send you down the road to steal from another unsuspecting employer. *I will prosecute you!*

I know most people understand that running a business should not be just about making money. A business must be profitable to survive, but a business should also be fair, generous, treat people honestly, be an asset to the community, and give good value to its clients. Although it has become trendy to criticize business owners for their devoted pursuit of the almighty dollar (as opposed to only being concerned with "giving back" and other lofty goals), I have noticed that even the most notorious anti-capitalist "business bashers" expect their paychecks to clear the bank, so making and protecting money must, of necessity, be pretty high up on the priority scale.

Some employees—or even partners—will be offended when you set up accounting controls; they may feel that you are being a nosey micro-manager, or that you don't completely trust everyone, sight unseen. It is a sad fact that not everyone is worthy of trust, and you need to protect your business assets accordingly.

As you read these statistics and start to understand the very real risk financial fraud poses to you, also keep in mind that those numbers represent the experiences of thousands of business owners—*just like you*—who suffered unimaginable financial loss and emotional pain at the hands of people they trusted. My accountant was—I thought—a close and trusted friend for over eight years. I never saw the embezzlement coming. I hope the information in *FraudPoints!* will help you be wiser than I was.

The facts, ma'am; only the facts.
—Joe Friday

I once heard a comedian joke about what it might be like to be Stephen King's kid. He said something to the effect of, "Can you imagine getting up in the middle of the night and saying 'Daddy, I can't sleep,' only to have Daddy King say (insert creepy voice and Vincent Price laugh), 'Would you like me to tell you a story? Ha ha ha ...' You then run back to bed screaming, 'No, no—I promise I'll stay in bed; no more stories—please!'"

Guess what … embezzlement is scarier than Stephen King ever thought of being because—unlike girls setting things on fire with their eyes, or evil cars that are out to get you—it can, and does, actually happen every day!

Although the facts listed here come from a number of different sources, many are taken from the *Marquet Report on Embezzlement,* which is well worth your time to go online and read in its entirety. Although it ceased publication in 2013, it still contains a great deal of relevant information. While there are other notable studies on fraud, this is the one that, in my opinion, cuts straight to the chase on the risk employee theft poses to businesses and doesn't cloud the issue with information on financial statement fraud, which, although a serious crime, may not result in any actual financial loss.

Financial Statement Fraud—Are You Guilty?

Many people have heard of financial statement fraud, but aren't really sure what it is. Below are three facts for you to consider, so that you—the business owner—do not find that the biggest fraudster in your business is YOU!

1. **Financial statement fraud** happens when you represent anything on your personal or company financial statements that is misleading or untrue. For example, if you have a receivable (money that is owed to you) on your books that you know will never be collected, or a vehicle on your asset list that has been destroyed or sold, but you leave it there because it makes your bottom line look better, you are committing financial statement fraud.

2. **It is often thought of as simply "creative bookkeeping"** but in reality, not only is it dishonest, it is a serious crime. As the owner, you must be familiar with everything that goes into the making of your financial statements and ensure that they are as accurate as possible.

3. It is generally done either by an owner, in an effort to make a business look better on paper than it really is (in order to obtain loans, favorable interest rates, credit accounts, or insurance), or by an accountant in order to cover theft.

Financial statement fraud is what brought down Enron, and put a lot of previously respectable business people and accountants in jail.

Financial statement fraud is a blatant act of dishonesty, and it is important that you, as a business owner, understand that. Go over your financial statements with a qualified CPA and make sure they provide a fair representation of the financial condition of your business. Although this type of fraud does not mean that anyone actually lost any money, it does mean that the people who loaned you money or insured you were probably taking a much bigger risk than they thought. (Interest rates and insurance premiums are frequently based on the financial condition of a company, so misrepresenting that condition in order to get better prices is fraudulent.)

It is a sign of poor business ethics to ask others to take a risk on your company based on information you know to be false. Additionally, you do not have the right to ask your employees to be any more honest with you than you are willing to be with your business associates and creditors. Honesty applies to all of us!

Furious activity is no substitute for understanding.
— H. Williams

Once you really understand the risk financial fraud poses to your business, you will never again allow yourself to be so busy *running* your business that you fail to take time to *protect* your business.

Below are the 10 scariest things I have learned about embezzlement:

Scary Statistic #1: *Embezzlement cases in 2013 were up 5% over 2012 and continue to increase.* Three out of five embezzlers are women. But, when men steal, they go for the gold—the average theft is $1.8 million versus woman's at $800,000. Sadly, embezzlement has been on the rise for many years, and it shows no sign of slowing down. This means that even if you have the same systems and employees that have served you well for many years, your risk of fraud is constantly increasing.

Scary Statistic #2: The *average loss for 2013 was about $1.1 million.* That will scare some of you to death, and give others a false sense of security. You may say, "My total gross revenues are only a small fraction of that, so I must be safe." If that is how you feel, let me ask you a question: How much money *can* you afford to lose? The big dollar amounts have a high "WOW" factor, but they represent only a small portion of the actual losses.

Cases involving under $100,000 are frequently not reported or prosecuted, as they are considered too small to be statistically

> **For nearly five years, someone you probably interacted with daily but never suspected was stealing you blind.**

or legally significant. Additionally, even those huge losses are often the cumulative total of a fraud that went on for many years, and not a one-time incident. Even worse, hidden behind the big cases are thousands of small stories that may have seemed minor to prosecutors and newspapers, but were devastating to the people involved.

Scary Statistic #3: The *average scheme lasts 4.6 years.* That means that for nearly five years, someone you probably interacted with daily but never suspected was stealing you blind. The really sad thing about this is that the average prison sentence is less than 4 years—about 44 months, which is significantly less time than the thief spent committing the crime, and probably much less time than it will take the business owner to recover —if recovery is even possible.

Scary Statistic #4: *Less than seven percent of the cases involved someone with a prior criminal history.* Background checks should still be done, but the reality is that a clean slate is no guarantee of an honest employee.

For most, embezzlement is a crime of opportunity, *not* a long-standing career choice.

Scary Statistic #5: *Low tech = BIG CHECK! One of the most common embezzlement techniques involve forged or unauthorized checks.* Check forgery is so quick and effective that it is mind boggling. In 2013, $140 million was taken by simple check fraud, representing 35% of reported embezzlement cases, and over 23% of reported losses. Even worse, that figure is just the tip of the iceberg and does not reflect the frauds that have not yet been discovered, were considered too small to prosecute, or that, for many reasons, went unreported.

Scary Statistic #6: *One U.S. Chamber of Commerce survey reported approximately one-third of business bankruptcies are due to employee theft.* This may be the scariest one of all. A business bankruptcy often results in people losing personal assets they may have worked their entire lives to earn, since these owners probably secured their business loans against their personal property. Even a "statistically insignificant" theft of $20,000 to $30,000 can cost business owners their company *and* their home. Their plight seldom makes the news and often receives no prosecution. Tragic!

The reported number of embezzlements represent only the tip of the iceberg.

Scary Statistic #7: *Most major embezzlers appear to have been motivated simply by the desire to live beyond their means, rather than by any true financial need.* That means that someone who just wants a cool car or some nice jewelry may be perfectly willing to financially destroy you in order to get it. This has changed over time, as in the past embezzlements most often occurred as a result of genuine crisis, such as threatened loss of a home because one partner was seriously ill and unable to work.

When you couple that with the fact that you probably consider this person a friend, you start to get a feel for the real impact of financial fraud. When reviewing the financial records of my embezzler I found that among other similar, frivolous expenditures, she and her family went out to dinner and a movie—complete with concessions—multiple times each week. Clearly, this was simple greed, *not* need or hardship, and it seems to have become the most common motive overall.

Scary Statistic #8: *A small business, one with fewer than 100 employees, is literally 100 times **more** likely to be embezzled than a large business.* People steal from large corporations and banks all the time, but many of these thefts are caught very quickly, because big businesses usually understand the need to protect themselves and have fraud prevention and detection controls in place … do you?

Scary Statistic #9: *Churches and nonprofit organizations account for over 11% of all embezzlements.* If people will steal from a church or a fund set up to help a child with cancer, do you think they will hesitate to steal from you? There is even a website devoted entirely to church and school embezzlement cases. Increasing at an annual rate of nearly 6%, researchers expect church financial fraud to reach the $60 billion mark by 2025. That's still not the whole picture. Experts estimate up to 80% of all church fraud cases go unreported and therefore are not included in statistics.

Scary Statistic #10: *The most common thing I have heard people say after an embezzlement is, "She/he was the most trusted person in the company— just like a member of our family!"* The very fact you trust someone so highly that you do virtually nothing to monitor or control their activities means that you have unknowingly created the perfect storm for your own embezzlement. It doesn't mean that you can't trust people, but you must do so in a cautious way; it is simply how business is done. Trust, *but verify!*

By compiling information from several large studies, it's revealed that the average embezzlement nets over a million tax-free dollars in under five years, and the thief has only a two to three percent chance of being caught, convicted, and going to jail.

Becoming a millionaire through financial fraud beats your chances of winning that big lottery prize hands-down! No wonder so many people try it.

Summing Up

Embezzlement is real, and it happens far more often than most business owners believe or think about. Rarely do they think of themselves as the recipient and therefore fail to put any safeguards in position for protection. Understand that all are not worthy of your trust. It must be earned. Today's business owner must protect his or her business assets—all of them.

CHAPTER 4

The Fraud Triangle

**Many embezzlement cases started with either
a very small theft or an accidental accounting error.**

A young woman I personally know was a teacher in a very expensive, private preschool. The parents paid a substantial weekly tuition rate, and were very limited in the number of days they could take as "no pay" days during the year.

In one two-week period of time, the school was closed twice due to blizzard-like weather conditions. The parents were not given any reduction in their tuition payments for the missed days, and several were unhappy enough about it to complain to the director.

She told them that the school still had to pay all of its monthly expenses, such as rent, utilities, and salaries, whether the students were there or not, so she could not reduce their tuition. Several of these parents also discussed the situation with their children's teachers. To their surprise, it was discovered that although the parents had to pay full tuition for the time the school was closed, none of the teachers were paid for those days. The result: The owner of the school netted a huge windfall profit by pocketing the wages withheld from the teachers.

I am not aware of any fraud that occurred as a result of an unhappy teacher or parent, but it is easy to understand how such actions could open the door for a disgruntled employee to justify "making things fair" by doing something to recover the value of pay she felt cheated out of. Sometimes major embezzlements emerge from such small situations.

What Is the Fraud Triangle and Why Should You Care?

Now that you know enough about embezzlement to be well informed, and more than a little nervous, what is your next step? It begins with understanding the cycle that is present in nearly all ongoing embezzlements:

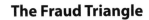

The Fraud Triangle

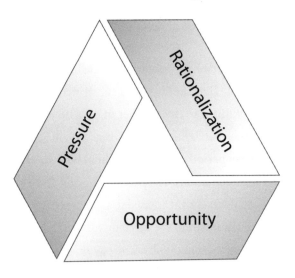

The Fraud Triangle, first identified by Dr. Donald Cressey, outlines three elements that must be present for long-term fraud to occur: Opportunity, Pressure, and Rationalization. Let's take a look at them individually.

Opportunity: The person truly believes he/she can commit fraud without being caught. Often, "the person" is right.

In the area where I live, there are several small towns who discovered that by running constant radar, they could earn a lot of money writing stacks of speeding tickets. One of the worst of these speed traps happens to be on the road to the church my family attends, so we drive it several times each week. Before the speed traps were set up, we were able to drive at whatever speed we chose. That opportunity changed quickly with introduction of radar, since none of us wanted to pay expensive tickets.

The knowledge that I will almost certainly be ticketed and fined for speeding has changed my driving habits considerably. Although I was never a speed demon before, you can be sure that now I never exceed the speed limit in that area, because I know the danger. In other words, my opportunity to speed without fear of a traffic ticket is gone, so I obey the law and drive the speed limit.

Most of us will be likely to avoid activities that can get us into trouble.

The point is, when you know there is a real danger of discovery and negative consequences, you will likely avoid activities that can get you into trouble. In fact, the negative consequences can be so sure and so unpleasant, that you never even consider breaking the rules (or the law). That means the perceived opportunity has been effectively eliminated. This is *exactly* what you want in your business. Your employees are no different from you in this matter; no one wants to suffer the painful and certain consequences of unlawful actions.

Many embezzlement cases start with either a very small theft or an accidental accounting error, which the owner never notices and which make clear there is a viable, low-risk opportunity to steal and not be caught. By setting up controls that let your staff know you are monitoring what they do, you have gone a long way toward eliminating the first, and most basic, part of the Fraud Triangle—*Opportunity*!

Pressure: This is the motivation, usually of a social or financial nature, that generates the action. It is often a "problem" the perpetrator believes cannot be shared with anyone; something they are ashamed of or embarrassed to admit.

When the original theory of the Fraud Triangle was developed, it was believed there had to be some sort of terrible pressure to steal, such as an expensive medical need, the possibility of losing a home to foreclosure, or some other catastrophic event. The thief could only avoid the crisis with a fast infusion of money that there was no other way to obtain. Most agree that stealing is wrong, but we can also have a degree of sympathy for a person in such a difficult situation.

The original theory, while accurate at the time it was developed, is frequently no longer the case. Contrary to the belief that fraud is usually due to a catastrophic event that seeded the theft, in the majority of cases today, simple greed is the primary motivator.

Just wanting better stuff is considered a good enough reason to steal.

There are many reasons for this, and I am not going to get into a lengthy analysis of our culture. However, consider how constantly we are bombarded with the idea that we must be beautiful, thin, drive the right car, have perfect homes, throw fabulous parties, wear the right clothes, etc.

One of the results is that many feel they can't be happy unless they have "those" things. We are encouraged by the credit card companies to get, with the use of their plastic, whatever priceless thing our hearts desire, as though the bill will never come due. State-sponsored gambling lures many to spend what money they do have—often the grocery money —on lottery tickets and online casino games. Is it any wonder that some of these people will take your money in a hopeless effort to buy happiness?

Motivation to commit fraud can still come from difficult, outside circumstances that leave the thief with few good options to resolve the problem. Yet the majority of the time, it now appears that just wanting better stuff is, for many, considered a good enough reason to steal.

Rationalization: Fraud can begin for any number of reasons, but for it to continue over the long-term, justifying the action is always in play. This rationalization is essential so the perpetrator can maintain his/her self-concept as an "honest" person caught in a bad set of circumstances.

For fraud to continue on an ongoing basis, the thief has to salve his conscience by incorporating the third corner of the Fraud Triangle: justifying (or rationalizing) the theft. There are some who consider the simple fact that you, the owner, make more money from your company than they do as sufficient reason to steal from you. Some rationalizations are truly twisted and are not due to any fault on the part of the business owner. They are convoluted excuses thieves invent to help themselves live with their own wrongdoings.

Other rationalizations actually make a degree of logical sense, even though they are still wrong. Some could even arise from unethical or abusive behavior on the part of a business owner. It can be quite easy for some to justify taking money to remedy a situation that is truly unfair. The caution here is to be mindful of how your actions may be viewed by your employees.

Defeating the Fraud Triangle
... Meet the Honesty Triangle

If Opportunity, Pressure, and Rationalization create fertile ground for fraud, how can you construct a work environment that discourages it? Simple: You set up your business controls based on the *Honesty Triangle!*

The Honesty Triangle incorporates three basic ideas:

1. Clearly understood, reasonable *Expectations*

2. Consistent, random *Verifications*

3. Fair, appropriate, effective *Consequences*

Let's consider how each works.

Expectations: What you expect, including deliverable time frames and boundaries, must be identified. Expectations need to be reasonable and clearly understood. Assuming that they will be met without clarifying what is expected will lead to failure.

If you are a parent, you have likely discovered that your idea of what constitutes a clean bedroom is somewhat different from the average child's (or the health department's) idea on the subject. Unless you have made it clear in advance that cleaning under the bed and emptying the trash are part of what you expect when you say "clean your room," those things are unlikely to happen. Years ago, I went into our kitchen after one of the kids assured me his cleaning assignment was done, only to find the dishes themselves had been washed, but the rest of the kitchen was a wreck. When rousted out from in front of the TV and confronted with the problem, he said simply, "You didn't tell me to clean the whole kitchen, only to do the dishes." I learned to be more specific about my expectations, and my son learned that smart-alec tricks resulted in loss of TV time.

The same idea is true of your accounting staff. It is important that what you expect of them be clearly defined. Even if they are not deliberately trying to put something over on you, your expectations of how things are to be done are probably different from theirs. If you don't know how to set up job descriptions, duties, and limits for your accounting staff, engage a knowledgeable, outside CPA to help you.

A nosey boss is Kryptonite to an embezzler—use it to your advantage!

It will be difficult for you to monitor or evaluate the accountant's actions if you have not taken the trouble to define what you want. Additionally, as the owner, your priority will be to keep your company safe and well run in a manner you can understand, while accountants may want to do things in ways they are accustomed to, which may or may not be in your best interests. It will also be tremendously helpful for you to understand what your accountant is doing, as well as where and how your records are kept.

Expectations must also be *reasonable*. Expecting someone to do things they don't know how to do (like requiring a bookkeeper to handle complicated tax filings) is not reasonable. Neither is demanding that a lengthy task be completed in a fraction of the time required for completion, or that multiple tasks be finished simultaneously. Remember that expectations are to be *clearly understood*, and *reasonable!*

Verifications: It would be nice to think everything in your accounting department is in perfect order, but don't assume it is. Business owners need to personally and continually verify that expenses, payables, reimbursements, etc., are valid.

Revisiting the analogy of a child cleaning his room, consider this: If your son knows that you may walk down the hall and stick your head in the door to verify the room is clean, he will probably clean everything visible from where you open the door and stand. If he knows that in the history of the world you have never gotten down on your hands and knees to look under the bed, that is where all things he doesn't want you to see will be shoved and hidden. It will quickly become a stinky repository for old gym socks, half eaten bananas, failed math tests, and so forth.

> **Remember what your grandmother told you about letting the fox guard the hen house!**

If someone in your company has something she wants to hide from you, she will also take care to keep the things you are likely to look at in good order, while hiding all of the "stinky stuff" where she knows you never check. If your accountant knows that you review reports with her monthly, but never look at source documents, she will know that she can do nearly anything she wants with the *real* paperwork, as long as the reports look good. Think about that:

Unless you have good prevention and detection controls in place, you are allowing the person with the most *access* to your money to be the only person in charge of what you *know* about your money.

Most people won't take advantage of that situation, but some will, and the results can bankrupt you. Remember what your grandmother told you about letting the fox guard the hen house? It turns out that Grandma was a pretty smart gal!

Besides determining what you should be looking at, you must be consistent and random when doing it. No, I am not contradicting myself. Everyone in your business should know that, sooner or later, you are going to personally have your nose in everything that is going on. They just don't know when. In fact, make it a habit to pull out random invoices, credit card statements, expense reports, etc., after everyone has left the office, and then ask questions about them the next day.

No questions? That's not the point. The point is to make it clear that you are a "loose cannon" about looking at your financial documents! If they know that the first Tuesday of every month you review the bank accounts, they also know that the day after the first Tuesday means they have nearly a month before you will look again. That is a lot of time to commit fraud and cover it up.

A nosey boss is Kryptonite to an embezzler—use it to your advantage!

Consequences: Actions have consequences; depending on what has happened, they can be positive or negative—but should be stated.

I love cake, and would eat it three times a day if it didn't make me fat. Why did I bring that up? Consequences. Wanting to maintain a healthy and attractive body weight is the primary reason I eat well. Getting on the scale and seeing a weight gain after a decadent weekend of eating out really motivates me to do some extra running and have a salad for lunch. It is an effective consequence for eating badly or over-indulging, and encourages me to get right back on the healthy-eating bandwagon!

Likewise, in order to be effective, a consequence must be meaningful to your employees. I once heard a child psychologist in response to the statement *my kids are driving me crazy*, respond with the observation: "Your children don't care about your mental health; they care about what you *do*." If they lose television or ice cream privileges for hitting their brother or (as my grandmother would say) for sassing you, they will probably take care not to do those things.

What is meaningful and matters to your employees? What would they not want to lose?

Perhaps you are uncomfortable enforcing consequences if that has not been a part of your company culture up until now. Get over it. Immediately set up positive consequences to reward and and encourage people who are doing well, and use negative ones to train or eliminate those who need improvement. Don't be afraid to change how you have done things in the past. Nagging people is not particularly effective, but sending them home on unpaid leave for a few days will probably get their attention.

Some actions should be clearly understood by all to be firing offenses. You will remember from Chapter 2, *Why I Was an Easy Target and You Probably Are, Too!* that dishonest employees can find many ways to obtain company checks and misuse them. Because of the risk this poses to your company, you should never let an employee destroy a check—that's your job. If everyone knows that you alone are authorized to destroy a ruined or voided check, and that it is a serious disciplinary offense for anyone else to do so, you will have come a long way toward safeguarding your check stock.

Even a warning intended to double as a training talk will be taken much more seriously if you put it in writing, along with the consequences for a future infraction. Because most fraud is simple, the solutions are also simple.

I am only one, but still I am one.

I cannot do everything,

But I still can do something;

And because I cannot do everything

I will not refuse to do the something that I can do.

—Edward Everett Hall, *A Year of Beautiful Thoughts*

Summing Up

Do not let yourself be deceived into thinking that fraud is so complex that you don't have the power to control it. You can—and you must!

CHAPTER 5

Money Leaks

**One of the primary reasons business owners resist
the use of controls is the idea that someone could—or *would*—
steal vast amounts of money right under their noses
doesn't seem possible.**

In our family, we have a weekly tradition of a sit-down Sunday dinner using my best china. Even though our eight children are grown and gone, my husband and I still enjoy doing it. Recently, during one of our nice dinners, I took a drink from a piece of vintage stemware and realized that some of the red juice in it had dripped on my white tablecloth. I wiped it up and went on eating.

A few minutes later, I took a second drink and noticed another drop of red had run down the glass. I blotted my lips, wondering how I could not have noticed that I was spilling my juice. A third time, I picked up my glass and saw a small pool of red dripping off the foot of the glass. It was at that point that I realized that I was not being messy; there was a leak in the glass. Because of all the etching, finding the crack was impossible. However, you can't argue with red stains on a white tablecloth; the evidence speaks for itself—there is a leak somewhere. And so it can be with a money leak in your business.

Just looking at the glass there is no visible clue there is a leak; the etching obscures the crack. Yet, I know the crack is there because the fluid inside is escaping. Red juice on a white cloth cannot easily be mistaken for anything else, but money issues are a different matter.

You may be aware of occasional financial surprises in your business, but unless you have educated yourself, you may not be aware that some of them may indicate the existence of fraud. You may experience the leak without realizing you need to look for a crack—potential financial fraud—before it becomes a massive flood. Leaks frequently look like simple cash flow or management problems: a high number of voided checks; vendors you thought had been paid calling for payment; an over-abundance of office supply orders; repairs on equipment you didn't think were needed; or a variety of other possibilities.

Your business is basically a bucket full of money.

My story is not one of hundreds; rather, it's one of millions. With the great majority of individuals employed by small businesses and organizations, the vulnerability and potential of being defrauded is exponential. The typical organization loses a median of five percent of revenues each year due to fraud. Keep in mind that, since fraud losses come directly off your bottom line, a five percent loss on total revenue may reflect lost profits of fifty percent or more. Now, look at the "soft" losses—the indirect costs: reduced productivity; low employee morale; and tarnished brand images.

The bottom line: Your business is basically a bucket full of money and you need to know exactly where money can leak out, and what the evidence of a leak is likely to be. Let's take a look at how an embezzler may be making or using cracks in your business.

Potential Money Leak #1

As a typical and often overwhelmed business owner, you delegate critical tasks to others in the name of efficiency, with no idea how, why, or if you should monitor them.

The embezzler thinks, "My boss loves it that I seem so dedicated and organized; he thinks I am the perfect employee! He never takes the time to look through any time-consuming piles of financial paperwork. He thinks I do it all to save him the trouble of reviewing it himself! He loves it that I sort it all out and compile beautiful, orderly reports he can review quickly. He thinks delegating important financial tasks to me helps him run the company more efficiently. He doesn't understand that this lets me rewrite the company records however I want. I make a bundle on the side, and he doesn't even suspect what I'm up to!"

When a trusting, and probably overworked, employer lets himself believe he is too busy to personally review and verify ordinary, everyday financial transactions, you can be assured his business is at risk. The distance this creates between what the owner sees, and what the accountant chooses to show him, is a danger zone to be avoided at all costs. A dishonest accountant can use feigned organization, efficiency, and helpfulness to manipulate a busy owner into giving him all the unsupervised access needed to financially destroy a company.

Behavioral red flags—like a minimum wage employee showing up with a new Porsche—should be obvious enough to attract some attention. But to the untrained eye, other activities can easily masquerade as great work ethics. Most employees who do the things listed on the following page are hardworking people and honest to the core. And yet, there are some who are not. Unless you recognize the potential danger these situations pose to your business, and you are prepared to either forbid these kinds of activities or closely monitor them, you may be giving your *perfect employee* a safe and easy opportunity to destroy your business.

A few of the most common "work ethic" imposters are:

- *He is so conscientious—he never takes his vacation days.* He may be afraid to leave because someone could discover what he has been up to unless he is there to keep it covered up. In fact, many embezzlements are caught in just this way—mine was!

- *She always comes in early and stays late.* She could also rely on those after-hours work sessions to give her the privacy to do things that she doesn't want anyone to see.

- *He even takes work home on the weekends—what a hard worker!* He now has an opportunity to freely alter your records and documents without the danger of anyone walking in and catching him.

- *She is always going the extra mile and taking on additional responsibilities without being asked.* In fact, we were able to cut back on our office staff because she works so hard. She now has access to more areas of your company, with fewer people involved to see what she is doing. This is very dangerous for your business.

- *He can find any records I need almost instantly, but doesn't allow anyone else in the company near his files because he doesn't want them messing anything up.* He is a total perfectionist about this! As in the other scenarios, the less transparency and oversight there is, the safer and easier it is to steal.

Potential Money Leak #2

The business owner adopts the attitude that standard business financial practices are an unnecessary waste of time. This is especially dangerous for innovative, life-hacking, young entrepreneurs who may feel that doing business in a modern way means abandoning "old-fashioned" business controls.

The embezzler thinks, "My ambitious young boss thinks all that fraud prevention mumbo-jumbo is for old-school Fortune 500 companies—not new entrepreneurial companies like us. I have access to everything, with no one looking over my shoulder!"

I know I have already said this, but it bears repeating: A *small business of less than 100 people is literally 100 times more likely to be embezzled than a larger company.* My questions for you are: Could that be you? Do you have less than 100 employees? And, what do *you* intend to do to protect your company?

In upcoming chapters, I will guide you to evaluate different areas of your business, looking for where you may be vulnerable to fraud, and setting up controls to protect you. To get you ready for that evaluation and help you become attuned to what to look for, first I'm going to cover two basic questions:

1. What are accounting *controls*?

2. Where are *money leaks* likely to happen?

Just as the name implies, an accounting control is a method of controlling how your financial instruments— cash, bank accounts, checks, credit cards, etc.—are handled. There are two basic types of controls: *prevention* and *detection*.

A prevention control is intended to prevent fraud, and a detection control is the failsafe to detect anything that might slip through. When

Some years ago, I had an accounting program in my office that I hated! I thought it was the most inefficient, poorly designed program I had ever used. Years later, and now a major embezzlement survivor, I understand that the things I thought were poor design were, in fact, accounting controls. For instance, once I completed making an invoice, in order to save it the system required me to "post" it. Once the invoice was posted, I could no longer edit it. If I needed to make an adjustment later, all I could do was void it and run an entirely new invoice. I couldn't even delete the invoice and redo it correctly using the same invoice number.

I didn't understand at the time that not being able to alter or delete posted invoices meant that many types of common fraud would be very difficult to conceal. Knowledge is power; be a strong and educated business owner.

you have clear, simple controls in place an embezzlement may not be impossible, but it certainly becomes a lot more difficult and dangerous for a would-be thief.

That all sounds pretty basic, and it is. But, and it's an essential "but," unless you are a trained accountant you probably don't really understand what comprehensive controls are, how to set them up, which specific ones are most critical for your business, or even what activities they are intended to prevent. Without that understanding, you will probably view controls as an annoyance and circumvent them on a regular basis, especially since some may seem redundant.

It is imperative as the owner, you understand the *why* of your accounting controls and become firmly committed to using them properly. If you don't understand clearly how controls protect you and what you are being protected from, you will use them carelessly, if at all. Let's be honest, controls take some time and effort to use. Setting them up may even be emotionally difficult for you because it means you are admitting that the people you work with and probably care about, could try to steal from you. I've got news for you: Dealing with the fact that someone you care about actually *did* steal from you is harder, so put on your grown-up pants and deal with it.

Common examples of *prevention* controls in sensitive areas where money may leak out include:

- **All checks are locked up in a secure place.** A single pilfered check can cost you thousands of dollars. Ideally, all checks should be in a locked safe.

- **Immediately log any check removed from the safe.** Knowing what checks are issued, outstanding, and reconciled will help protect you from one of the most common and expensive types of fraud—simple check forgery.

- **Get your own mail.** Get your own mail for one week, and as you go through it ask yourself, "What could a dishonest person do with this?" You will be amazed at how sensitive your mail really is.

- **Reconciling bank statements should not be done by the person who issues the checks** (unless that's you). This is called "segregation of duties" and it prevents someone who is stealing or altering checks from falsifying your books to cover it up. In a small business such segregation may not always be practical, but it does mean that you will need to be especially careful about your detection control procedures.

- **Have a system for setting up new vendors.** Setting up a vendors in your system is a big deal. It means that those persons or businesses are authorized to receive payments through your accounting system. Once vendors are entered in your system, processing a check to them is usually a piece of cake. *Before* they are entered in your system make sure that vendors are legitimate, not shell companies for dishonest employees, their family members, or businesses willing to pay kickbacks.

As you can see, these systems are intended to *prevent* fraud leaks from occurring in the first place. Next come *detection* controls.

- **Regularly compare your check register**—which you verified was correct at the time you signed the checks—with your online bank statement. If someone managed to get past your prevention controls for authorizing checks, this will detect check forgery or other electronic fraud schemes that steal money directly from your bank account.

- **Always be the first person to review your monthly bank statements.** Look them over carefully. Review the copies of your cancelled checks and see if anything looks as though it has been altered. In my situation, my accountant was showing her forged checks in our check register as transfers to other company accounts or payments to legitimate vendors. She had a complex shuffling system that was intended to confuse anyone who took just a quick look. Had I cross-checked the bank statements and required authorization for transfers, I would have caught the fraud in its early stages.

- **Review incoming invoices and your Accounts Payable carefully prior to paying them.** Go over them with people in your business who can confirm anything you are not sure about. Additionally, never be afraid to go to multiple people within your company, or to call the vendor directly, to confirm what you are told. Verifying that a bill is legitimate before paying it is not an insult—it is good business! Someone else may detect a fraudulent invoice or overpayment that you missed.

Set up your controls in such a way that:

- You clearly understand what specific kinds of activities you are looking for, and what a red flag could mean.

- They are simple and efficient enough that you will commit to consistently following them.

- Your employees know that you are continually looking at things, even if they don't know exactly what or when. Be proud of being called a nosey boss!

Even if you don't prevent a theft, you'll probably detect it.

Potential Money Leak #3

Allowing yourself, the business owner, to believe people you care about would never steal from you. The most horrific thing about this situation is when the embezzlement occurs, you lose not only your money, but also your friend!

The embezzler thinks, "He'll never check on what I'm doing. We've been friends for over thirty years!"

The Three F's: Friendship, Faith, and Family

Friendship

One of the primary reasons that a business owner resists the use of controls is the idea that someone could—*or would*—steal vast amounts of money right under his or her nose doesn't seem possible. Particularly in a small business where employees are likely to be friends and family members, it can seem almost insulting to set up systems that make it clear you are watching what people are doing. Some of you aren't going to like this, but the fact you consider someone a friend does not mean you should automatically trust them. Ouch!

Without having standards to measure against, you may not even know what to look for.

Like most people, I have friends whose marriages have broken up over marital infidelity. Sadly, it is a common problem. If you find yourself falling into the trap of thinking you don't need accounting controls because of the relationships you have with your staff, remember this:

> If someone will casually violate what many people consider a sacred vow and betray a loved one over basic physical gratification, why would you be surprised to have someone with whom you have a much less formal and committed relationship betray your trust because they want money—yours?

A true friend will understand and support your desire to protect your business. Keep in mind that the very fact you consider someone a friend probably means you would never think to look at what they are doing, unless you have a professional system that requires you to do so. When you set up a formal system that requires you to review all aspects of your company's financial transactions on a regular basis as part of your normal business procedures, you make it clear that this is a professional practice, done by businesses everywhere. It is completely impersonal; it's business.

Without a system, you put yourself in the position of having to walk into your accounting office and randomly start looking through things. This will feel far more like snooping for both you and your accounting staff. Furthermore, without having standards or processes to measure against, you may not even know what to look for.

If you think that setting up controls and reviewing your accountant's work sounds uncomfortable, just picture instead sitting in a courtroom with your former "friend/accountant" and her crying family while she is sentenced to years in prison for a crime that could have been prevented if you had known what to do to. Take it from me: *it stinks. And no amount of time or discomfort spent on financial controls could possibly be worse!*

Faith

Just as faith is the bedrock of many people's lives, shared faith is the foundation of many personal and business relationships. We feel safe and secure in a community of others who are committed to the same things we are.

This is not limited to a shared religious faith—it could be a causation —a charity, a booster club, an HOA, even a school fundraiser. You let down your guard. Without question, you assume that people who say they are committed to the same principles you are will conduct their lives in ways that reflect that commitment.

Many times that is a correct assumption, but consider this: Churches and charities that experience financial fraud are nearly always victimized by members, their own. Such embezzlers are frequently leaders or treasurers, holding positions of trust within those organizations.

If people will steal from their own churches or their children's clubs, why would you assume your business is safe from theft just because your accountant goes to church on Sunday or supports the local sports team?

In 2013 just under four percent of embezzlements targeted churches, and eight percent involved nonprofits. That means that religious groups and organizations who exist to serve others represent nearly 12 percent of reported fraud cases. Additionally, *the average loss for a nonprofit was $673,884.* These organizations suffer a real double whammy from such a theft. Not only do they lose money to the embezzler, but most exist almost exclusively on donations, many

> Increasing at an annual rate of nearly six percent, *Sharefaith* magazine revealed in September of 2015, researchers expect church financial fraud to reach the $60 billion mark by 2025.

of which dry up when donors find out their hard-earned contributions have been stolen through what may be viewed as carelessness or neglect.

In a church embezzlement, the thief may be the young minister with a lovely wife and three beautiful children; the woman who has been the church secretary and ladies' auxiliary chair for over 30 years; or a respected local banker who is also head deacon and in charge of counting the weekly offerings. In a business embezzlement, the fraudster could be someone who has prayed with you, brought in meals when your father died, or worked tirelessly with you on fundraisers.

Sadly, people who will work for good causes and are very sincere in their beliefs, may also steal from you or your organization. Religious people are not perfect, and they deal with the same problems and temptations that nonbelievers do. You cannot assume that outward faith is a guarantee of inner honesty. In both our churches and businesses, we need to be responsible stewards of the resources in our keeping, and we can use accounting controls to fulfill those obligations in a loving and respectful way.

Family

When one of our younger daughters was preparing to take her driver's test, her big brothers decided to play a trick on her. I am not sure who started it, but one of the four boys told her that the stop signs with white borders around them were optional—drivers only had to slow down and check for traffic before rolling through them. Because they had been playing practical jokes on each other for years, they spun this story like professional actors.

When Brother #1 started the story, she didn't believe him so she asked Brother #2. Brother #2 was not even in on the joke at this point, but when she told him what Brother #1 had said, he already knew the gig and played along. When she verified the story with Brother #3, he fell right in line, confirming what the other two culprits had said, and so on with Brother #4.

When I happened to accidentally overhear her informing a friend of her newfound knowledge about traffic signs, I hit the roof! If you remember mom Lois from the TV series *Malcolm in the Middle*, you will be pleased to know that I did her proud! I was floored my daughter would believe her big brothers over the written information in the driver's manual.

Next, I got those boys by the ears (figuratively speaking, since they were all over 6 feet tall by this point) and demanded to know what the *heck* they thought they were doing. Didn't they realize that she would flunk her driving test? (Snicker, snicker…) That she could get a ticket? (More snickering…) That someone could be hurt or killed by a car rolling through a busy intersection? (Goofy silence, as they started to finally think about it.)

When I yelled, "What in the world were you thinking?" the only response I got was the universal excuse for every bad decision since Adam ate the apple, "I don't know …" And they probably didn't know; it just seemed like a good idea at the time.

They didn't mean any harm; they were just playing a joke without thinking through the ramifications. And, by the way, not only are these guys extremely intelligent, they were all grown men when this occurred, and one was married and had a young child!

Too often, people do dumb things without considering what the eventual consequences for themselves or others are likely to be. When it comes to embezzlement, the idea that someone could end up bankrupt or in jail is not often considered during the thrill of grabbling a little extra cash. And in reality, the "E" word (embezzlement) isn't in their vocabulary. Most don't start with the thought, *Hmmm, I wonder how much I can steal today?*

Friendship, Family, and Faith are not accounting controls—they are relationships and you must never confuse them!

No, it often starts with a small "borrow"—a few dollars to tide them over, then a few more. It rarely occurs to them to hang the label "thief" around their necks.

Even worse, people who are in business with family members often ignore even the most basic advice about adopting accounting controls, just as my daughter ignored the driving manual. They do not believe a family member would ever deceive them. I wish this were true, but it is not.

Actor Dane Cook hired his half-brother to handle all his business affairs in the 1990s. Over a four-year period of time, the brother and his wife siphoned off more than $12,000,000 from Cook. That abruptly ended when a $3,000,000 check the half-brother wrote to himself caught the attention of the actor. After an extensive investigation, his half-brother pleaded guilty to 27 counts of larceny over $250 each, three counts of forgery, embezzlement and other charges.

Interestingly, he was a former corrections officer. After completing six years of jail time, he will serve 16 years of probation; his wife was sentenced to three years in prison and 13 years probation. They have also been ordered to repay Cook the money they stole. Cook was someone who made significant amounts of money and could have taken greater steps to protect his assets, yet he didn't. He assumed the same level of trust that you and I do when it comes to family members.

Real statistics on the involvement of family members are hard to come by since this is considered by many to be the most under-reported of all fraud crimes. Some sources estimate that at least a third of all embezzlements involve family members. There is a whole different level of complexity involved when a family member steals. These relationships span a lifetime and can be filled with unresolved issues.

The devastation caused by financial fraud within a family business can easily destroy the business *and* the family.

Some may feel they are righting wrongs from the past by evening things up. Others, that they are entitled to share in your success and that it is all "family money" anyway. Maybe that was the motivator for Dane Cook's brother. Additionally, a family member may feel a deep level of shame at needing money to resolve debts, which may be the result of irresponsibility or bad decisions. They may even intend to pay you back someday, just like in sixth grade when your brother borrowed your bike without permission, but then wrecked it on the way home and couldn't buy you a new one.

The devastation caused by financial fraud within a family business can easily destroy the business *and* the family. Money can be replaced; family cannot. Just try to imagine having Christmas dinner with your siblings after one of them has bankrupted your business because their spouse had a gambling problem you didn't know about, and they cleaned you out to try and save their home.

These scenarios happen every day. In a family business the *family* is the most important asset; protect your family relationships by making sure that they are never destroyed by theft.

Get Your Thinking Cap Out and On

Years ago I read an article that listed funny answers children gave in response to questions about their mothers. My favorite was, "Why did your mom marry your dad?" The child answered, "Well, Grandma says she wasn't wearing her thinking cap."

Out of the mouths of babes comes wisdom. When you set up the running of your business, were you wearing your thinking cap? For most small business owners, an amazingly small amount of attention is paid to the details of financial management. It is so much easier to just hire someone to do all the nitty-gritty for you. After all, you want to put your energy into the growth of the business, right? Plus, since most of us have limited (or perhaps nonexistent) business training, we probably don't know what procedures we need to set up in the first place.

If that is you, as it used to be me, don't worry! Safeguarding your business doesn't have to be difficult or confusing. Just follow the guidelines in the upcoming chapters and you will be well on your way to a safe and secure management plan. You have probably invested a sizeable chunk of your life, as well as your financial security, in your business. Start guarding it as though your life, or at least your lifestyle, depended on it. It does.

Summing Up

Since my experience, I have studied fraud cases where the victim company had a good control system set up. However, because it was not *used*, embezzlement occurred anyway. Accounting controls are like seatbelts; they work only if you use them.

CHAPTER 6

Red Flags
and Tornadoes

As a life-long Missourian, not only am I a self-proclaimed connoisseur of great barbeque, I can smell a tornado coming from miles away.

I grew up smack in the middle of an area in the Midwest that is universally known as Tornado Alley. We have a lot of tornadoes, and we have them on a very regular basis. In fact, we have them so often that many of us get pretty casual about the whole thing. I have been known to point out in jest that in Missouri when a warning siren is heard, it is time to get your video camera and go stand in the front yard—where most of your neighbors are—and wait for something exciting to happen!

In reality, a tornado is a deadly event, and you had better know when to be on the lookout and how to protect yourself; your life, and the lives of your family members, may be depending on it. Although we joke about it, probably as a coping strategy to deal with a dangerous situation, tornadoes are no joking matter.

There are two levels of tornado alert. The first is a tornado watch, meaning no tornadic activity has been detected yet, but the conditions are ideal for one to occur. Although you do not need to take cover, it's wise to be on the alert. The second, a tornado warning, is serious. It means that an actual tornado has been spotted and if you are in its path, take cover immediately. Huddling in a dark basement with sirens blaring and a house-rattling storm going on overhead is a terrifying experience.

Anyone who has spent much time living in this area doesn't need the weatherman to know when conditions are ripe for a tornado. The color of the sky, the sounds outside, the feel of the air, all tell you that the weather is becoming unstable; it's time to check the weather radar and see what's up. You can simply feel it in the air. Even if there is no storm going on, you can step outside and know immediately that trouble is afoot. A trained meteorologist can give you all sorts of scientific facts coupled with the barometric pressure readings and so forth. Interesting, but not necessary. All you need to know is that it's tornado weather.

Financial Fraud Is Like a Tornado

You may be wondering if this can possibly have anything to do with financial fraud; I assure you it does. When you read any standard accounting books about fraud, they will all give lists of Red Flags, which are warning signs that fraud may be occurring. This is good information to know, but keep in mind that in fraud, just as in tornadoes, there are different levels of alert.

Conditions conducive to fraud always existed prior to the occurrence of fraud.

A red flag is like a tornado warning; it means that fraud may have already occurred and you are seeing the evidence of it. Like a tornado, financial fraud is deadly and can quickly suck the life out of your business. What is left is devastation. Sometimes, total destruction. You should be very familiar with red flags and what they can mean. But, understand this: A business fraud red flag is ultimately a sign of failure.

Just as a tornado warning (meaning a tornado has occurred) is always preceded by a watch (meaning conditions were ideal for one), when financial fraud occurs, conditions conducive to fraud always existed prior to the occurrence of fraud. A red flag, or occurence of fraud, is always preceeded by a yellow flag, or opportunity for fraud.

Because preventing fraud is always better than detecting fraud, I'm going to expand your understanding of accounting flags to include green, yellow, and red flags. As you learn to evaluate the financial security of your company, you will be looking at the ways you do many things and determining what level of financial security you have in each area. Most likely you have not given extensive thought to either. As you do your analysis, you will be rating these areas with different colored flags to denote your level of security in each one.

> I realized that I had paved the way for this crime to happen right under my nose.

- **Green flags are used to indicate that an area is secure.** It means that you have looked at it carefully, considered whether any opportunities exist that a thief could take advantage of to do you harm, and you have set up controls to manage any potential risk. *A green flag means that you have consciously and deliberately looked at this area as with the eyes of a thief and taken effective steps to protect your company.*

- **Yellow flags are used to indicate that an area is not secure.** It means you have found conditions that are ideal for fraud to occur, or in other words, a fraud tornado watch. Once you start thinking like a thief, you will probably be amazed at the opportunities that you have unknowingly left wide open for dishonest people to take advantage of. *A yellow flag means there is work to be done to ensure the security of your company.* Turning your yellow flags into green flags will be your primary goal in implementing the FraudPoints System.

- **Red flags mean you may have a real problem on your hands.** It means that you may already have a financial tornado on the ground, sucking the cash flow, and life, out of your business! Not all red flags will turn out to be actual fraud, just as not every tornado warning means that your house is going to wind up blown into the Land of Oz. It does indicate you are dealing with a major risk factor that must be taken seriously, immediately.

I believed my embezzlement came out of the clear blue sky. I was wrong, and was amazed at the yellow flags that had been waving in my face for years. In fact, many of them were red ones that I had ignored—and didn't want to believe were flying high, even after revealed in our investigation. Had I understood the yellow flags that existed everywhere in my company and changed them to green ones, I would never have been faced with the catastrophic results of my ignorance. I cannot even tell you how stupid I felt, sitting across my desk from an FBI agent, as he asked me question after question about how I handled financial processes in my company. What I realized was that I had paved the way for this crime to happen right under my nose.

The areas you will be evaluating for risk are areas I also evaluated, but my evaluation was part of a gut-wrenching federal investigation into a Class A felony. I promise that changing your yellow flags into green ones will be much easier than digging to the roots of the red flags, and sending someone to prison in the process.

Get Ready for the FraudPoints System (FPS)

To prepare you to start setting up your own FraudPoints System, I want to take you through a brief assessment of how you are doing things in each of three designated areas: Mail, Accounts Payable, and Accounts Receivable.

Pick the options that are closest to how you do these things, and be totally honest. It is essential that you carefully evaluate your fraud exposure in these areas if you are going to be able to set up a more secure system.

Mail

Who handles your incoming mail?

☐ The accountant always gets the mail, opens it, distributes it, and processes it.

☐ Whoever happens to be around when the mail comes, gets it and puts it on the accountant's desk.

☐ I always get my own mail, and review everything before releasing it to the appropriate members of my staff.

☐ If none of the above applies to you, what are you doing?

Who takes your outgoing mail—which includes checks—to the post office?

☐ The accountant mails everything herself, because that way she knows it has been done.

☐ All of the outgoing mail goes into a basket, and whoever is going to the post office takes it.

☐ I mail all payments myself, but allow staff to handle regular daily correspondence.

☐ If none of the above applies to you, what are you doing?

Accounts Payable

How do you approve the bills that need to be paid?

☐ I ask the accountant to figure out what bills need to be paid and tell me how much it will cost.

☐ The accountant brings me a list of everything that needs to be paid, and I review her recommendations before authorizing the payments.

☐ I review and verify all of the bills before giving them to the accountant to enter into the system, and then carefully review a current AP report before authorizing which bills I want to pay.

☐ If none of the above applies to you, what are you doing?

How do you store your blank checks?

☐ They are in the accountant's desk drawer.

☐ The accountant keeps them locked up in a file cabinet and gets out what she needs when I tell her to pay the bills.

☐ I lock the check stock in my safe. I log the check numbers when I remove them, and I verify that each check I remove from the safe and give to the accountant to process comes back to me to sign.

☐ If none of the above applies to you, what are you doing?

What do you do if someone you know you sent a check to calls and says they never received it?

☐ I ask the accountant to make sure the check didn't clear the bank, and then have her issue a new check and stop payment on the lost one.

☐ I look online to be sure the check never cleared the bank, then give the accountant a new check to pay the bill and ask her to stop payment on the old one.

☐ I review my AP report from the previous payment period to verify the payment was processed, I check my online bank account for the missing check number, I personally call the bank and stop payment on the check, and then remove and log a replacement check, which I sign and mail personally.

☐ If none of the above applies to you, what are you doing?

Accounts Receivable

What do you do with payments that come in the mail?

☐ The accountant enters and deposits them, then tells me what the bank balance is.

☐ The accountant shows me all the payments that came in the day's mail, and then she takes them to the bank for deposit.

☐ I separate the checks when I open the mail, mark each one off on my AR report, stamp them with my personalized company "For Deposit Only" stamp, add them up, note the total amount in my Business Bible, give them to the accountant to drop off (or I do it myself, if possible), and then watch the online bank account for the deposit to post.

☐ If none of the above applies to you, what are you doing?

What do you do with delinquent accounts?

☐ After having the accountant call and send them a final notice or a nasty letter, I have their account sent to a collection agency.

☐ I send the company a letter myself, asking it to contact my office and make payment arrangements with my accountant.

☐ I personally call the manager or owner of the business, asking him to research the bill and contact me directly with what he finds. I keep a copy of the unpaid invoice in my private files so I am able to follow up on it myself.

☐ If none of the above applies to you, what are you doing?

That took just a few minutes. Did any of the questions start you thinking? Have you determined if you are a "hands-on" or "hands-off" person? Are there areas that you should be more involved with? All of the answers to the above questions contained either red, yellow, or green flags; were you able to see them? Now consider your own business practices; what flags do you see there?

Summing Up

No one wants to go through a financial fraud. Ironically, most fraud is easily prevented. It starts with your business mail, your accounts payable, and accounts receivable. When these areas are addressed and essential systems are put in place, you will reduce your vulnerability significantly.

CHAPTER 7

An Ounce of Prevention: The Business Bible

The Business Bible is a simple idea that is so powerful, gives you so much security, and saves you so much time, I am still amazed it is not taught in every business school in America.

I have a good friend who is a professional architect and works for a large company. Several years ago he and another architect decided to form a partnership and start handling small private clients on the side, with the intent of growing into a full-time practice. He handled some of the initial expenses personally, paying for all of their office rent, phone, and internet services.

One day he asked to speak to me privately in regard to a business issue that he was obviously upset about. He shared that a client he had contracted with and his partner had done most of the work for, had paid the partner directly for the design services. Rather than depositing the payment into the checking account set up specifically for the LLC, the partner simply deposited the funds into his personal account. (In fact, my friend discovered this payment completely by accident when, during a design meeting, he asked the client what arrangements he would like to make to handle his bill and was told it had already been paid in full.) No money was paid into the partnership bank account to cover future expenses, nor was there any offer to reimburse my friend for expenses he had already paid personally. Since I have run a business for over twenty years, he wanted my opinion about what to do. I was happy to oblige and so I asked him some questions.

First, I asked what the written guidelines of their partnership agreement were. They didn't have any. Next I asked how they intended to distribute income. They had not discussed it. I asked for the details about how he was to be reimbursed for the expenses that he was paying on behalf of the partnership. Again, there were no plans for repayment. And so it went for every question I had. Although an LLC (Limited Liability Corporation) and a business bank account had both been set up, the financial planning had pretty much ended at that point.

There were plans about what kinds of clients they wanted, what their various income and professional goals were, and so forth, but no financial management plans. This is not an unusual scenario, and there are many reasons for it. To begin with, we tend to plan the things we like or are good at, but skip over the things we do not enjoy, or are just not comfortable with.

Planning how you will *spend* money is a lot more exciting than planning how you will *manage* money. You can easily develop a "someday there will be a lot of money and we will all live happily ever after" attitude that leaves you wide open for serious problems, of which financial fraud is only one.

Another reason for not planning is that discussing money can be uncomfortable, particularly with friends or family. This is especially true when discussing fraud prevention. Or in other words, dealing with the fact that you are openly acknowledging people you care about could steal from you, and you want to make it difficult and risky for them. It can feel a little like a friend asking if she can use your bathroom, but you insist on doing an inventory of your medicine cabinet before letting her close the door. Awkward, to say the least.

A financial loss could crush a small company. That means yours.

Finally, most small business owners do not have much, if any, formal business training, and even less fraud control training, so they don't know what to plan or why they should plan certain things in the first place. They wrongly assume that financial controls and formal business agreements are reserved for huge corporations, when in fact, a large company can easily weather a financial loss that would crush a small company. That means yours.

Don't let yourself fall into the trap of having your financial arrangements—whether with your business partner or your accounting staff—be vague, haphazard, or nonexistent. If you do not currently have a financial management plan that includes well-thought-out fraud prevention processes, ask yourself why.

- It could be you don't know what to do. The solution for that is simple: Educate yourself.

- It could be the possibility of encountering financial fraud is not on your radar. Few think that someone would try to steal from them. Yet the probability is, someone will.

- It could be you don't want to be the "bad guy," bringing in experts to help implement formal controls. But preventing fraud doesn't make you a bad guy—the only real bad guy is the thief.

- Perhaps the real reason is less obvious: You aren't really comfortable being *The Boss*. It is easy to fall in love with the status and perks of being "The Big #1," without feeling confident enough to accept the full spectrum of *responsibilities* that come with the position.

If you are not able to sit down with a partner, whether a family member, a friend, or a random hire, and discuss money management in a detailed, professional, no-nonsense way, you probably shouldn't be in business with him or her.

If you are not comfortable giving clear, non-negotiable instructions to your office staff, then you may want to consider whether or not you should be running a business in the first place.

And, if you are not willing to educate yourself about how a business should be run, and discipline yourself to do it properly, then you should probably go work for someone who is. That may sound harsh, but without being committed to running your business according to sound business principles, you are opening yourself up to a world of trouble.

Willingness to change is a strength,
even if it means plunging part of the company
into total confusion for a while.
—Jack Welch

Ultimately, my architect friend left the partnership, as he felt that he had been dealt with unethically, if not downright dishonestly, and he never recovered a dime of the money he had invested. I don't know if their small business would have succeeded in the long-run, but I do know that a failure to set up and adhere to a clear financial management plan ended it before they had a chance to find out.

Get your own mail and open it yourself, every single day.

Now that you know the importance of having a clear, effective financial management plan, where do you start? The answer:

- You start where you are. Don't make yourself crazy trying to jump in and change the way you do everything all at once. I tried that; it was *not* fun or effective, and no one liked me very much for a while.

- You follow the plan laid out in this book, and you do it methodically and consistently. *It is a process, not a quick fix.*

For those of you who are ready to take action on something immediately, here are three things you can do today to get started:

1. Get your own mail and open it yourself, every single day.

2. Lock up your check stock and track every check you remove.

3. Look at your online bank accounts every day.

Do not be deceived by how simple those tasks seem—they are very powerful! Each of these actions will be covered in much greater detail in their own section of The Business Bible, which begins in the next chapter. Additionally, these actions are not secretive; you *want* your employees to *know* that you are reviewing these areas. Several important things are going to happen as a result.

Lock up your check stock and track every check you remove.

There's a huge payoff for you personally and for your business. First, you are going to be in much closer touch with the inner workings of your business. You will have your finger on its pulse every day, and will no longer need to rely on others to tell you what they think is important, or be at the mercy of those who will only tell you what they want you to know.

And second, your employees will know you review the mail *before* anyone can touch it; that all checks have to be physically obtained from you; and that no matter how well things may be covered up in the office, you will be using the online bank account (which cannot be altered) to monitor and confirm all transactions. You will be the first person to see bills, past due notices, tax related communications, bank statements, credit card applications, and so forth. A great deal of the opportunity to covertly interfere with your financial affairs will disappear if you consistently do these three things.

Look at your online bank accounts every day!

That was easy and fairly painless, wasn't it? Now, you are ready to build on those basic practices and start putting together the two systems at the core of your business and financial management plan. Although each of these processes will be dealt with in detail in their own section of this book, here is an outline of what you will be putting together.

The Business Bible

The Business Bible is a simple idea which is so powerful, gives you so much security, and saves you so much time, I am still amazed it is not taught in every business school in America. The first system consists of three volumes of business documents:

1. Permanent Records

2. Annual Records

3. Working Records,

All of which you are going to keep in your office safe where they will be protected from fire, water, and dishonest people.

Start with a Full-Sized Safe... It's Not Just for Gun Freaks Anymore!

One of the first things I did after my embezzlement was to invest in a large gun safe and start locking things up. As I continued to uncover the full scope of the crime, every time I found a new way I had lost money, I looked for a way to keep it from happening again. Since check theft and forgery comprised a huge portion of my losses, checks were the first things I locked up. Over time, I developed a system to track the checks

Be sure to purchase a safe that is larger than you think you will need. Once you start "thinking like a thief," you'll be amazed at the things you want to lock up!

after I released them, which you will learn in Chapter 13, *FPS: Keeping a Check Log*, but the first step was simply to lock them up.

My purchase was a full-sized safe, and even though it seemed a little excessive at the time, now I am glad I did it. As I continued to develop my awareness of what I wanted to have personal control of, I discovered the perfect place for a number of things was a safe.

Volume One: Permanent Records. Documents you will rarely change or add to will be contained here. This is where your Articles of Incorporation, Corporate Bylaws, Stock Certificates, Partnership Agreements, Succession Plans, proof of initial financial investment, and other records relevant to the legal structure of your company, are kept. Unless you rewrite your bylaws or issue more stock (mine have not been changed in over 24 years), they never expire.

These documents are the proof that your business is actually a business. Banks, taxing authorities, attorneys, etc., may ask for these

These documents are the proof that your business is actually a business.

documents at any time, and you want them readily available. Personally, I chose to purchase a large, high quality leather notebook to house these records. It looks permanent and important, just like the records inside.

Volume Two: Annual Records. This volume contains your legally required corporate meeting records, business licenses, insurance policies, continuing education certificates, year-end financial statements, and certain tax records. Records of things which occurred during the current year, some of which you will need to keep forever, such as corporate meeting notes, as well as licenses and certificates that you will renew periodically should be filed here.

A new volume will be made each year with the previous year's volume archived. Talk to your attorney about what records you may safely destroy and when. You will not need most of these documents often; but when you do need them, you are likely to need them quickly and you will be glad to have them where they are easily located.

Volume Three: Working Records. The heart of your daily financial management plan is contained within Volume Three. By having current information on everything you need to monitor—such as log on and password information for your bank and credit card accounts—as well as a designated place to quickly save important records where they can be found later, you have set up a system that will greatly simplify your daily monitoring. This volume will increase your company's security in general. Your sensitive information now has a secure place to land, where it can easily be found when needed, and kept safe from prying eyes.

This volume includes current check registers, payroll records, credit card information, a comprehensive password list, tax deposit and filing information, payroll specifics, current accounts receivable and payable, current financial statements, a daily check-off sheet to implement your plan, and other items that are relevant to your business.

All three volumes of the *Business Bible* need to be securely stored in a fireproof safe. Volume Three: Working Records is the one you will use the most often, and which you must handle the most carefully. It can never be left out for anyone to have access to, even for a moment. And, if having all of this information in one place makes you nervous, just think how unsecure a lot of that information may be now. Your current method for storing passwords and security questions

Over 90% of the population carries a phone with a camera in it.

may be to keep them on scraps of paper in desk drawers, sticky notes, or even on rolodex cards on the accountant's desk—where I found many of mine!

Today, over 90% of the population carries a phone with a camera in it—that means you are vulnerable. Think of it: An embezzler with only a minute or two of access could photograph logon credentials for every bank, credit card, and account you have.

Most likely, since you won't want to get into your safe the multiple times a day you will probably use your Business Bible, you may want to have a desk drawer that locks so you can quickly access it as needed during the workday, while still being secured in your safe whenever you are away. Having everything at your fingertips is great for you—but just imagine how convenient it would be for a thief to have it! This way you are in complete control of who has access to this information, and can secure it appropriately.

FIFI – File It. Find It.

The second system, which allows you to quickly file and easily find important, but less sensitive information, is called *FIFI – File It. Find It.* It is a system of organized piles.

Organized, in that there is enough structure to file and find things quickly without having to hassle with a time consuming, complex system; and piles, in that you are able to put miscellaneous papers into designated places with little effort.

Once set up, it is almost as easy to put a document in an "organized" pile, where it can be quickly located as it is to throw it in a stack with a multitude of other unrelated documents. Once a paper is tossed into a random (or catch-all) pile, it may take a tremendous amount of time and effort to find, even if it is sitting on top of your desk. It also solves the problem of having an assigned place for things that you want to keep, but don't really have a formal location for.

Ask yourself: Does anyone really have a complete file set up for potential colors you might want to paint the conference room; a place to hold a company event in the future; a business article with information you want to implement; or a website that may be worth checking out whenever you have the time? What about a credit card bill with an error on it that

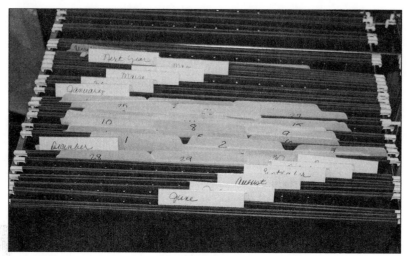

My file system with months, individual dates.

you have called about but need to remember to follow up on, or a travel document you will need three months from now?

Now, you can have all of those things at your fingertips. Properly used, this system will eliminate piles of random things on your desk (or floor) that you will need soon or might want in the future. It will enable you to have a nearly effortless way to keep temporary or permanent track of miscellaneous scraps of papers. Plus, you will have an efficient way to follow up on tasks without even taking the trouble to write them down anywhere.

You will have 12 folders, each labeled with the name of a month. You will also have a folder for each day—labeled 1-31—which will rotate behind the monthly folders, in which you will place items needed on a given day. You will also set up a place to store folders for any project or idea on the planet, including completely random and unrelated ideas. Once you *File It* in an organized pile, you should be able to—*Find It*—or lay your hands on anything you want within minutes, or even seconds. If that sounds too good to be true, keep reading!

You may be asking what any of this has to do with financial security.

A lot. Some of the systems initially set up to manage accounting controls also apply to a broad range of other business tasks. The FIFI system gives you a way to quickly file action items in such a way that you will have needed items at your fingertips in each day's file.

Each of the Business Bible volumes and the FIFI files will be covered individually in the following chapters. This way you can set them up one at a time and customize them so that they work perfectly for you. The ability to track company finances effectively, easily follow up on important tasks without searching for relevant data, and lay your hands on diverse pieces of information quickly, are now completely within your reach simply by setting up this system to manage them.

> **No institution can possibly survive if it needs geniuses or supermen to manage it. It must be organized in such a way as to be able to get along under a leadership composed of average human beings.**
> **—Peter Drucker**

Summing Up

Albert Einstein said, "Everything should be made as simple as possible, but not simpler." Ideally, knowing what should be coming into your business—and what does—must be simple; and knowing what should be going out of your business—and what does—must also be simple. Fraudsters count on business owners not wanting to know what's really going on, or being too busy to look closely. I've made the FraudPoints System as simple as possible, but not simpler. You will thank me.

CHAPTER 8

Business Bible Volume One: Permanent Records

These documents are essentially the birth certificate, driver's license, and immunization records of your business.

Welcome to the core of the FraudPoints System—your own custom Business Bible! It will save your business butt along with your emotional and financial life. Within the first few chapters of *FraudPoints!*, you discovered that embezzlement and fraud doesn't happen just to others ... *you could be next*. As a business, your vulnerability is high and will remain so unless you (and it is up to you) set up the watch dog alerts.

At first glance, *Permanent Records* may not seem to have a lot to do with financial fraud. You will discover it has a significant connection once you understand the purpose of your company records and how they can be used. Lending institutions, credit card companies, and tax attorneys routinely require many different types of official documents, or the information in them, to handle your financial and legal affairs. If you are sued, you will need many of these documents to help preserve your corporate veil and protect your personal assets. These items may also be required in the event of a tax audit. In fact, not having them may enable an aggressive auditor to disallow your business deductions, since you can easily be determined to not be a "real" business.

Be mindful that under certain circumstances an IRS agent can walk into your office and demand that you present specific documents immediately. Additionally, an attorney can subpoena them as part of a lawsuit. If you do not have them on file and up-to-date, you may not be able to repair the damage later.

Having this information secure, organized, and in one place probably puts you in the top one percent of all small businesses.

Getting Started

Your Business Bible volumes are best kept in separate 3-ring binders, with often-used documents kept in sheet protectors, where they can be easily viewed and protected from damage. Keep a dry erase marker handy for making notes without damaging the documents, as well as a pad of sticky notes to leave quick reminders like "Bob took this title to the license bureau on 7/15/17" or "Credit card checked out to Leslie 9-22-17." This way you can remove records as needed, and never lose track of where they have gone. When I check out a record to someone, he or she knows know that I have done this, and that when the record is returned, the person watches me replace it and destroy the note.

Permanent Records

Not only is it critically important for you to have these corporate records available when needed, you must understand what a dishonest person could do with them and protect yourself accordingly. With your information, any fraudster can make legal and financial commitments on behalf of your company that can destroy you. Even if you are eventually released from liability through court proceedings, the immediate consequences may be fatal to your business. Additionally, it may be difficult to get a court to absolve you of responsibility if your handling of these sensitive items is deemed negligent. A business is expected to be businesslike, and should not be operated in a casual or slipshod way.

Although you should review this list with your business attorney and CPA to determine exactly what needs to be included for your particular jurisdiction and occupation, below is a list of items for you to begin with.

Gather these things up into one place, organize them, and then lock them safely away. Although not all of the listed items

Any fraudster can use these records to make legal and financial commitments on behalf of your company that can destroy you.

will be applicable to your business, most will. Talk to your CPA or attorney to find out which are most important for you to have on hand. Additionally, many of the items on this list are for a Sub-S Corporation, which is the most common structure for small businesses. If your business is organized under a different designation, such as LLC or PC, remember that similar record-keeping requirements exist for all of them, they may just be called by different names. For instance, an LLC will have an Operating Agreement instead of Corporate Bylaws.

An online search for the record-keeping requirements for your business structure, and a quick review by your attorney, should give you the essential guidelines for your business.

To get started, print out this list, put it in the front of your Volume One notebook, add whatever additional items your business advisors feel are necessary, and check items off as you put them in. Make notes on the list about the status of certain items, such as "requested a copy from the Secretary of State's office on June 4; follow up in 30 days," or "asked CPA for this information on 8/2; call him back next week," or even "I have no idea where this is; I asked the secretary to look for it. If we can't find it by the end of the month, ask attorney how to get a replacement."

Label notebook divider tabs for each section, and then put things in their proper place to make them easy to find when needed.

As you locate these items, take the time to read them. Check them against each other. Make sure that the stock certificates issued are in compliance with your bylaws and stock ledger. If you are like many business owners, the last time you looked at these documents was probably when your attorney filed them, and you may not even have read them carefully then.

Ensure that your lists of directors and officers are up to date, and that all changes have been properly documented and filed with the Secretary of State's office. Check the schedule and notification requirements for your corporate meetings and be sure you are holding and documenting them properly. Ask your attorney to help you bring all of your current activities into compliance with your bylaws, and make proper amendments if you need to change anything. In *Volume Three: Working Records*, the notebook one you will use most often, you will have a list of what you need to do on an ongoing basis to keep your business records up-to-date.

It is *your* company, so take charge of it!

It is *your* company. You have a great deal of latitude in how you manage these details, but they must be managed. Bear in mind it is critically important that your regular business activities are in compliance with your corporate documents, and that you use the proper procedures to make changes. Not doing these simple things correctly can allow someone to pierce your corporate veil and go after your personal assets. Since asset protection is one of the most common reasons owners form corporations, not doing the little things that keep that protection in place doesn't make much sense.

Most of these requirements are fairly simple. You just need to understand which documents and procedures are required, whether you are currently in or out of compliance, and be sure that you have a plan to keep everything in order.

Once you have compiled all of the necessary documents, reviewed them, and made a written list of all questions and concerns, you will be prepared to sit down and have a productive, efficient meeting with your attorney and/or CPA. The bonus: Having your documents already put together with action items noted should help you to minimize the professional expenses required to get everything in proper order. The internet is a great place to get a lot of questions about corporate record-keeping answered for free before you start paying your attorney or CPA for his or her time.

Suggested Documents List:

- Company information sheet, with company name, address of record, any Doing Business As (to register a fictitious name), date of incorporation, state of incorporation, other states you are registered to operate in, registered agents, business license number, etc.

- Certificate of Incorporation.

- Articles of Incorporation.

- Any amendments to your Articles of Incorporation.

> **The typical executive wastes 150 hours a year (almost an entire month), searching for lost information. – *Forbes***

- Minutes of Initial Meeting (when you formed your corporation).

- Corporate Bylaws (or for an LLC, an Operating Agreement).

- Amendments to your bylaws, if any.

- Stock Certificates: Make sure that number of shares you have issued does not exceed the number stated in your bylaws. If you have questions about this, talk to your business attorney. Errors may allow your corporate status to be challenged.

- Stock ledger: Must match what is stated in your stock certificates and bylaws.

- Notice of Transaction: or whatever form is required in your state, for every issuance of stock. Many small businesses will only make a change in their stock ownership if they are selling the company, so it is entirely possible that you will not have any transactions after your initial issue.

- Shareholders agreement.

- Any fictitious name registrations (DBA - Doing Business As).

- List of Corporate Officers: This may change from time to time, but keep the original list, as well as the revised forms showing that you changed or added new members. This way you can always show the history of your corporate officers, as well as your current roster. (You will keep a list of current officers in your *Volume Two: Annual Records*, but this permanent record will show a complete history.)

- Board of Directors, and all changes to the board.

- Proof of initial investment - A cancelled check and proof of where the funds came from. Include loan documents if funds were borrowed.

- All tax identification numbers such as your FEIN and SEIN (Federal or State Employer Identification Number).

- Succession Plan: and other instructions for company management in the event of your death. Update as necessary, and file all current information here. Be sure the people who will need this information know where to find it. This is incredibly important to do! Do not think that you will live forever, because you won't. Since many small businesses support children and grandchildren, you must do all you can to make sure that your death does not inflict a mortal blow to your business, or destroy your family as they fight over what they think you wanted. Additionally, having dishonest people use fake documents to try and take over the business of a person who has died is not all that uncommon. Being a dead fraud victim is pretty much the only thing worse than being a living one.

- Corporate Seal, which should be locked up securely in your company safe.

Give each item its own tabbed section, and keep an accurate index.

Having this information secure, organized, and in one place will put you head and shoulders above most other small businesses in terms of professionalism and security. Why do I say that? I recently attended a seminar for small businesses that dealt with how to obtain small or disadvantaged business certifications—such as WBE, Women's Business Enterprise—through governmental entities. One of the presenters, who sat on the board of a certifying agency, spent considerable time discussing the documents required to submit an application.

Her list included most of the documents listed above, plus additional current year information that will be included in your *Volume Two: Annual Records,* such as financial statements. As she went through the list of necessary corporate records, people started groaning and laughing about what a hassle putting together an application seemed to be and how hard it would be to find all of the necessary documents. She stopped in the middle of her certification instructions and spoke to everyone quite pointedly about the importance of maintaining all of these documents in one place, emphasizing that everyone should already have them readily available.

Real businesses recognize the importance of keeping these things secure, on hand, and organized. If you value your business, so will you!

NOTE OF CAUTION: Do not let getting the ideal binder, setting up the sections perfectly, or obsessing over exactly how to organize the book become ways to procrastinate getting this done. If you currently have these things jammed in the back of old files, scattered around your office, or in an old safety deposit box somewhere, it will be frustrating to pull all of this together when a crisis hits. Just do it now and be done with it.

Give the list to someone on your staff and have them play hide and seek for any missing documents, if necessary. If some of your corporate records are missing, contact your Secretary of State's office to get copies—most of them are now online and you can print from their website; the same with tax records. Contact the IRS if you are missing information. Requests for missing forms and filings can usually be done online.

Having this information secure, organized, and in one place, probably puts you in the top one percent of all small businesses.

These documents are essentially the birth certificate, driver's license, and immunization records of your business. All essential. I know everyone laughed when Mitt Romney quipped, "Corporations are people, too!" but in many ways, it is true. Your company is a legal entity that is authorized to act and be acted upon, and will continue to exist after your death.

A company can earn money, file taxes, be sued, audited, fined, or killed. It is required to comply with the law, and will be punished if it does not. Properly set up and maintained, a corporate veil will protect your home and personal savings from being taken to satisfy business debt. Trying to operate your business in a safe and legal way without the required documents is like trying to travel internationally without a ticket or passport—it is chancy, at best.

Definitions and Terms Every Business Owner Should Know

These definitions are not meant to give you a full legal description, but to help you have a general understanding of what the terms mean. As always, talk to your legal professional to determine exactly how any apply to your business, and what your unique circumstances require.

Corporate Veil: a legal concept that separates the identity of a business from the identity of its owners and stockholders. It protects the owners from being held personally liable for the company's debts and actions. Although an owner can still be held responsible in cases involving negligence or criminal activity, a properly formed and maintained corporation offers a lot of protection from business debts and lawsuits. Holding an owner personally responsible for the actions of the corporation is referred to as Piercing the Corporate Veil.

Personal Assets: the personal property or bank accounts of an owner or stockholder, which are separate from the property or bank accounts of the business.

Certificate of Incorporation: this is essentially the birth certificate of your corporation, and lists its legal name, date of formation, registration with the state, etc.

Articles of Incorporation: together with your Certificate of Incorporation, this establishes the charter that gives your business legal standing as an independent entity.

Corporate Bylaws: a document that defines what a corporation does, its purpose, how it will run its affairs, and the duties and responsibilities of people who own and manage it. The basic information about your company is included in your Articles of Incorporation, but bylaws are much more detailed. They describe how the shareholders, officers, and directors are expected to run the business. They set forth how stock will be issued,when meetings will be held, how officers are appointed and dismissed, and so forth. It is a detailed plan about how the company will operate.

Amendments: a document that formally establishes changes made to the Articles of Incorporation or Bylaws. For instance, if your bylaws say your company will engage in personal fitness training activities, but you later decide to go into real estate development, you may need to file an amendment.

Board of Directors: the governing body of a corporation, with the authority to make decisions on behalf of the company.

Corporate Officers: the executives of a corporation who are charged with specific responsibilities in running the corporation. They include titles such as President, Vice President, Corporate Secretary, Treasurer, etc. The officers of the corporation may be fired by the Board of Directors who manage the affairs of the company in a more general sense.

Shareholders or Stockholders: they own shares of stock in the corporation, and may be entitled to vote on important matters, be paid dividends, and to sell their shares.

Stock Ledger: shows how much stock the company has issued, and who the owners are.

Corporate Seal: although a corporation may enter into a legal agreement, it has no ability to sign its name. A corporate seal is used to stamp or emboss the legal signature of a corporation onto official documents.

FEIN/SEIN: Federal/State Employment Identification Number is a 9-digit code that is assigned by the IRS, and is used by a business to identify it as a taxpayer. It may also be called an EIN—an Employer Identification Number. Although an unincorporated business may use the Social Security number of the owner as identification, a corporation is assigned a number that must be used for tax filing and business banking activities.

Summing Up

The nice thing about *Volume One: Permanent Records* is that once it's done, it is finished. You will very seldom make any changes to it. Additionally, the ease of being able to produce all of this information whenever it is required far outweighs the possible inconvenience of putting it all together. Having this information secure, organized, and in one place, probably puts you in the top one percent of all businesses. Putting this volume together should only take two to four hours—and much of it can probably be done by others. Get it done, lock it up, and pat yourself on the back for achieving this monumental step!

What's your maintenance after it's created? Nearly none. Just add documents that actually change your corporate structure, such as changing officers or directors, issuing new stock, or amending your bylaws.

CHAPTER 9

Business Bible Volume Two: Annual Records, Current Year

What could you do with an extra six weeks?
Multiple surveys have revealed that business executives
lose six weeks a year looking for items. Six weeks!

Now that you have your permanent records and corporate documents organized, it is time to start keeping a book of annual records. Many of the reasons for this are the same as for the others: Important records must be up-to-date, secure, and easy to find. You will love having important documents at your fingertips, and will quickly develop the habit of storing—not stuffing—important information easily and efficiently.

Although the records in *Volume One: Permanent Records* will be largely consistent for a variety of companies, *Volume Two: Annual Records* is much more individualized. You will create a snapshot of your company activities for the current year, and much of it will be archived or destroyed at the end of each year to make room for current information. Your volume will contain a mix of standard documents along with items which are completely unique to the nature, function, and location of your business. It will include industry-specific licensing and continuing education requirements, insurance binders, records of official corporate actions, various items required by your local jurisdictions, and so forth.

Ask your business consultant how long you should maintain this volume but, with the exception of corporate records (you will transfer to either *Volume One: Permanent Records* or a designated Corporate Minutes notebook at year end), at least three and up to ten years is a good storage guideline. Since they represent your company history you don't have to destroy them, but should keep them in a secure place—this volume does it.

Additionally, these notebooks are compact. If storage space is an issue, you may want to scan the records to a flash drive and shred the hard copies. Realistically, many of these records may exist in other places in your business, but having them all in one place can help you in any number of situations.

After my embezzlement, I discovered that many essential records were missing, misfiled, or nonexistent—some critical tax records had even been forged! The hours that I would have saved during the criminal investigation by having my original, intact copies easily available would have been a godsend. The hardest thing for me was that my embezzler knew exactly where all of the items I needed were located, but under the circumstances, I couldn't exactly call and ask her.

Much of the next year was spent searching for and attempting to duplicate, correct, or replace critical information. For example, I had changed my commercial insurance broker and policy several times during the years my embezzlement was occurring. This meant that I could have potentially filed claims with several different companies, depending on who carried my insurance and what my losses during that coverage period were.

Many essential records were missing, misfiled, or non-existent—some critical tax records had even been forged!

Looking for the name of multiple insurance providers from the past six to eight years was very difficult given the state of my internal records. Having a record of my insurance policies, financial statements, tax returns, etc., at my fingertips would have made my life much easier, and possibly have resulted in additional insurance payments, which I desperately needed.

Over the years I have had other less frustrating, but still problematic, issues which involved not being able to quickly lay my hands on important documents. The time spent compiling and maintaining an annual record is tiny in comparison to the problem of not having important items readily available. If you have ever had to search for a record of continuing education credits, tax filings, or a specific financial statement, you will understand. If you have not had to look for important documents yet, you are either very lucky, or you haven't been in business very long! But be mindful, your day is probably coming, so be prepared.

Remember, this volume will include things relative to the current year, but which are typically updated annually and not used daily. These things are often kept in various places around the office, and can be a terrible nuisance to locate in an emergency, if you can find them at all.

Do you know *who* has access to accounts, credit cards, and passwords?

Below is a list of corporate records that nearly all organized businesses will maintain permanently; your particular type of business or its location will influence which documents you choose to keep on hand. In the second section of this chapter is a detailed list of business-related items for you to consider storing, with recommended "maintenance" for each.

Corporate records that nearly all organized businesses will maintain forever:

- Minutes of official corporate meetings, such as the Annual Shareholders Meeting. (Since I am still the only shareholder for Obermiller Construction, it is a short meeting that includes chocolate!)

- Board of Directors meetings. (Since my daughter, her husband, and my son are the only other board members, these meetings are also short, and include even more chocolate!)

- Minutes of any other meetings that involve making important decisions for your company, such as approving large purchases, hiring management personnel, or taking out loans.

- Any issuance or sale of company stock.

- Changes to your Board of Directors or Corporate Officers.

- Registration of a fictitious name for your company (Doing Business As) and proof it was filed with your Secretary of State.

- Any records recommended by your CPA or business attorney, based on the organization of your company—LLC, Sub-S Corp, etc.

Not having your corporate records or minutes up-to-date and accurate—as directed by your legal or financial consultant—can be a huge problem for your company! Review your record-keeping requirements with them, and then follow their advice. Your Business Bible Volume Two is the perfect place to store the items they recommend for your business!

Unique business-related items to consider storing

You will also need to consider what other items you may want to store in Volume Two. This section lists a variety of documents that contain information about important activities within your business. Go through this list and consider which of the following ones apply to your situation. Skip the ones that don't apply, and add whatever else you consider important to your individual circumstances. Stop and think about important documents that you have had to look for or replace in the past and consider if they should have a place in your book.

Each item listed here also includes a maintenance note with ideas on how to handle this information at the end of the year. The following items are suggestions, but are not by any means an exhaustive list, for you to consider including in your own annual book:

- **Proof of continuing education credits earned during the year.**
  Maintenance: Move into the next year's book, so you can always prove you are current, and note when they will expire. (Check with the certifying entity for information about how long certificates should be retained.)

- **Key employee agreements and related insurance policies.**
  Maintenance: Transfer each year unless abandoned. If that happens, note the date the agreement was cancelled, and keep it in the archived book for that year.

- **Your personal financial statement: quarterly, semi-annual, or annual.**
  Maintenance: Ideally, you will update it in January after your business financial statements for the year are done. In any case, always make sure you have one that is less than a year old. You may want to leave a year-end statement in your archives for future reference.

- **Complete end-of-year business financial statements for the previous year, and monthly or quarterly ones for the current year.**
  You need to understand the difference between a Balance Sheet, a Cash Flow Statement, and a Year End Financial Statement, and whether they are based on cash or accrual. Discuss this with your CPA.

  Maintenance: Update annually, and at desired intervals during the year. I used to do annual and quarterly, but as my business has grown I changed to monthly. Make sure you have the most recent of both annual and periodic on hand, as those will be the ones most often required for financial transactions. Move a copy of the year-end statement to the current-year book when you archive the past year.

- **Copies of your current business and personal tax returns.**

  Your business returns will likely be quite lengthy, so you may want to consider keeping just the first few pages in your book and storing the schedules in your accounting office.

  Maintenance: Leave the past year's copies in the book you are archiving, and put copies of the current returns in the new book as soon as you file them. Remember, the taxes you file in the current year reflect your activity for the past year, so, for example, the taxes you file in your 2015 book are your returns for 2014.

- **A copy of your current company insurance policy.**

  Maintenance: Put a new copy in when you renew your policy, and move the old policy to the past year. If your policy is too large to include in the book, keep it in a notebook of its own and store it in the safe next to your Business Bibles.

- **Professional licenses or business permits.**

  Maintenance: As you renew them, move old copies to the archived book and file new ones in the current book. You can destroy the expired ones immediately if you choose, but it is nice to have the ability to prove you were in compliance with what was required in the recent past. A good policy is to keep at least the most recent year's documents.

- **Any documentation of physical condition or medical treatment relevant to your business activities.**

  For instance, if you have a commercial driver's license, you probably have to have an annual physical. If you have had to have drug tests, vision exams, range-of-motion evaluations, and so forth, you may want to keep a copy here. You can also keep these things in your own employee file, but if it's really critical to have on hand, a copy here might be a good idea. If your employees are required to have these evaluations, keep a copy in their employment file.

Maintenance: Keep in the archived book and file new ones in the current book.

- **Credit information, such as a Dun and Bradstreet number and your rating.**
Maintenance: Make sure you keep the Company Information sheet referred to in the previous chapter with your account number in your current book. If desired, check your rating periodically and keep a copy.

- **Proof of forgiveness of a debt, or correction to an improperly reported debt.**
This is especially important if taxes were involved (one copy here, one in accounting files).

Maintenance: Keep in archived book for the year it occurred.

- **Certificates of small or disadvantaged status for your business.**
Maintenance: Keep a current copy in this book, and move expired certificates to your archived book. If you are often asked for copies of your certification, you may choose to keep the current year in Volume 3, or keep a scanned copy on your computer. I have had to prove past certification before, so I never destroy these.

- **A list of all active bank accounts, including names of all those authorized to speak with or conduct business with the bank on your behalf, as well as contact information for your personal**

representative at the bank. Make sure your internal records match the information the bank has.

Maintenance: This will remain in the book being archived as a record of banking activity for that year. At the end of each year, make a copy of it, along with any corrections, and keep in your current volume. This is a great time to make sure no past employees are still authorized to speak to your bank regarding your accounts.

- **A list of tax filings and proof of payments made during the year.**
Maintenance: You will keep your list of current year tax filing requirements and payments in your *Volume Three: Working Records.* At the end of each year, you will move that information to your archived annual book as a permanent record.

- **Loan Documents.**
These can be large, so you may want to keep only the relevant pages, or even compile a list of loans, including the name of the lending entity, loan number, payment amount, payoff date, etc.

Maintenance: Update annually and move to current year volume.

- **List of major purchases.**
Although you have already noted the approval of major purchases in your corporate meeting notes, having a list to use when updating insurance coverage or asset lists is a real time saver.

Maintenance: Move to archived storage and start a new list for the current year.

One more, which few companies do, and even I sometimes struggle to keep accurate:

- **A list of who has access to accounts, credit cards, and passwords.**
Do you know who has keys to your office? Was issued a credit card? Has a code to your alarm system? Can make purchases from your suppliers? Document the access employees have to your physical and financial assets, and be sure to terminate the access if they leave.

Maintenance: Review and update at least annually, and store in current year book.

Take time to think about what else you want to include as you compile these items. If you aren't sure, ask your CPA, attorney, and possibly your insurance agent, for suggestions. During the year as you process information, ask yourself if it is something that should be included in your Permanent or Annual records. If you find you are looking for the same type of information more than once, especially if you have had a hard time locating it, that is a good indication you should consider setting up a permanent place for it. If it is sensitive financial information, it probably belongs in your Business Bible. If it isn't sensitive, but is still important, file it in your FIFI system that is covered in Chapter 11, *FIFI: File It. Find It.*

As you assemble your Business Bible, strike a balance between keeping so much that it becomes unmanageable, and keeping so little that it is not useful. This is a work in progress and can be customized in whatever way best serves your business needs. What is essential is to make it work for you. As you become more conscious of the activities you want to keep track of, you will likely add some records and delete others.

At the end of each year, you will take an hour or so and look through this volume. Some items will be copied and transferred into the new book, such as bank account information, and others will remain in the

> **If it is sensitive financial information, it probably belongs in your Business Bible.**

expiring book as a record of business activities which occurred throughout the year. The old book will be moved to your archived files, or broken down with important information filed separately.

Having this information at my fingertips, rather than depending on others to manage it for me, has both saved both my time and my sanity! I know where critical information is and how to access it, and no longer feel totally dependent on my accounting staff to provide information I need.

The end result was that I was the one in control of my important information, instead of always relying on others to handle it properly. It also added a level of security that lets me sleep better at night. What I've shared with you is an integral part of really owning and managing your business as a competent professional, rather than being at the mercy of others to show you what they want you to see. It made me feel like I was really running my company, instead of pretending. It made me feel like a grown-up.

Optional Additional Volumes

You may choose to set up separate volumes for bulk items, or records not easily categorized. Because my company owns numerous titled vehicles and pieces of untitled heavy equipment, I keep a separate book for vehicle titles and equipment bills of sale that don't easily fit into archive, annual or working files. They still need to be secure and accessible. Additionally, my commercial insurance policy is quite large and is kept in its own binder, rather in my Business Bible. Don't feel that you have to go overboard with individual binders, just do what works best for you. If you have a locking file cabinet in a secure place, you may choose to designate a drawer just for these important, but bulky, records. In the end, you can combine or eliminate records as you wish.

Summing Up

When compiling this volume, keep Goldilocks in mind; you don't want to have it be too large and cumbersome, or too small and incomplete, but just right for your business and its needs. As I cautioned before, do not let this become so complicated that you don't get it done. You can always add another tab if you have forgotten something, or eliminate one if you feel it was unnecessary. Just do your best and make changes or additions later, as needed.

What could you do with an extra six weeks every year? Multiple surveys have revealed that business executives lose six weeks per year looking for items. Six weeks! Imagine what an extra six weeks could deliver to you—the brainstorming and seeding of a new product, time to reach out to your customers, even an amazing no-stress vacation. Having a number put on the amount of time I probably wasted looking for important records really got me inspired to get things organized.

Having easy access to documents which allow you to quickly prove that you did indeed get the required Continuing Education Units two years ago, review the terms of a loan that you want to pay off early, or prove your taxes were paid timely in the past, can be a life saver for a business owner! Rather than having files for each individual type of information spread throughout your office, the yearly snapshot provided by Volume Two of your Business Bible may be just what you need. You may also want to include a list or spreadsheet of where other items relative to this year are stored.

Ultimately, you, your attorney, and possibly your financial advisor will be the best judges of what is important for your business. Ask them.

CHAPTER 10

Business Bible Volume Three: Working Records

The investigation into my embezzlement changed my business life and opened my eyes to a whole new—and dark—reality about being in business. Over time, I became slightly less shell-shocked by the whole thing; uncovering the various ways Tammie had stolen money became morbidly fascinating. Over and over again, I found that fraud had occurred right under my nose in such obvious ways I couldn't believe I had missed it.

After a while, I moved past the shock and the fascination, and started getting angry. Not just mad, but deeply angry on a level I didn't realize was possible. Every day I went to work and spent hours talking to people I owed money to. Some were understanding, some were threatening, and others were hateful and insulting. I talked with my bankers every few days about late payments, cash flow projections, and the progress of the investigation, knowing full well that they were within their rights to call in all of my loans, an event which would have bankrupted my company. I dealt with IRS personnel who were so ruthless that their actions, words, and behavior still leave me stunned. After all, the tax issues were the result of a federal crime!

All of these gut-wrenchingly stressful issues were the direct result of illegal actions by a person I had treated very well. I know many people believe business owners get rich off the backs of their poor, downtrodden employees, and in some cases it is true, but not in this one. Tammie was paid generously, and never had to worry about losing her job for taking time off to care for her family. She brought her daughter to work with her on days school was out, and I even paid her daughter to do little things like empty the trash, or help her mother file papers.

I dealt with IRS personnel who were so ruthless. Their actions, words, and behavior still leave me stunned.

Even now, years later, I cannot think of a single thing I could have done to provide her a better job or a more flexible, positive working environment. Knowing how well I treated her, and that I had given her no cause for the way in which she treated me in return, was eating me from the inside out.

I had panic attacks in the night, and went for months without a full night's sleep. My family became worried about my mental health, as I was clearly buckling under the stress. I would randomly burst into tears at the dinner table and be unable to eat. As I read case histories of other embezzlements in order to learn more about how this had happened, I saw it was not uncommon for people suffering the kind of business losses that I had experienced to commit suicide. At this point, I realized I had to do something to change course.

Tammie had stolen my money, but I was not going to let her steal my happiness or my life. My husband was my greatest support, and often said to me, "It will be interesting to see how the Lord will use this to bless us." Finally, I accepted that on an internal level and started looking for constructive ways to deal with my emotions. That "light in the darkness" moment is when the idea for my first Business Bible began to shine.

As I analyzed the ways I had lost money, and saw my experiences were consistent with many small business embezzlements, I started to make a list of the things I needed to monitor and how to do it.

- I did online research and looked for books that dealt with different fraud prevention strategies, but nearly all of the information available was written for accountants, not business owners.

- I realized I was on my own, and would have to come up with something myself.

- I started watching how money moved through my company, and creating systems to track it.

- I did consult with accountants, attorneys, and business consultants—but much of what I really learned came from what I discovered on my own.

- I read books and case studies on financial fraud until I felt I really understood how I as a business owner—not an accountant—could manage my company finances in a secure, professional way.

And I started sleeping at night.

The Core of Fraud Defense Is the FraudPoints System

The heartbeat of your company lies within your financial management plan. Outlining your daily financial management routine, your *Working Records* allow you to intercept, manage, track, and verify all critical financial functions. As with the other volumes, you may find sections that do not apply to you (although most of these probably will) as well as processes peculiar to your business that you want to add a section to monitor. Each of these modules—except mail, which is a standard operating procedure (SOP) and feeds into all of the other sections—will have its own section in your Business Bible, and its own SOP to handle and track activity.

At the beginning of each module, a list is included to help you evaluate how you are currently managing those activities within your business.

You probably already have some procedures for handling many of the areas, but unless you have started thinking like a thief, you probably haven't plugged all of your potential money leaks.

To be truly effective, a system must:

- Carefully consider the potential risks in an area and establish clear objectives needed to safeguard it.

- Provide an efficient way to prevent and detect the fraud risks associated with that area.

- Give the owner knowledge and skills required to take effective control of it.

Each FPS module has its own *specific objectives*. Be very mindful of these and be sure you understand them! I may recommend that you perform a control in a certain way, but you want to change it. This could be due to personal choice, or a basic difference in your business that makes another method preferable. The system can be customized to work in whatever way best suits the unique needs of your business. However if you make changes, be sure they meet all the objectives for that module.

Without clearly understanding the objectives, you may guard one part of your business while leaving another completely unprotected. You may add additional objectives if your business calls for it, but be very careful about eliminating any. They have all been carefully considered, and the methods deliberately constructed, to prevent and detect specific and common ways people can commit fraud within this area of your business. If I have listed a particular objective and a method to achieve it, it is because someone just like you has lost a lot of money in this area.

It is not an attitude of distrust, but of realism.

After several years of trial and error, I developed the Business Bible to track the *daily movement of money* through my company; from coming in the front door to clearing the bank, I know where every dollar is. When I took control of the mail coming in, monitored every financial process along the way, and then closed the loop by confirming that what came out of the bank was consistent with my intentions, the success of my company skyrocketed, quadrupling in revenues and profits over the next few years.

The Business Bible put all of the tools I needed to monitor my money and financial processes quickly and effectively into one place at my fingertips. It is such an indispensable part of my daily routine now, I do not know how I ever managed without it.

This is the most critical part of your financial management strategy, and I have done all that I can to make it easy for you. Each FraudPoint System (FPS) module will provide you with:

- Definitions of basic accounting terms you need to understand.

- An introduction to the topic, and how fraud can occur in this area of your business.

- Objectives for the FraudPoints controls in this area.

- Where to file the information in your Business Bible.

- Concepts of Forms to help you easily organize and access your information.

- Instructions on exactly how to monitor and protect your company's assets.

As you begin to set up each FPS module described (each is outlined fully in the following chapters), take a moment to consider how you are currently managing those activities within your business. Consider if any procedures you currently have in place are truly secure, or if they are based more on convenience than security. Unless you have started thinking like a thief, you probably haven't organized your daily activities in a way to ensure all of the potential money leaks have been plugged. For any system to be effective, it must:

- recognize potential fraud risks in an area;

- establish clear objectives to safeguard it;

- provide an efficient process to prevent and detect fraud; and

- give the owner the knowledge and skills required to take efficient, effective control of it.

Critical Sections to Include

Listed here are some of the sections you will be setting up in your Business Bible, along with a short explanation of each. As you read them, remember to think about how you currently handle these activities in your business, and how someone could abuse them to commit fraud. It is very important that you start looking at all the activities within your business for Fraud-Points so that you will be able to set up systems to safeguard them.

It is not an attitude of distrust, but of realism. You may feel that additional areas need to be monitored, so make a note of them at the end of this chapter. You can use the same process as I have to set up a list of Fraud-Points, Objectives, and Controls, in order to safeguard them.

Some modules, like mail, are procedures with no record keeping section required. Most modules include prevention and detection controls over specific financial processes, which could prevent most fraud before it occurs, and catch items that may slip through the cracks. Others contain information you will need to keep secure and on hand in order to perform your prevention and detection controls quickly, like your password list and credit card information sheets.

By setting these all up in a single binder, using a daily checklist to help you stay on track, and scheduling a regular time to do your processes, most can complete their daily control checks in an average of under 20 minutes per day. Remember, this is a subjective estimate, and will depend how your company does things and what your internal schedule is.

Get a 3-ring binder to house this information. This will give you room to add sections if needed. You will use it daily, so be sure it is sturdy. Add at least 12 tabs. As you set up each section, you will insert the necessary information as described, and learn exactly how to establish your controls in this area. Don't jump the gun and set up a section for every area listed below, as some of them are supportive procedures you will use that do not require their own record keeping area.

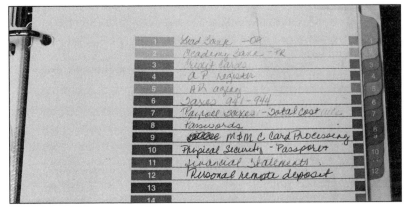

My Business Bible

Procedures and Records. As you read through the following FPS modules, think of how you currently handle your various finance procedures and maintenance of records in your business. Think about how someone could abuse them to commit fraud. You may not currently have any specific structure for things like getting the mail, or follow practices like keeping check logs. That's OK! This is a learning process.

Throughout, I will consistently stress how important it is that you be on the lookout for FraudPoints within your business. You want to be able to set up systems to safeguard them. It is not an attitude of distrust, but of realism.

Some modules, such as mail, are procedures with no record keeping required. Most modules are prevention and detection controls over financial processes, like accounts payable and receivable, which will help you stop most fraud before it can occur, as well as catch anything that might slip through the cracks. Others contain information you will need to keep secure and on hand in order to perform your prevention and detection controls quickly, like your password list and credit card information sheets.

- **FPS: Mail** The first Standard Operating Procedure under the FraudPoints System you are to implement is *Mail*. It supports the other modules and does not require its own records section. While the mail itself is not a part of a daily tracking system, what comes in the mail is. Invoices, payments, tax notifications, etc., all belong to different modules and will be tracked as part of those.

- **FPS: Accounts Payable** Incorporating two different and essential monitoring systems is the *Accounts Payable* (AP) task. First, you will review all incoming invoices and verify that they are legitimate. This should happen before they are passed along to your accountant and entered into your AP system. Second, you will establish a system in which you approve items for payment, select how they are to be paid, and then—through your banking controls—confirm that those payments have correctly cleared your bank or credit card account.

- **FPS: Accounts Receivable** Monitoring and confirming that everything which is invoiced is also paid—AND that those payments are deposited in your bank, is what the *Accounts Receivable* undertaking will accomplish. Because you are now getting your daily mail, you will intercept all payments which come that way, and you will document them. By using the Objectives for this method, you will look at all of the ways your business receives payments and determine how to best monitor and verify each one.

- **FPS: Check Log** You will have your own record book, which is kept in the safe with your check stock. You will learn how to set up a *check log* to track what checks you have released as well as the purpose for each.

- **FPS: Payroll** You will review your weekly payroll and tax obligations, confirming that the people being paid are being paid correctly, there are no "ghosts" (employees that don't really exist, but still receive a paycheck), and that your taxes are paid timely and in full. Nonpayment of *Payroll* taxes can allow the IRS to blow through your corporate veil and seize your personal assets in order to satisfy the debt. Not only will confirmation of these tax obligations protect your business, it may save your home!

- **FPS: Daily Banking** Within the *Daily Banking* step, you will discover that it ties together all of the methods discussed. It is here you will confirm that everything you have approved has come out of your bank account correctly, and that nothing you haven't approved is siphoning off your cash.

  By keeping a confirmed check register, and checking it regularly against your online account, you will catch fraud and errors quickly. A vast number of frauds involve forged checks or unauthorized electronic transfers—all of which come out of your bank account. Daily Banking is one of the most important areas for you to watch like a hawk.

- **FPS: FIFI - File It. Find It.** Now that you are starting to monitor your mail, checks, and banking activities, you need a filing system that gives you a simple, organized way to store information you need to track or follow up on. The *FIFI* method of filing is as easy as putting papers in a pile, but now you can find them when you need them. I don't know how I ever lived without it!

- **FPS: Credit Cards** Today, a commonly used payment tool for most businesses is a credit card. It is essential that you monitor yours, and the obligations they put upon your business, often and accurately. *Credit Cards* have a lot of purchase and fraud protections built in, yet they are commonly and easily abused. You will monitor them in much the same way you do your banks, and your employees will know that you are doing so. Sometimes the simple knowledge you are watching is the best prevention control of all!

- **FPS: Taxes** Very few things are more likely to be completely and gladly handed over to an accountant than preparation and payment of *Taxes*, and yet few things are a greater danger to a business than unpaid taxes and unfiled returns. In this section, you will compile a list of all the taxes your business is required to report and pay, and you will verify that all are paid correctly and timely.

    Not only are mistakes in this area just as dangerous as deliberate noncompliance, many embezzled companies wind up with serious tax issues as a result of the crime. In fact, it is not at all uncommon for a company to survive an embezzlement, only to be put out of business by tax problems that are the direct result of the crime.

    Whether a dishonest accountant or payroll service is stealing your tax payments, or just not doing them correctly, you will now be able to proactively monitor this critical area of your business finances and protect yourself.

- **FPS: Passwords** A major problem I discovered as I uncovered and investigated my embezzlement involved missing *Passwords* and logon information for bank and credit card accounts.

Because Tammie had set up the online access procedures for most of these accounts, the security questions had been answered from her perspective. Just try calling one of your credit card holders to obtain information about an account when you do not have the username or password and you can't answer any of the security questions. It was a nightmare! Having an up-to-date password list of access information for every account for which you are financially responsible is critical these days. Now you will keep a current list securely at your fingertips.

If the idea of tracking all of this information seems overwhelming to you—*don't worry about it!* This system is designed to make it simple and efficient. Having done it myself for several years now, I don't know how I ever managed to sleep at night when I was relying on an accountant to tell me everything I knew about my finances. I didn't realize the risk I was taking then, but I do now. I have learned that ignorance may be bliss, and realization may be hell, but knowledge and action are peace. I will never again go back to my old management style of "I can't be out of money—I still have checks!" That is an exaggeration—I did monitor my finances, and I thought I was being careful. But I didn't realize at the time that nearly all of the information I relied on had passed through the hands of an embezzler by the time I saw it. I now manage my multi-million dollar business with the respect and attention it deserves, and in turn, it supports me and my family in the way a business that size should.

As I studied embezzlement cases, I realized that even though they sounded very different, when you came right down to it, the basics were quite similar. Although accountants describe the methods with phrases like, "misappropriation of cash receipts," as well as other terms which are not understood by non-accountants, there were three common threads running through most cases:

- **Shoplifting:** stealing payments when they come in, before they enter your accounts.

- **Lying:** deceiving you into authorizing payments for fraudulent expenditures.

- **Robbery:** getting money or goods directly from your bank or other credit accounts.

Although the tactics used to commit these crimes may differ somewhat, the basics are the same. The good news for you as a business owner is that the ways to prevent and detect these frauds are also very basic, which means that a few simple procedures will prevent a multitude of fraud crimes.

Summing Up

Typically, when most people hear about fraud and theft, they think about the extreme cases at both ends of the scale. They have read about highly sophisticated crimes and heists, such as what occurred at Enron which shut down the accounting firm of Arthur Andersen and sent several to jail; the fake bank accounts that Wells Fargo created; or high profile robberies, like crashing into Tiffany's with large caliber weapons. When asked about how to prevent those types of crimes, I tell people the truth—I have absolutely no idea!

Most of us aren't in much danger from those crimes. The most dangerous threat to your business may be the accountant who looks like your grandmother and brings homemade cinnamon rolls to staff meetings, or the bookkeeper who has been your father's best friend for over 25 years.

The beauty of this system is that it allows you to protect your business daily in a few minutes, without destroying those relationships. Openly closing the window to your money will stop the majority of fraud crimes before they ever start.

So let's get started!

CHAPTER 11

FIFI: File It. Find It. The Last Filing System You'll Ever Need!

FIFI is the down-and-dirty guerilla filing for busy people who hate paperwork, but still need to deal with it.

The point of setting up a filing system is to be able to put stuff away quickly; to put it where it can be found when needed; and to do both with as little effort and thought as possible.

I don't know about you, but I always had at least one big pile of papers on the corner of my desk— a black hole for items that needed some sort of action. That's not counting the other piles in various locations throughout my office. How much time do you spend looking for misplaced papers or lost files? I used to be afraid to answer that question!

Sharon Mann, an organizational expert at Esselte, the makers of all things Pendaflex, disclosed:

A cluttered workplace is not only aesthetically unappealing it also is an element that usurps company time and money. Unfortunately, people often don't realize how fiscally damaging disorganization can be.

According to a variety of time management experts, American workers spend nine million hours collectively searching for misplaced information, which in turn costs companies billions of dollars each year.

Before FIFI, my junk mail, to-do notes, important invoices, and highly sensitive information all sat in piles on my desk—and became lost in plain sight. Finding any important item was time consuming and frustrating, and the related deadline often passed before I got around to addressing it.

There are some important questions to ask yourself if you don't already have a solid organizational structure in place:

1. *How organized are you about managing and protecting your business?* Dishonest employees, like sneaky children, know that disorganization and distraction can effectively keep you from getting to the bottom of things they don't want closely examined.

2. *How likely are you to check your credit card statement next month to confirm if a questionable charge was resolved or a refund was posted on an account?* Out of sight, out of mind!

3. *Will you remember to follow-up and verify if the bank corrected a check paid in error?* Unless it was a really big check, you probably won't.

4. *If an issue arises, will you be able to find the documentation you need to resolve or confirm these issues—even if you DO remember to follow up?* Remember, in most of these situations, the person with the biggest pile of papers is likely to win the dispute—whether they are right or not!

Sure, you can put a reminder on your phone or calendar, but where will you put the paperwork needed to resolve the issue? Scanning items and attaching them to electronic calendars may not always be practical.

Additionally, in many cases original documents are required and copies are not an acceptable substitute.

If you're like I used to be, you don't want to put things away until outstanding issues have been resolved. I lived in fear I would put something away and forget to deal with it, or be unable to locate critical documents at the appropriate time. So, the pile of "important stuff that I really need to take care of" grew daily, with no real mechanism to reduce or organize it.

> **Get ORGANIZED: Divide the towering pile of paper overflowing on the desk into three ... throw the bottom third directly into the recycling! Don't look at it ... everything has resolved itself and those people hate you!.**

Maintaining a logical organizational system is imperative to the success of your business.

- Items will be at your fingertips, exactly when you need them.

- Sensitive information will be securely filed where you, and only you, can access it with ease.

- Most importantly, a system is not only essential to the professional management of your business; it is a critical piece of your fraud control plan!

As you begin to store and monitor information in your Business Bible, get ready for a surprise. Not only will you find things that need to be set aside for action or follow-up, you will also become aware of items piled on your desk that should instead be stored securely.

I once heard someone say that organization experts can be the worst hoarders of all. They encourage people to keep things they don't really need, and set up high-maintenance systems to store them, as though beautifully organized stuff—rather than simplicity—is the end goal. My advice: Go for simplicity.

Blogger Victoria Elizabeth Barnes, who describes herself as a dictator, procrastinator, and hoarder, offers tidbits about a variety of topics—from house remodeling and kittens, to reducing paper. Her advice:

> *Divide the towering pile of paper overflowing on the desk into three*
> *... throw the bottom third directly into the recycling! Don't look*
> *at it ... everything has resolved itself and those people hate you!*

A definite high-five to Victoria for creativity! However, FIFI will save your sanity without driving you to such desperate measures.

An unfortunate temptation with a simple filing system is to refile things you no longer need, simply because you created the file in the first place. Just because they're easy to put away doesn't mean you should keep papers you no longer use. An important part of managing any filing system is being selective about what is valuable enough to save in the first place.

There's no shame in purging items that are no longer useful. If you saved an article in a FIFI file and then decided not to use it, do NOT file it neatly away. Draw a line through the item's description on the front of your folder, and then throw out the unwanted paper.

The trash can—not the file cabinet—is where you store papers that are no longer needed!

For instance, if you set up a folder for "Remodeling Ideas for the Conference Room," don't be afraid to throw the entire file away after completing the project, unless you have plans to use the information elsewhere. No matter how easy refiling is, unwanted items should be purged or your system will collapse.

Unnecessary clutter wastes time and space, creates the feeling of being continually overwhelmed—and makes it more difficult to find the things you need.

I recently helped clean out my mother-in-law's home. She prided herself on maintaining thorough financial records. However, forcing your children to throw away your 1971 check registers and tax returns in 2015 is not filing—it is hoarding! Be orderly with your filing, and ruthless with your discards. Remember—the ability to put something away easily does not mean it is worth putting away. Additionally, the clutter may make it more difficult to locate things you really do need. Be wise!

The trash can (also known as the circular file) is where you store papers that are no longer needed!

This is where File It. Find It. (FIFI) comes in.

FIFI is the solution to the problems I encountered with other systems. It is down-and-dirty guerilla filing for busy people who hate paperwork, but still need to deal with it. It is the only paperwork organization system that has ever worked for me, instead of making me work for it.

I can find important papers more quickly and easily than I ever could before. This is not to say that I never get behind or have a pile of work on my desk—*I do*—but in just a few minutes I can get everything where it belongs so I can deal with it at the appropriate time. Coming into work in the morning to a disorganized desk is so overwhelming that I typically dedicate five minutes to FIFI before leaving the office.

FIFI allows you the mental and physical space needed to deal with what is important right now, secure in the knowledge you're prepared for your next steps!

When using *FIFI Action Files*, the papers themselves serve as your follow-up reminder. When using *FIFI Random Files*, the information on any given topic will always be available in a single location. Your days of searching for lost paperwork have come to an end!

You and your employees can save your company thousands of hours and dollars by learning how to find and follow-up on important items that are hard to categorize for filing purposes. "The High Cost of Not

Finding Information," an International Data Corporation white paper by Susan Feldman and Chris Sherman, discusses the exorbitant costs of NOT maintaining a solid system. It's a systemic—and expensive—issue that's plaguing businesses across the globe.

After you teach the people in your office how to use this system, you will be amazed at how much easier it will be for them to find documents and meet deadlines. Now the only time I have a pile of unorganized papers on my desk is if I've been out of the office and other people have put them there. Even dealing with the pile is not nearly as daunting as it used to be, since I now have a fast, easy way to sort, throw away, act on, or file papers for action at the appropriate time.

The point of setting up a filing system is to be able to put stuff away quickly, to put it where it can be found when needed, and to do both with as little effort and thought as possible. It is NOT to set up a monument to beautiful filing that requires a daily sacrifice of maintenance time—this is strictly guerilla filing!

FIFI will allow you to:

- Find nearly any paper with ease just by glancing down the list on the front of a folder, or by going to the relevant dated folder. No more sorting through mounds of paper to find a single lost item!

- Know exactly where to refile something if you have gotten it out to use or loan to someone.

- Quickly file a wide variety of information with minimal effort.

FIFI delivers the mental and physical space needed to deal with what is important right now, secure in the knowledge you're prepared for your next steps!

As a personal example, once I finished the outline for this book, I set up a special file drawer to hold all the information. I knew it would be a large project, so I designated a folder for every chapter. I then printed the outline for each chapter and taped it to the outside front of the appropriate folder. Information in that folder was then labeled and filed. (You will learn exactly how to do this in Random Files section, p. 136.) I also set up folders for more general information, such as "Interesting Fraud Cases," "Statistics on Fraud," "Personal Stories," which I wanted to use at some point, but was not sure where.

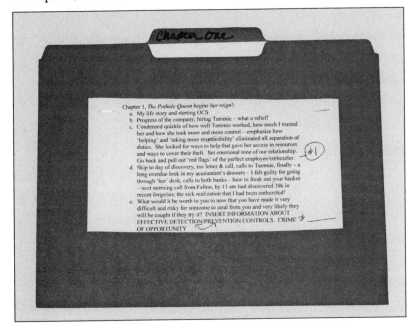

I clearly labeled the exact information in each file. Months later, finding the relevant information was simple, as opposed to digging through large, unorganized piles of "important stuff I saved because I know I want to use it in my book." If I couldn't find something quickly, it was because I had neglected to follow my process.

As an added bonus, I only needed my laptop and folder for the chapter in progress to work from anywhere. I was good to go!

I taught a church scripture study class for many years, and we always had a short devotional at the beginning. I started a folder of "Devotional Ideas" where I kept inspiring or interesting things to use for that purpose. I eventually saved and stored several hundred ideas in four different folders, any of which I can locate in under a minute, just by skimming the lists on the outside of the folders.

Additionally, I set up a lesson folder for each week of the study year and wrote the topics and scripture references to be used during that week on the outside of each one. My lesson manual was then torn apart and the applicable pages placed in the folder for that week. If I saw a quote, visual aid, or inspiring story in October that I knew would be wonderful for a lesson being taught the next April, I had a designated "pile" to put that information in, where it would be at my fingertips at the time I was preparing those lessons.

If you have ever wondered where on earth you could put a scrap of paper torn out of a magazine in a place where you can find it in six months, you should be having a real "aha" moment about how useful this system can be.

As a bonus, FIFI decreased my tendency to become distracted and wind up working on something that was not planned—or even important—but which caught my interest while searching for something else. Am I the only person who has ever gone into a big box store for a gallon of milk and come out an hour later with a pair of shoes, a new movie, and a family-sized tent that was on clearance—but no milk? Why does that happen? Because the path to the dairy case is lined with attractive displays, sale advertisements, and ladies giving out samples of food.

Although you can't put on blinders in the store, you can do a great deal to control distractions at work. When you reduce your opportunities to be sidetracked by unnecessary and unimportant things while searching for what you need, you increase your likelihood of staying focused and completing your most important tasks.

Read through this entire chapter before you start setting up your files. As you read, make notes about things that you have trouble filing, locating, or remembering to do on time. I think you will find this system can help you solve most of those problems. The system is very flexible, which means it can be adapted to work for nearly all people under nearly all circumstances. Just remember the basic guidelines and use them in the ways that best serve your unique situation.

Consider the following points:

- Which important things often wind up being lost in plain sight?

- What types of piles make sense to you? Could some be based on their use rather than their topic? For example, an organized, numbered "Management Ideas" file may be best for long-term ideas, but a brief management idea you want to cover in a staff meeting may work better in an unstructured "Staff Meeting" file, or a date-specific Action File.

- How often will you need to use or add information to a file?

There are two different types of filing systems in FIFI—Random Files and Action Files. Random Files are primarily a storage and organizational system for information related by topic, while Action Files are intended to work with your calendaring system by filing items based on when they will be needed.

Neither of these filing methods will replace large specific files that need their own place—such as payroll records, project files, or tax filings, many of which are permanent records. FIFI files serve the purpose of giving you a way to manage the information you use on a regular basis, which you therefore must efficiently file and find.

Random Files

The Random Files system gives you a place to organize information that is hard to categorize and store using traditional filing methods. You can set up files like "Inspiring Quotes," "Decorating Ideas for the Conference Room," "Business Management Methods," "Tax Planning Articles," or "Possible Locations for the Office Christmas Party."

NOTE: don't try to store things in your Random Files that are better suited in the time-sensitive format of Action Files, which will be explained next. Remember, things related by topic belong in a Random File; things you need at a specific time belong in an Action File.

How To Set Up a Random File

- Start by selecting a type of information that often winds up being lost, misfiled, or in a pile on your desk. Decide whether the information is topical or time sensitive; set time sensitive items aside for your Action Files.

- On the file folder tab write the name of a topic, such as Management Ideas.

- On the outside front cover write #1 and a title for the item, such as *Forbes* article, "Searching for the Right Leadership Style."

- On the top right-hand corner of the article, write #1 and circle it.

- Continue in like manner with the other items you want to file on this topic, listing and numbering them sequentially.

Using single sheets of paper, you should be able to store 25 to 50 items per folder. If your folder gets full but you want to continue saving articles on a topic, add a letter designation to the file folder tab so that you now have "Management Ideas A," "B," and so forth. Remember that the simpler and clearer your system, the easier it will be to FIFI!

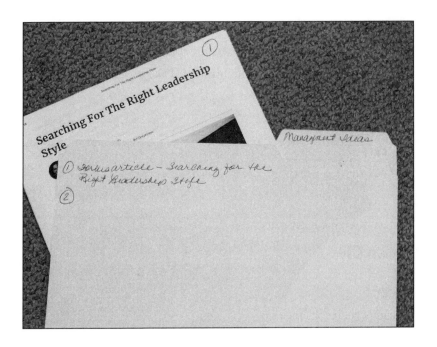

Additionally, you can make the folders as general or specific as you like. If your Management Ideas files get too large to handle or you just want to refine it further, you can divide it into smaller, more niche topics. For instance, you may want to set up folders on topics like "Management Techniques for Women Who Manage Men," or "Management Ideas for Difficult Employees."

Store your Random Files folders in hanging files, which can either be grouped together by general topic, alphabetically, or simply in the order you created them. As long as you can find them, you're doing it right! The less critical the filed items are, and the less volume you are dealing with, the less structure you require. Don't go crazy setting up a detailed system to contain small amounts of non-critical or infrequently used information.

What if some of the items you want to save are on sticky notes or small scraps of paper? Just tape or staple them to a sheet of plain paper before numbering and filing them. What about items that you will use soon but don't want to keep long-term? Set up a file with the topic, such as "Staff Meeting," and purge unwanted items each week after your meeting. In that instance, you can probably skip listing and numbering the information altogether. But, if you are collecting information for a major quarterly meeting that requires a lot of preparation, you may need a way to file and locate critical items. Itemizing and numbering them as you would with any other major topic so they can be located with ease may make sense.

Action Files

You will utilize Action Files to organize information that will require action on a particular date or time period. By assigning specific files to the different months and days of the year, you create an orderly sequence of streamlined file-piles that contain the papers you need, at exactly the time you'll need them. I was good about using an electronic calendar to schedule important appointments and tasks before implementing this system. Yet, I habitually struggled to locate the documents I needed relative to those activities. That was before I started using Action Files. No longer!

How to Set Up Action Files

First, choose a dedicated file drawer which you can easily access while sitting at your desk. You will then make the following files:

- Twelve monthly files, with one month of the year written on each tab

- Thirty-one daily files, numbered 1–31

- Six hanging file folders to hold the monthly and daily files

1. Start by removing the folder for the current month and putting it in the first hanging file. Behind it, insert the numbered tabs,

starting with the current day of the month. Then insert enough additional numbered files so the last one represents the date for the end of your week.

As an example, if today was Tuesday, November 3, your first hanging file would start with the November monthly file, and would be followed by files #3 through #8. Files #1 and #2, for Sunday the 1st and Monday the 2nd will be placed behind the December file. This gives you a place to start storing papers and other information that you will need to access during the upcoming week.

2. In the second hanging file, place files #9–15, which are for the days of the next week. The third hanging file will contain files #16–22. The fourth will hold #23–29. The fifth hanging file will begin with file #30, the last day of November, which will be followed by the monthly file for December and files #1–6. The file numbered 31 will not be used, since November has only 30 days. Don't put anything in it, and rotate it at the same time you move file #30. The sixth monthly file will hold the remainder of the monthly files, which will be rotated as time goes by.

3. Assuming today is November 3rd, if you have a contract you need to follow up on in two days, place it in the #5 file, where the information will be at your fingertips on Thursday the 5th. You will be reminded to act on it when you check your action file that morning. If you are unable to speak to the client on Thursday and want to try again the next day, place the contract in the folder for day #6. If you call the client on the 6th and he wants to wait until January to make a decision, place the contract in the January file, where you will find it at the beginning of

that month. If he wants you to call on January 15th, you will put that information on a sticky note and attach it to the contract, since you do not yet have any daily files rotated behind the January file. As you can see, items with a specific date go in a daily file, while items to review during a future month go in the monthly file.

4. At the end of each day, review that day's action file and move any uncompleted items to another day's file. Now rotate the empty file for the current day to the back of the line, which in this case will be behind folders #1 and #2 for the month of December. This way your daily files will always start with the current day's date, you will always have 31 daily files available to store items needed during the upcoming month, and you can file items needed at any time during the next year in a designated monthly file.

If you need to file items that will exceed the twelve-month capacity of this system, you can also set up yearly files for upcoming years. I personally found that I didn't use them, but to each his own. Set it up any way you like! It is your filing system to set up however you feel it will serve you best.

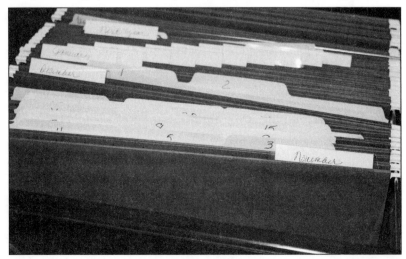

Inversely, if you do not deal with many papers, you can choose to eliminate the step of dividing the daily folders into weekly groups and just rotate them behind the upcoming monthly folders. For me, that didn't provide enough space for weekly items. A single hanging file with up to 31 folders in in quickly became overstuffed, and sometimes even collapsed the hanging file where the folders for the month were stored. You choose which method will work best for you.

High maintenance filing systems rarely work.

Fingertip Versus Stored Files

Action Files—which are used daily, as well as certain Random Files—that contain information I use often are kept in a Fingertip File location. Information I use less often is placed in a Stored File location. I do not formally use these designations to label my files; this name simply deals with whether I choose to store them in a desk drawer (at my fingertips) or in the filing cabinet a couple of steps away from my desk (in storage).

A file folder may change from a Fingertip File to a Stored File—or vice versa—depending on how you are using it at the time. For instance, in July when you are actively looking for places to hold the office Christmas party and need to make a decision by August, the file with information on potential locations may be needed at your fingertips. After the decision is made and the file is no longer in frequent use, you may choose to move the file to your stored file area so you can refer to it next year, and still easily add information on other potential locations until that time.

Just be mindful that any file can change in importance and use over time. If you have run out of room in your fingertip file area, or are constantly getting up to find files in your stored file area, consider reevaluating where the best place to keep them may be.

Summing Up

There you have it—a piling system, rather than a filing system, but one that allows you to find things! I once heard a home organizer say, "Contrary to what your mother may have told you, not only is everything not worth doing well; some things are barely worth doing at all!" A great deal of information storage falls into the latter category. High maintenance filing systems rarely work. Often the effort required for upkeep exceeds the value of the papers themselves.

Without an Action File, an important paper with unresolved issues may be lost while waiting for you to deal with it, or you may not be able to locate the documents you need to take care of a calendared item at the time required. Without a Random File, information you need may continually play Hide and Seek on your desktop. As a successful business owner, you want information readily available at the time needed so you can move forward!

There is no scorecard and no measure of getting it right or wrong. If you can easily store and locate the information you need, then it is working as intended. Let FIFI be a tool to make your life easier.

CHAPTER 12

FPS: Mail

**As a business owner,
one of the most important things
you can do is get your own mail.**

When FBI Special Agent J was first assigned to my embezzlement case, he interviewed me at length in my office.

At this point I was still in shock; not yet calm enough to step back and analyze how the fraud occurred. After he reviewed a lot of the hard evidence, including forged checks and concealed tax notices, we sat down to talk. Agent J truly helped me, both emotionally and practically, during the investigation and prosecution. Notwithstanding my positive experience with him, one of the top items on my bucket list is to never again be involved in anything that requires having my own, personal FBI agent!

He asked me, "Who paid the bills?"

"Tammie," I responded

"Who balanced the checkbook?"

"Tammie."

"Who processed payroll?"

"Tammie."

As Agent J brought to light the pattern of inter-connected duties that had allowed her to steal so much money, I could see how it had happened, but I didn't know what to do about it. I felt completely overwhelmed, thinking about how many of those duties I would have to take over myself.

Then he asked, "Who got the mail—Tammie?"

I exclaimed, "Of course, Tammie got the mail! Why in the world would I not have the person in the front office get the mail? What is the point of having office help at all if you can't even let them do something as simple as getting the mail?"

He kindly looked out at me over the top of his glasses and said, "Her complete control over your mail allowed her to be involved in many dishonest activities and hide them from you. She hid the bank and credit card statements, unpaid tax notices and late notices from vendors. As a business owner, one of the most important things you can do is get and open your own mail."

I was stunned.

As the pieces of the puzzle finally fell into place, I connected the dots in processing her deception. I realized mail is the major hub where pieces of sensitive information vulnerable to fraud constantly moves in and out of my business. I could have caught it at any time, if I had known to look.

While discussing this later, the Assistant US Attorney prosecuting the case apologized if it made me feel bad when Agent J pointed out my negligence regarding the mail. She said, "Investigators who regularly deal with fraud, and see the amazing amount of damage employees do with mail-tampering, often forget business owners are generally unaware of the threat."

Contrary to what the attorney thought, it didn't make me feel bad. It opened my eyes. I saw the process of deception as a circle, which could have been interrupted and stopped at many points. Taking charge of my mail would have been the simplest and most effective action of all.

Collecting mail gives an employee enormous control over much of the information and resources your business receives every day. It is not uncommon for mail to be lost or stolen once it enters your internal systems. In fact, your mail is generally safer on its journey from Timbuktu to your office than it is once it comes through your front door. An accountant who gets the mail stands in a unique position. Tammie not only intercepted and misused a variety of sensitive communications, she altered the records of my company to cover her actions.

The simple task of opening the mail is one of the easiest and most effective things you can do to fight financial fraud.

A dishonest accountant can interrupt the flow of mail going in and out of your company. He or she can:

1. Steal incoming payments, and then delete the related invoices out of your Accounts Receivable. You won't see the unpaid accounts.

2. Steal incoming invoices for unauthorized personal purchases, enter them into your Accounts Payable in a misleading way, and then trick you into making payments for them.

3. Hide unpaid tax notices, so you don't realize the money was stolen instead of paid to the appropriate taxing authority.

   Both tax payments and benefit account contributions, such as 401k deposits, are easy marks for embezzlers. They involve large sums of money which are transferred on a regular basis into accounts an owner seldom monitors. Missing tax payments and unfunded employee benefit accounts are huge problems for a victimized business. They present serious legal problems, in addition to the financial ones.

4. Hide financial statements from retirement or other investment accounts, then pocket the intended deposits instead of making payments to those accounts.

5. Conceal and alter bank statements to hide evidence of forged or altered checks, fraudulent electronic transfers, unauthorized credit accounts, or secreted withdrawals.

6. Order and accept additional checks for your business, then use them without your knowledge, even if you keep your authorized check stock secured.

7. Deliberately send a large payment with the wrong address on it to a vendor. The check will be returned to your office, where it can be intercepted and altered for personal use.

8. Obtain unauthorized company credit cards and use them for personal purchases.

9. Steal the convenience checks, which are often included in your credit card statements, and use them to transfer personal balances onto company accounts.

10. Steal incoming credit card statements that show personal purchases.

The simple job of opening the mail is one of the easiest and most effective things you can do to fight financial fraud. Examining, confirming, distributing, and following-up is also critical. When your Business Bibles and FIFI systems are set up, you can start processing your mail more effectively than you ever thought was possible—or even necessary.

Although this is a FPS with specific procedures to be followed, it does not have its own special section in the Business Bible. It feeds into and supports the other modules by ensuring the information going in and out of your company is protected and tracked. The other modules are only as effective as the information traveling in and out of them, so an ongoing flow of unaltered mail is the foundation of your fraud control plan.

When I started to pay attention to what came in my daily mail, I quickly discovered that the United States Post Office had become an unsuspecting accomplice to my vulnerability. In one week alone, I was inundated with mailbox offerings—offerings that in the wrong hands can create a snowballing financial crisis. My mailbox contained:

1. Two credit card bills with cash advance checks attached.

2. Three applications for new credit cards, with minimal information required to apply.

3. One credit card bill with a helpful Add an Additional Cardholder space.

4. A bank statement for my main operating account.

5. Over $200k in invoices from various suppliers.

6. Two checks for small projects (over $1,500 each) whose contracts had not come across my desk and so I was not expecting the money.

7. A solicitation from a discount check printing company offering to print company checks.

Can you imagine the number of ways that any of the above could be misused and lead to financial fraud?

Getting Started:

It starts with your taking control.

- **Inform everyone in your office that you will handle all the mail in the future.** No one should helpfully get it and put it on your desk, without your direct instruction.

If you feel this will be difficult to enforce, either get a locking mail box for your office or rent a post office box.

- **Place a shredder close to your desk.** Destroy anything that could be removed from the trash and abused.

- **Start opening everything and really examining it.** Anything offering you credit, financing, or other paid services should be shredded!

After You've Sorted Your Mail into Piles:

- *If it's junk*: Throw it in the trash or shred it.

- *If it's a payment*: Set it in a pile for deposits.

Once you have removed all payments, stamp the checks "For Deposit Only" to your business account before placing them in your safe to wait for processing and deposit. I will expand on this later.

- *If it's an invoice*: Look it over and identify it. Like the deposits, I will expand on this process later. For now, just review each invoice carefully and ask questions if something doesn't make perfect sense to you.

- *If it's a tax letter*: Be sure it's not a past due notice or filing. If it is, follow up—personally and quickly!

Read all other correspondence and make sure you're clear on everything you read. Ask questions, if necessary, and do not be afraid to insist on answers.

After You've Sorted All Items:

- Distribute action items to the appropriate employees.

- Place follow-up items into the correct FIFI daily file so you will remember them at the appropriate time.

- Research any suspicious items, and don't be afraid to go to an outside source for answers.

- Make copies of items you need others to follow-up on. Keep the original in your FIFI files, and give a copy to the person asked to investigate. Verify the answers you get by checking with the source.

Looking back, Tammie answered many questions in ways that didn't seem quite right, but I wasn't aware they were clear signs of financial fraud. She told me credible lies, that I accepted with no verification, simply because I trusted her. Be mindful.

You might be asking an embezzler about his or her own activities!

Ask yourself how a dishonest person could abuse each piece of mail. Use those thoughts to determine how to protect yourself.

If an invoice from a supplier is marked past due, but you are certain you paid it recently: Call the supplier and ask. Someone might be redirecting your payments or altering checks.

If you receive a check from an unfamiliar source: Call and ask them what invoice they are paying. Someone in your office could be sending out invoices and stealing payments for services being kept off the books. In short, become familiar with everything the moment it enters your business, *not* after someone else has already gone through it, passing on only what he or she wants you to see.

From Cheryl's Desk

Just this week, as I was opening my mail, I discovered a check for trucking services from another company in the amount of $1,462. I did not have any corresponding invoice issued to that company, so I immediately spoke to both my accountant and my truck boss. I let them know I expected answers about the situation ASAP, and I would personally verify the information they provided.

The accountant stated we had issued no such invoice. The truck boss couldn't explain it off the top of his head, but said he would check it out immediately.

It turned out we had issued an invoice for trucking services to an asphalt supplier for hauling material to one of his clients. The asphalt supplier issued an invoice to his client, which included both the material and the trucking, and included a copy of our bill as back-up. The confusion came about because his client—whom we had not invoiced—paid the material and trucking to each company separately.

Nothing dishonest occurred; we were just paid by a different company than we had invoiced. I was all over it until I knew exactly what had happened. Why? Because having money come into your business, without a matching invoice in your system, can mean someone is providing "off the record" goods or services and intercepting the payments as they come in.

My employees took no offense at my inquiries. They know I ask questions and expect answers. They do not take it as an insult, but as an indication that I am firmly committed to keeping the company that pays their wages on solid financial ground!

As with any other new habit, it will seem awkward at first. It may even seem like a waste of your time. I struggled when adding this new responsibility to my other tasks. Now, after five years of handling my own mail, I can't imagine letting someone else take over the responsibility.

At Obermiller Construction, my husband goes to the mailbox and brings everything directly to me. Occasionally, he'll forget and pass the mail to accounting. I immediately retrieve it, reinforcing that no one opens the mail but me. The longer I open my own mail and see what comes in it, the more devoted I am to never delegating this task again. When I am away from the office, I make provisions so I can follow up, even from halfway around the world.

Summing Up

Checking the mail—just like the other FraudPoints Systems I have implemented—is something I do myself. My business has tripled in size since my embezzlement. I employ over 30 people. I have devoted untold hours to writing this book. I am active in my church. I spend a great deal of time with my family, including a newly retired husband who likes to travel and spend leisure time with me. In short, I am busy! But I make time for these modules every day, even if I don't do them perfectly.

Although I don't have an advanced university degree, I paid a million dollars in tuition for an intensive home-study course in "Why Embezzlement Stinks!" I learned my lessons well.

It's your turn to do likewise.

CHAPTER 13

FPS:
Keeping a Check Log

You must track a check through its entire payment path,
or it can be intercepted and misused without your knowledge.

In his late teens and early 20s, Frank Abagnale cashed $2.5 million in fraudulent checks in every U.S. state and 26 foreign countries. Among his many identities, he masqueraded as an airline pilot and a physician, and then landed in prison for five years. That was more than three decades ago. Since then, he wrote *Catch Me If You Can*, his best-selling autobiography that Steven Spielberg turned into a movie.

His expertise: why theft and fraud, of course. And who better to teach about fraud prevention than a reformed master. Today, he consults with the U.S. government on identity theft and fraud prevention, and works with the FBI as a consultant. As he says in the movie, "I can't be over-drawn, I still have checks left!"

Despite a variety of different estimates of how often fraud occurs and how much it costs, nearly all researchers agree on one thing—check forgery is the simplest and safest form of fraud.

It costs businesses millions of dollars each year, it is so easy nearly anyone can do it, and it can kill your business before you know what hit you. Banks often resolve cases of check fraud to some degree, but if they can prove you were negligent in handling your checks, they can legally refuse to replace the stolen money. There is also a strict time limit of how long they are liable for improperly paid checks.

Business owners use different tactics to safeguard their checks. Even the best techniques fail if they address only one or two potential types of misuse. For instance, purchasing checks that cannot be altered is a good start, but they can still be stolen and forged. You need a system to keep those checks locked up and accounted for.

Since check fraud is very low tech and simple to commit, it is also low tech and simple to prevent.

You must track a check through its entire payment path, or it can be intercepted and misused without your knowledge. Your simple check-monitoring process includes:

- Taking control of your mail

- Monitoring critical FraudPoints in your AR and AP processes

- Confirming authorized payments cleared your bank properly

This process is the single best way to both prevent and detect check fraud. A fraudster who deposits a forged check into a personal bank account, particularly if that deposit is made via an ATM, is quite likely to get away with it, *UNLESS* you are monitoring your company's FraudPoints.

Unless someone without an account at your bank takes a check from your company and presents it in person to a teller for cold cash, it is unlikely the signature will be verified. It is your responsibility to watch for check fraud! Don't rely on the security of signature cards—it doesn't exist anymore!

Most business owners have no idea how many of their company checks are "in play" at any given time.

- Do you know how many checks have been issued, but have not cleared your bank?

- Do you have a list of checks your records show as voided?

- Do you have a way of tracking which checks you have authorized for use?

You will now! It is as simple as setting up a check log.

There's good news. Since check fraud is very low tech and simple to commit, it is also low tech and simple to prevent.

Never forget how easy it is for a dishonest employee to take a piece of paper in the form of a blank check and turn it into cash, and do it right under your nose!

1. Set up a check log using the example shown on the next page.

2. Record checks as you use them.

3. Print enough pages to last you six months to a year, depending on how often you issue checks.

4. Bind or staple the pages together.

5. Put your check stock in a secure place, and then place the check log and a pen directly on top of it, so what you need is at your fingertips. Since you will have to move the check log to get to the checks, you should never forget to record the checks you remove.

Because I have multiple checking accounts, I use stacking file trays to hold the different checkbooks, and I keep a separate check log for each account. Once a check log is full, I simply make another one and start again.

I retain a record of the most recent checks, which may not yet have cleared the bank. I save the last page of the old log and insert it into the front of the new check book.

Here is an example of what your check log will look like:

Date	# of checks	Begin-ning #	Ending #	Checked out by	Given to	Notes
12/14	3	1246	1248	CJO	LS	Paid Weekly Bills
12/14	1	1248	1248	CJO	n/a	Returned to Stock
12/14	1	1248	1248	CJO	LS	Void – Printer Error
12/17	1	1249	1249	CJO	n/a	Lawn care – Hand-Written Check

Maintaining a check log only takes a minute, and it will quickly become second nature.

> *"... they (criminals) look at check forgery and they know that for every 1,400 forgers arrested, only about 123 get convicted and about 26 go to jail. So the rewards are great, but the risks are very slim. So that's one of the reasons that make it very popular."*
> — Frank Abagnale, *Catch Me If You Can*

A few hints to get you started:

- **Create a work surface next to your safe, so you have a place to count out checks and write in the check book with ease.** This is one of those simple things that proved to be immensely valuable to me. When I first started keeping a check log, I was getting really annoyed with the process. Whenever I needed checks, I pulled the check log out of the safe and tried to write in it by pressing it up against the wall while holding the checks under one arm, which was terribly awkward and usually resulted in a pile of checks on the floor.

Due to the layout of my office, I had no place to set down the tray with the checks to count out the number I needed, and no hard surface to set the check book on so I could write in it neatly. I quickly became frustrated with this important part of the system. Once I realized what the problem was, I rearranged two pieces of furniture and the problem was solved. By moving a lateral file cabinet next to the safe, which I keep clear of decorations or other items, I gave myself a convenient work space. This simple furniture shift changed keeping a check log from an annoyance to a simple, low maintenance habit.

- **Whenever you remove a check, look at the last entry in the check log to be sure none are missing.**
  If the next check in the tray is 1247, then the last check in the log should be 1246. If it is not, immediately find the lost check or personally call the bank to stop payment on it. Never allow anyone else to call the bank for you. It gives them the opportunity to steal the check, pretend the payment was stopped, and use the check later for unauthorized purchases.

- **Inform your employees that any damaged or ruined check must be brought to you for disposal.**
  Note the check number in your log, and then shred the ruined check. Never allow anyone to tell you they destroyed a check! Make it very clear to your accounting staff that you're the only person authorized to do so. If someone forgets and tells you that they destroyed a ruined check, call the bank and stop payment on it. Then, write up the employee for violating your company's security policy. Never let your check stock get out of your direct control!

- **Keep all checks–including unopened boxes–locked up in the safe.**

  Do not order more than you can safely lock up at any given time.

- **Keep a separate check log for each bank account.**

  For instance, I have an operating account for bills and non-payroll taxes, and a separate payroll-only account for paychecks and related taxes. Tracking two accounts with different check numbers could make things confusing, and confusion is a fertile field for financial fraud! Even now that we use direct deposit for our paychecks, the money comes out of the payroll account, where it is easy to track without the confusion of being mixed up with numerous payments coming out of the operating account.

- **Always keep a pen on top of your check log.**

  Never let something as simple and easily managed as your check log be bypassed for lack of a pen to write with. Always keep one with your register.

- **Last, but not least, never remove a check without logging it!**

  On the few occasions—and I mean count-them-on-one-hand few—I have been in such a hurry I didn't log a check, but I still created a record. I tore off the bottom section of a three-section check. I wrote my initials, date, amount, and payee on it. I set it on top of the check book, where I would see it the next time I got in the safe. Do that only in an emergency, as a pile of unentered check stubs can easily turn into a complicated task which you are unlikely to complete.

It is critical that you are so committed to this process it becomes second nature.

Your objectives are simple:

- Record the checks you removed from your stock, so that you can monitor them as they transition from paper to real money.

- Personally shred all ruined checks, then document their destruction.

By simply implementing this basic control, you have not only made your company much safer from check fraud, you have also laid the groundwork to accurately monitor all of the transactions that flow through your bank account.

Never forget how easy it is for a dishonest employee to take a piece of paper in the form of a blank check and turn it into cash, and do it right under your nose! Controlling and monitoring your check stock is as powerful as it is simple. Don't just take my word for it; check out these examples of every day, ordinary check fraud cases.

Here's Why

I read a lot, always with an eye out for the latest I can find on fraud and business theft. Some of the classic examples of check forgery that caught my eye include:

#1 Virginia Woman Charged with Embezzling $469K from Local Architectural Firm reported via the *Virginian-Pilot* on 3/21/2015.

A former employee of a prominent Virginia Beach architecture firm was arrested Thursday regarding an embezzlement scheme that cost the company nearly a half-million dollars.

Katherine Albert-McNaughton, 36, of Virginia Beach was charged with one count of making a forged security and two counts of engaging in monetary transactions relating to criminally derived property.

According to the indictment, Albert-McNaughton worked for HBA Architecture & Interior Design. It alleges she forged the signature of one of her bosses on 83 checks between October 2011 and June 2014. The checks totaled $469,831.89 and ranged in value from $768 to $9,987.

The theft was revealed last year during an internal audit, according to an affidavit for a search warrant filed in Virginia Beach Circuit Court.

Albert-McNaughton was responsible for handling the firm's accounts, making bank deposits and distributing petty cash and charitable contributions, the affidavit said. She also was required to make monthly reports to the firm's financial manager regarding discrepancies between the company's bank statements and general ledger.

The affidavit said the financial manager found a check missing and asked Albert-McNaughton for the statements. Albert-McNaughton became nervous and started crying, and claimed she had just received a call about a family member who had been in an accident. She said she needed to go to the hospital and left, the affidavit said.

#2 Pennsylvania Woman Sentenced for Embezzling $600K from Auto Dealership repored via the *TribLiveNews* on 3/11/2015.

A Lawrence County woman's request for home confinement as punishment for stealing nearly $600,000 from her employer was bold if not bordering on delusional, a federal judge said Wednesday.

U.S. District Judge Cathy Bissoon sentenced Deborah Cassini, 62, of New Castle to 3 1/2 years in prison and three years of probation.

The former office manager for Three Rivers Volkswagen of South Hills, Cassini pleaded guilty in August to four counts of wire fraud and three counts of filing false tax returns.

Her thefts nearly drove the dealership out of business, said Kathi Tennant, president of the company.

"We almost got padlocked three times," she said after the hearing. Bissoon ordered Cassini to pay $250,000 in restitution to the dealership's insurer and $397,000 to the dealership to cover her thefts and the cost of an audit that uncovered them.

"The dealership is still recovering. It hasn't returned to the financial position it was in before Cassini began stealing," Tennant said.

"We've gotten through the worst," she said.

Cassini apologized for her crimes.

"I never thought it would come to this," she said. "I never thought it would be this much money."

While Cassini worked at Three Rivers Volkswagen, she lived in Peters. Between 2006 and 2011, she used her online access to the company's bank accounts to make 163 payments to her credit cards and six payments on her BMW, prosecutors said.

She issued herself additional paychecks 98 times, regularly skimmed cash and wrote business checks to herself and to cash, prosecutors say. She concealed the thefts by making false entries in the dealership's accounting system and preparing false financial statements, prosecutors said.

"This was a long, destructive course of embezzlement and lies," Assistant U.S. Attorney Lee Karl said. "And it nearly destroyed Three Rivers Volkswagen."

"Cassini embezzled money so that she could play slot machines to forget her depression and other problems," said her attorney, Douglas Sughrue.

"Instead of cognitive therapy, she went to the casinos," he said.

Sughrue said Cassini didn't set out to steal $600,000. Most of the thefts were in small increments, and his client didn't total them to see how much she was stealing, he said after the hearing.

"The vast majority of them, in fact, are what the government and I would call cash-skimming," he said.

The evidence in the case showed she spent money on a lot of things other than gambling and generally was living beyond her means, Bissoon said.

"The defendant stole until there was nothing left to steal," the judge said.

For more information, including similar cases, reference *The Fraud Talk blog archives* by Chris Marquet, with SunBlock Systems, Inc. SunBlock is a leading computer forensics, e-discovery, cyber-investigations and digital security firm. Marquet leads its expanded Investigative Services Division.

Summing Up

A small percentage of thieves are caught; an even smaller percentage are prosecuted and pay any consequences for their actions. Setting up a system that monitors which of your checks have been issued and what they have been used for will significantly reduce the risk of fraud happening in your business.

CHAPTER 14

Daily Banking Review

**In terms of financial fraud,
low tech = big check,
but low tech is easy to catch!**

aily Banking Review completes the three basic pillars of financial security you must implement to protect your business:

- Get your own mail.

- Lock up your checks.

- Check your online bank accounts every day.

Other aspects of the FraudPoints System will help you set up additional controls to protect your business against a variety of common schemes. But, if you do nothing else, these "Big Three" will go a long way toward helping you prevent and detect the most common types of fraud.

When I say, "Check your online bank accounts every day," I mean check them every day. The ability to log online 24/7 allows you to verify whether or not the activity in your accounts is legitimate. This daily banking review is another of those simple, yet deceptively powerful, activities you must engage in.

Rosana Privitera Biondo owns Mark One Electric, a major electrical contractor in the Kansas City area. As a friend of many years, she once told me she looks at her bank accounts at least two to three times daily. It takes under a minute to log in and examine your accounts. If a person with a business the size of Rosie's can do it multiple times a day, the rest of us have no excuse to not do it at least once a day.

Although the FraudPoints AP and AR processes, which are explained in upcoming chapters, will build on the way you review your bank accounts, the first thing to do is just to start looking at them daily. As this becomes a habit and you become more familiar with important items—as well as the logistics of how your bank's online site works—it will become second nature to you. In fact, when I travel outside the country and don't feel confident about the security of my internet connection, I may miss doing my daily review—and it drives me nuts! Even though my adult daughter, whom I trust implicity, oversees the banking during my absences, it is very stressful if I can't access it as well.

You'll know your system is a success once missing your account review for a day becomes an annoyance for you—or if you catch yourself pulling out your smart phone to check before falling asleep! Taking ownership of your position as the person who is ultimately responsible for the financial well-being of your company is a great place in which to find yourself.

Before we move on, I want anyone who feels this practice constitutes a borderline obsession with money to consider one simple question: *How easy would it be to run your business without any?*

If everything you value in life hinges on money; if you would do anything—even if it was wrong—to get more of it; and if you neglect your family to earn more than you need, then you have a destructive obsession with money. If you keep your priorities in line with your principles, you'll recognize you must be ever-vigilant about protecting the financial resources of your company. If it benefits everyone who depends on you, then you have accepted your responsibilities as a wise steward. See the difference?

Where to File It in Your Business Bible

You'll set up a tab in Volume Three: Working Records, and insert a current copy of your inhouse check register. In my Business Bible, my main account is Tab Number One. If you have multiple accounts, set up multiple tabs. Since I have both an operating account and a payroll account, I have two tabs that are set up in an identical manner—one for each account.

I also have a holding account, which is interest-bearing. I sometimes move large sums of cash into it that will be held for more than a month. I do not have a separate section in my Business Bible for that, since there are never more than two or three transactions per month. It is easy for me to know what I have approved in that instance. But I look at it every day when I check my other accounts, just to make sure there are no unauthorized transactions.

Getting Started

> Taking ownership of your position as the person who is ultimately responsible for the financial well-being of your company is a great position in which to find yourself.

1. Review the most current copy of your bank statement, or wait for your new statement if it is due in a few days. In order to do your daily online account review effectively, your inhouse register must be as accurate as possible. Because of that, we will cover how to review your monthly bank statement.

2. After sorting all your mail, review the bank statements before anyone else touches them.

3. Remember, a dishonest accountant can Photoshop and alter bank statements to hide fraud, so look closely before turning them over to accounting.

If you have never reviewed a bank statement in a meaningful way before, you may not know what to look for. Here are the steps to take:

Step 1: Carefully Examine Each Check

Copies of cleared checks are usually located on the last few pages of your statement. Carefully examine ALL information on every check. Period. The five bulleted points below are invaluable for catching anything fraudulent.

1. **Skim down the page and check the signature on each check.** Is the signature yours? This only takes 5-10 seconds per page.

2. **Review each check, ensuring the payee and the amount on each check is accurate and confirming each check appears unaltered.** Does that make sense? In other words: Does the name of the payee and the amount of the check pass the smell test? A check might look OK, but ask yourself, "Did I really make a $4,058.27 payment for lawn care?" Additionally, anything that looks smudged, written over, or whited out should be checked on immediately!

3. **Do you recognize the person or company?** Modern technology gives people the ability to change a check in ways that look nearly perfect to the eye, but can still be easily detected if you just think about the information on it. *If you see a check made out to a company or person you have never heard of, you better find out why!*

4. **Review all the check numbers—both cleared and outstanding.** Look for out of sequence or duplicate check numbers. If your check log shows the next available check is #5678, you should not see check #2345 on your current statement; it should have cleared the bank long ago. Likewise, check #8901 should not have been issued yet. Additionally, no check number should appear more than one time!

   Follow up on any checks that have been outstanding for over 30 days. Call each payee and ask if they have an uncashed check.

If yes, ask to please have it deposited immediately. If not, explain that you'll stop payment and reissue the check, so no one thinks you wrote a bad check if someone finds it in a desk drawer and tries to cash it later.

If you do discover checks that begin with numbers you have not yet issued, it may indicate someone has found a way to take checks from your check stock. It's also possible they ordered unauthorized checks to use on your account. Check it out!

If you find duplicates or out-of-sequence checks, don't panic—just investigate.

- **First,** look at your check log to see if there is a reason a nonsequential check was issued. For instance: Did you open a new box of checks and use one before discovering there was already another box open?

- **Second,** look in your check stock to see if the check in question is there or not. If check #8901, which is way out of sequence, is missing from a box of checks you had not yet started to use, someone may have gained unauthorized access to your check stock. If check #8901 is still in the box, someone may have ordered extra checks you didn't approve. If you cannot solve the mystery quickly, call your bank and discuss how best to handle the matter. You may need to destroy your existing checks and order new ones.

One thing to keep in mind is that discovering duplicate check numbers or gaps in the numerical sequence could mean there is a defect in the checks themselves that causes the bank computers to read the numbers incorrectly. This happened to me once when I ordered checks from a discount company. But be careful—it might also mean someone is ordering unauthorized checks to steal money from your account.

5. Look at all other transactions, especially electronic ones.

Are there payments you didn't authorize? Are there transactions missing, such as regular tax or loan payments? Are there transactions you don't recognize, or which do not seem like normal amounts for the entity being paid? Are there deposits missing? Does your bank balance look a lot higher or lower that you thought it was? If there is anything that doesn't look right to you, investigate it!

Never be afraid to question—and confirm—any concerns you have about these transactions.

For instance, if you issued a check to Smith Concrete, and you see the name of the payee was changed to ABC Enterprises, find out why. If your accountant says Smith Concrete is a division of ABC Enterprises and they must have changed the name before depositing the check, verify it. You can easily look up ABC Enterprises online. If that doesn't tell you what you need to know, call Smith Concrete directly and ask to speak to the owner.

This may sound like a lot of trouble, but remember: You will almost never have to do it! You just need to know how and why in case you do find something amiss. It is also vitally important that your accounting staff knows you will do it.

Remember, this is a matter you must personally address. Sadly, although most accountants are honest, they are also the people in your company with the easiest opportunity to commit financial fraud and to hide it. Asking the accountant to solve a discrepancy is like asking the proverbial fox to take inventory of the hen house.

It is your responsibility, no matter how busy you are. You cannot delegate this oversight to anyone else. My accountant lied to me repeatedly when I asked her about accounting irregularities, and I always believed her. If someone else has managed to steal or alter a check, you will not only lose the stolen money—you will still owe Smith Concrete. Pay attention!

This basic review should not take you more than ten minutes a month. Ten minutes is nothing if it triggers the alarm that something could be wrong.

If I had done this, I would have caught my embezzlement the first month, simply by looking at the signatures on the checks. It is a very effective fraud protection strategy. If you do a daily review of all online account activity, you will automatically see each transaction when it occurs. This applies to missing deposits, as well. My primary purpose in reviewing my statement, since I do not look at the electronic copies of every check when doing my daily online review, is to confirm the checks are intact and contain my real signature. Then I account for all outstanding checks. Anything else: Missing deposits or tax payments, unauthorized withdrawals, out of sequence checks, or unusual transactions, should have been caught during the daily review.

> I want anyone who feels this practice constitutes a borderline obsession with money to consider one simple question: *How easy it would be to run your business without any?*

Step 2: Monthly Bank Reconciliation Report

This should be provided by your accountant within a week of receiving your monthly bank statements, if not within a couple of days. Many of you will have never thought to ask about it before. It tends to fall into the category of "stuff my accountant does that I don't pay attention to but goes in the files." That's what I used to think.

I considered reconciling the bank statements to be accounting housework—something to verify all the math was correct. Boy, was I wrong! The bank reconciliation will tell you several things:

- The amount of money withdrawn from your account during the month and the types of transactions: A check, an electronic withdrawal, or a transfer.

- Whether checks you issued during the month cleared the bank in a reasonable amount of time.

- If deposits, including loan proceeds, were properly credited to your account.

  This once caused me a huge problem when purchasing a piece of equipment. After signing the loan papers, I was given the all-clear to issue a check to the seller. There was only one problem—the loan officer forgot to transfer the money to my account. I discovered that when you write someone a check for over $10,000 and it bounces they get terribly cranky—no matter whose fault it is.

- If your inhouse records mirror the bank's records.

In short, it is an inhouse analysis that compares your internal accounting with the actual bank transactions. If you look at it carefully, it is also where you will find loose ends such as lost checks, bank errors, accounting anomalies, and financial fraud. Although only one of these is an intentional, criminal act, all of them reflect the fact you may not have as much money in the bank as you think you do. You had better figure out what is going on—and fix it!

Step 3: Match Your Records with the Report

- Compare your reconciliation report with your inhouse check register, which will be kept in your Business Bible back to the oldest outstanding check. You can either ask your accountant to reconcile the statement, which you will then carefully review and confirm, or you can do this initial reconciliation yourself, just to be sure no one has been pulling the financial wool over your eyes. When you do your initial reconciliation, mark your inhouse register as follows:

- Circle the check numbers that have not yet cleared the bank.

- Draw a line through the check number of all cleared checks.

- Mark off all checks which have cleared during the time between the issuance of the bank statement and the reconciliation report, up to the current day. You will do this by checking your online bank account.

- Make a list of all outstanding checks and review them for anything out of the ordinary.

- Investigate any anomalies. You are looking for a complete and accurate list of all checks issued on your account, and their current status.

You will accomplish two things during this process. First, you require accurate information on your inhouse register in order to conduct effective daily monitoring. Second, you need to account for and resolve any open transactions.

If your accountant has not been doing regular reconciliations, there might be a rough transition. You shouldn't automatically assume this is a sign of fraud, but it is certainly an inviting place for it to happen—a Fraud-Point. If it is impossible for you to resolve a particular issue, ask your bank for assistance. Since they can be liable for accepting forged checks or other fraudulent transactions, they are usually very willing to work with you.

The way you mark your check register will change slightly once you have implemented the FraudPoints Accounts Payable System. What you are doing right now is reconciling your bank statement to ensure you have an accurate point from which to start your daily monitoring.

Step 4: Pick a Regular Time to Review Your Online Accounts

Determine the best time for you. I find that first thing in the morning works best for me. Open your online account, with your Business Bible in hand, and review everything that has cleared since the previous day. Mark off all cleared transactions by drawing a line through the amount of the transaction in your register. I know this sounds like the opposite of how many of us were taught to balance our checkbooks, but there is a reason for it.

As you continue to implement additional FraudPoints systems, you will mark off the check number at the time you approve the transaction, and the amount of the transaction at the time it clears the bank. This allows you to confirm that the check register accurately reflects the checks and other transactions you approved. It also confirms those transactions cleared the bank properly. This two-step process verifies both approval and completion of your transactions.

As you review your daily banking activity and mark off transactions that cleared the bank, you will sometimes find things that are not accurate. For instance, you might learn the bank misread a check and paid the wrong amount. This is most likely to happen with handwritten checks, often involving money in the cents area. A check for $25.52 could clear the bank as $25.57. These numbers look very similar when written by hand. If something is obviously a small posting error you may choose to leave it, but you should still note the discrepancy on your check log.

You may also discover transactions like automatic minimum credit card payments, which have cleared the bank but were not listed in your register. When that happens, you should do two things:

1. Handwrite the transaction details on your copy of the check register: **O - 2/15 Citibank auto pay $52.00**

   The O indicates the transaction has not been recorded in your internal register. The date the transaction occurred and the payee are both noted, and the strike-through amount indicates it has cleared the bank. When you get your weekly copy of the check register and see that this has been entered in your internal balance, you will mark through the O.

My general rule: Markings on the left side of the register confirm internal verification, and markings on the right side confirm bank verification. In other words, I mark the left side of the register when noting I processed the transaction correctly, and the right side to confirm the bank cleared it correctly.

2. Notify your accountant to enter the transaction in the register. You can email, text or make a written list of corrections to the account. I always do this in writing.

Step 5: Do a Quick and Dirty Bank Balance

Deduct the outstanding transactions from the bank balance, add in any unrecorded deposits and verify your bank balance and internal balance are a close match.

If they aren't, find out why not. Personally, I may have the accountant look for discrepancies, but I always verify the information she brings back to me. If she recorded a deposit in the check register, but it hasn't posted to the bank account yet, I will make a note and watch for the deposit. Or, if I notified her the day before that two automatic credit card payments cleared the bank and she hadn't entered them yet, I would remind her and note it.

It is very important your accounting staff knows you will verify information they bring you. Keeping a bright light on all your accounting functions lets everyone know it will be next to impossible to hide anything. This will go a long way toward stopping fraud before it begins.

Verifying a match between the contents of your internal records with the bank records will both prevent and detect some of the most expensive and common fraud risks your company faces.

Remember, if I had implemented this system before my embezzlement, and spent the 20 to 30 minutes a day required to monitor my finances, it would have been worth over $2,500 an hour to me. By taking the time to do these small things, you have become your very own high-dollar financial consultant. Take your responsibilities seriously and let your business reap the rewards!

Definitions: You Need to Know and Understand

Bank reconciliation or reconciliation detail report:

A monthly report created by your accountant after your bank statements are received. It is like balancing your personal bank account, but with more detail. It should be a printed report you review and store. Personally, I do not routinely keep a copy of the bank reconciliation in my Business Bible, except when it contains information I need to follow up on.

Your report should include the numbers and amounts of all transactions: checks, electronic transfers or payments, deposits, and adjustments. It will provide you with a list of checks that were issued but have not cleared the bank, and outstanding transactions that occurred after the statement was issued. It should print directly from your accounting program.

Summing Up

My friend Jeffrey Combs, author of *The Procrastination Cure* as well as many other books on business and personal success, likes to say, "Low Tech = Big Check." In terms of financial fraud that is very true, especially given the massive amount of money lost to simple check fraud each year. But inversely, low tech is also easy to catch! Imagine how much safer and more secure your company will be when you implement these simple steps to handle your daily account reviews. It takes just a few minutes each day to complete this process. Once you create a routine that works for you, a habit is formed that will ensure you know exactly what is going on financially with your company at any given time. Talk about peace of mind!

CHAPTER 15

Passwords

As the owner, you must keep all passwords and logon information for every account, even though you will probably share them with some of your employees.

For many years, I was in the same boat as many other business owners. I stored a few passwords on a sticky note by my computer, and my office accountant solely possessed the rest. Since Tammie controlled all financial processes, I asked her for whatever information I needed, rather than using the passwords and looking for myself. She produced beautiful, completely organized reports, so looking at the original source documents seemed like a total waste of my time.

Tammie's setting up all the passwords wasn't even the worst of it—in the process she also set up all the security questions and listed her email as the address on file. Without knowing the name of the street she grew up on, where she'd met her husband or her father's middle name, I couldn't open the accounts. I later found much of this information on Rolodex cards in the file on top of her desk, where I—or anyone else who wanted to—could have seen it at any time!

I spent a great deal of time convincing the people at the credit card companies I owned the accounts, so I could set up new passwords—and view my own accounts!

Although they were very helpful, and I ultimately got all the necessary information, the process was difficult and time-consuming. I also felt incredibly stupid about yet another critical aspect of managing my business. Knowing what I know now, I realize it was more naiveté than stupidity, and I realize I am in good company. Many business owners find themselves in exactly this position when trying to get into their accounts, if the person who set accounts up is unavailable.

As the owner, you must keep a master list of all password and logon information for every secure account your business uses, even though you will probably share some of it with select employees. You need a comprehensive list of **You need a way to keep your passwords easily accessible, yet highly secure.** the information, which you keep under lock and key. Give it out on an "as needed" basis only, and note who you give access to. If you choose not to share logon information with anyone else, I understand, but you must realize that decision will shift certain tasks to you that could otherwise be delegated to someone else. It will likely become unrealistic if your organization grows.

My personal decision is to allow my accountant to know passwords, but not the answers to security questions. Additionally, I carefully monitor the transactions on each credit and bank account. I am continually on the lookout for irregularities of any kind, whether they be fraud or simple mistakes. Ultimately, you will have to decide what method works best for you.

I store my logon information and passwords in two ways:

1. A spreadsheet with the logon information.

2. An encrypted password storage program on my electronic devices.

Spreadsheets

Include:

- Account name, such as ABC Bank, CitiCard, or Amazon.

- Last four digits of account number, if applicable—to help identity the specific account.

- Username—also known as logon.

- Password or PIN. Some accounts require both.

- Security image, if required.

- Security questions and answers.

- Email address associated with account.

- Physical address associated with account, if you have more than one.

- URL: Where to find it on the internet.

- Notes

For instance, I have a credit card that requires different usernames and passwords to view the account activity versus to pay the account. I leave a note to remind myself. You could also list a contact name and phone number or other related information here.

CREDIT CARD LOGON

Card Name	Last 4 Digits	Username	Pin	Password	Email	URL	Notes
Chase Visa	1234	Owner	4567	Safe101	me@abc.com	chase.com	No security image

The document should be password protected, so no one who happens to get unauthorized access to your computer can open it. Spreadsheets allow you to remove extraneous information if you want to print a copy for someone who needs only limited information.

My spreadsheet separates bank accounts, credit card accounts, vendors, tax accounts, and any other sites or accounts I need a password to access.

Encrypted Password Storage

These programs give you the ability to electronically store information you don't want to share, such as the answers to security questions. You hold important passwords at your fingertips, wherever you go. I personally use an encrypted password storage application on my phone called Keeper®, although many other programs are available. Keeper is free to use on one device, and there is a small annual charge for multiple devices. A top IT specialist recommended a similar app: Lastpass®.

I spent a great deal of time convincing people at the credit card companies I owned the accounts, so I could set up new passwords—and view my own accounts!

Because I travel, as well as occasionally work from home, I like the portability of an electronic program to manage this information. It's beneficial, as well, to store confidential information on a private device. I am in no way tech savvy, so I read up on different programs and rely on good reviews from knowledgeable individuals.

Business Bible Location

Place a current spreadsheet in its own section, under a tab labeled "Passwords."

As you update your sheet, place the new copy here and shred the old one. NEVER, under any circumstances, leave this document where anyone else can see it. Anyone with a smart phone—and five seconds alone—can simply photograph it and have access to everything you are trying to guard.

How to Get Started

Compile a list of every account which requires logon information to access.

Include:

- Credit Cards
- Bank Accounts
- Email Accounts
- Merchant Accounts
- Tax Payment or Filing Accounts
- Travel Account Memberships
- Credit Card or Other Reward Partners
- Anything Else with a Password

Start fresh, by setting up new passwords for every account.

Share the new passwords only with employees who really need them. Don't use a password anyone in your office already knows. If your middle name is Alice and you were born in 1965, and you have always used variations like Alice1965, 1965Alice or 19alice65—do a total change. Don't make it hard—have fun with it! Since your passwords are usually entered multiple times a day, use positive reinforcement words or phrases, like *#1FITnessQueen!* or *wOrlds#1mOm*. By doing this, you will keep your accounts secure, and give yourself a boost at the same time!

Use a mixture of upper and lower-case letters, as well as symbols.

Make it nearly impossible for someone to guess the correct password.

Change the answers, on all accounts, to your security questions.

Make sure no one can go behind your back to reset passwords or transfer money. Store the new security questions and responses ONLY on your personal encrypted password application or master password list.

Important things to consider as you start this process include:

- Approaching the subject with your current employees.

  If you have worked through the other security measures, like getting your mail and locking up your checks, your office staff already knows you are establishing security controls. Changing passwords for accounts and locking out anyone who doesn't need the information could make some of your employees feel you no longer trust them.

  While you should never let yourself be manipulated by someone trying to send you on a "Don't you trust me?" guilt trip, you must be sensitive to the feelings of your employees. They may not yet realize these controls are not a reflection on their performance, but a system designed to protect their jobs from fraudsters. Realize that anyone who fights you too hard on establishing better financial controls could have a selfish—or even dishonest—reason for doing so. Clearly communicate the goal behind these changes, then be mindful of how people respond.

- Committing yourself to investigating anything that seems fishy, no matter where it leads.

A woman business owner, who wishes to remain anonymous while her case is under investigation, recently shared a financial fraud and password manipulation experience with me:

> *When my former CFO—we'll call him George—created passwords for the company online bank and credit card accounts and did not share them with me, I didn't think twice about it. After all, I wasn't managing those things. It was his job.*
>
> *Later, when I suspected something was wrong and couldn't check my own accounts without his assistance, I realized it was because he didn't want me to have access to them. When I asked*

him for the passwords so I could see the accounts for myself, he not only refused to give me the usernames and passwords—he tried to make it seem like I was being unreasonable, and accused me of not trusting him!

When I called him into my office to fire him, it was a closely orchestrated dance in which all passwords were changed as he was being terminated. We changed log-in account names as well as passwords. In under 15 minutes, we had locked him out of all accounts. I chose passwords that did not have to do with me personally or with the company, and discarded the triggers used during his tenure.

We could not change any secure information before he was physically in my office because he had alerts on his phone that notified him when anyone got into the bank or credit card accounts. We didn't want to tip him off, because we were afraid he would go in and cover up evidence of possible fraud before we could see everything for ourselves.

George figured out he was going to be fired that day because the managing director of the company and I had a meeting at the bank about potential problems with my accounts. His banker—who is also our banker—tipped him off that trouble was afoot. Ultimately, he hijacked his own firing in such a way as to draw attention away from the potential fraud issue, and divert it to poor performance. He said he could understand why he would be terminated, since he hadn't paid the taxes, and it would be difficult to continue to pay him the large salary he was making.

At the end of the meeting, he said, "Oh, by the way, I was wrong. I thought I repaid the cruise expenses you gave me permission to put on your AMEX card. But, I actually deposited those funds into the company account."

The accountant who sat in on the meeting looked at me incredulously and just kept shaking his head. Finally, George said he had to leave immediately to pick his child up at daycare and would not be able to give us any QuickBooks information for several hours. In the end, he did not give us the information for almost 18 hours. We are currently investigating our books to see what changes he made during that time. How much fraud he committed remains to be seen.

Knowing what I know now, I would never have let him—or any other employee—be the only one with passwords to my accounts. Additionally, I wish I had understood how important it was for me to monitor the activities of anyone with access to company accounts, and to continually review source documents.

Looking back on everything, sometimes I feel a little stupid, but stupid women don't build successful businesses. I simply never realized how easy it is to commit financial fraud, or how important it is to proactively prevent it. I didn't know what to do then, but I do now. I run my company in a much more careful and secure way. This will never happen to my business again!

Controlling your passwords is no different than using a house key; I have great neighbors whom I trust, but I still lock my house and give keys only to those who need them. To keep your accounts secure, complete the primary objectives of this module:

1. Change all passwords and security questions, so you know exactly who has access to each account.

2. Compile a spreadsheet with account information, which can be given out on an "as needed" basis.

3. Set up an encrypted password system to hold all additional security information, including answers to security questions.

4. Going forward, proactively change the password to any account account you suspect has been compromised. Be sure to store all updates on your Password Master List and your encrypted system.

Realize that anyone who fights you too hard on establishing better financial controls could have a selfish—or dishonest—reason for doing so.

Summing Up

Knowing who has access to your passwords is essential. Having a master list of all passwords PLUS related security questions is critical for the financial protection and preservation of your company. In many companies it is common for employees to come up with their own unique password and/or security questions, if they are given access to an account. If that is happening in your company, stop the practice immediately! You create both so you can delete them as necessary. And, if the employee leaves for any reason, change it yourself.

As the owner of the company, the password buck needs to stop with you!

CHAPTER 16

Accounts Receivable

**Accounts Receivable is the heart of your business.
It is the invoicing, collection, recording,
and depositing of money owed to you.**

Accounts Receivable (AR) can be an enormous temptation for dishonest accountants, since it presents numerous opportunities to commit fraud. The multitude of ways businesses receive and record money make it difficult to design a single, one-size-fits-all fraud prevention system. You may have to spend a little creative time analyzing how money flows into your business—and how you can protect it by identifying key FraudPoints.

When you think like a thief, you will be able to find the FraudPoints in your AR system.

By using your "thinking like a thief" skills, you will design a customized method to protect your cash flow.

I repeat: Accounts Receivable is the heart of your business. It is the invoicing, collection, recording, and depositing of money owed to you.

This section addresses invoices and corresponding payments, which are probably being processed almost entirely by your accountant. Accounts Receivable payments generally process through mail or EFT, and not point of service or retail cash sales. If your business engages in the latter, I recommend working with an accounting consultant who specializes in point of sale fraud prevention, to design a series of prevention and detection controls to protect you from theft in those areas.

By using your "thinking like a thief" skills, you will be prepared to help your consultant design a customized method to protect your retail cash flow. Remember, you still face risk from accounting fraud, so don't eliminate or neglect your accounting controls. Always add point-of-sale controls to your system. Controls in these areas work hand-in-hand to protect FraudPoints in your business.

Accounts Receivable fraud is a common and expensive way for businesses to lose money, since incoming payments are easy to steal and can be difficult to track. In accountant-speak, this type of theft is generally known as "asset misappropriation" or "skimming." In layman's terms, it's effectively "shoplifting," since it means someone pockets your payments and walks out the door with them without your knowledge. Specifically, AR fraud refers to the interception of money coming into your business before it can be recorded or deposited as a company asset. Luckily, there are ways to both prevent and detect this type of fraud.

Invoicing stands as the foundation of your AR process. It is imperative you oversee the accuracy and completeness of this process. I will provide examples for companies similar to my own, but you will need to customize your own invoicing system based on how your company does things. If you invoice multiple clients electronically or by mail each day, you will handle invoicing very differently than someone who sends bills to a small number of clients on the 15th of every month, or who personally delivers them upon completion of a project.

Before you begin setting up the controls in the FPS Accounts Receivable module, you need to examine your current invoicing system.

- Do you know precisely how your system works?

- How often do you invoice?

- What steps are involved in your process?

- What information do you provide to accounting?

- Do you track invoices by number?

- Can anyone revise or delete an invoice? This is controlled by a setting in your accounting software.

- How do you handle invoices you choose to write off for nonpayment?

- How could a dishonest person manipulate your invoicing system to steal from your company?

Think like a thief and look for your FraudPoints.

Since you are now watching your bank account on a regular basis and handling your own daily mail, the easiest way for someone to steal your money may be the interception of payments—such as an office visit copay, a retainer for future services, or an invoice paid in person—and then delete the corresponding invoice. The invoice simply disappears, nothing ever shows up as past due, the books balance, and the business owner is none the wiser.

AR fraud is a common and expensive way for businesses to lose money, since payments are easy to steal and can be difficult to track.

As an alternative to deleting invoices, your accountant may tell you she sent the client numerous bills and called them repeatedly with no results, and recommends you write the accounts off or sell them to a collection agency. If you request she send the past due accounts to collection, and you don't have a clear list of these accounts to verify with the collection agency, she can remove any accounts with stolen payments before sending them. That way, no one who really paid their bill will contact you to complain about calls from a collection agency, and you will be led to believe that a good client is really a deadbeat.

From Cheryl's Desk

A friend's husband is a chiropractor. He discovered a massive insurance copay theft at his office. When patients came in and paid for their copays or noncovered treatments by cash or check, the accountant pocketed the payments. Then she issued internal invoices to balance the books, but never sent the invoices to the patients. She deleted invoices from the system, a few at a time, or wrote them off as uncollectable.

In a little over a year, the doctor lost an estimated $100,000. Since no one monitored either the issuance or deletion of invoices, it was a simple theft for the dishonest accountant. Additionally, deleting the invoices hid nearly all proof of the crime, since there was no way to track the missing cash.

The chiropractor could not prosecute the accountant, since she carefully destroyed all evidence on an ongoing basis. They could look back and see that they had not received payment for many patients, but could not see where the money had gone, so they had no way to prove the accountant was responsible for the missing payments. Easy as pie, and very profitable!

Along with the basic objectives for sound invoicing, I will list some potential dangers. Do not be afraid to call in an accounting consultant to assist you if you feel overwhelmed, or if you just want some professional expertise. Be sure to go over all the listed fraud prevention objectives with your consultant, including any FraudPoints you know exist, but you don't know how to handle. Since this person is only consulting, and not actually handling your books or payments, it is unlikely you have any significant fraud risk from this engagement. However, always be on your guard!

If you do choose to call in a consultant to help set up a more secure invoicing process, there is something important you must keep in mind—you are not trying to learn how to be an accountant! You are learning to manage an accountant, and that is a very different thing.

- *Do not let any consultant leave you feeling confused or stupid because you don't understand accounting terminology or acronyms.* Stop him or her every time something is said you don't understand. Ask to have it explained in layman's terms. Anyone who is working with you needs to be reminded to keep it simple. The only thing you should require is assistance in setting up an invoicing system and meeting the objectives listed here.

- *Do not let yourself be pressured into setting up an invoicing or management system so complex only an accountant or someone with an advanced degree can manage or implement it.* If you are paying a consultant to set it up, you need to understand the concepts behind it, the basic operations, and who you can contact for assistance if you have questions. You are paying them ... they work for you, not the other way around. *Do not let yourself become discouraged because you don't understand things they have spent years learning.*

You have probably never considered how easy it is to use an inaccurate invoice to commit fraud.

Remember, your consultant is probably not an expert in your field, either. You are on a path to learning more about business financial management, and that is something you should feel great about!

Objective #1: Ensure all invoices are accurate.

I know this sounds obvious, but you have probably never considered how easy it is to use an inaccurate invoice to commit fraud. You need to receive all the money clients owe you without offending anyone by overcharging them.

If your accountant undercharges an invoice, they may receive kickbacks from dishonest clients who are saving money by being billed less than they owe you. When issuing inaccurately high invoices, a fraudster can trick your clients into paying more than they owe, collect the higher payment, delete the old invoice and issue a new one for the correct amount. Then they pocket the difference!

As an alternative to deleting invoices, your accountant may tell you she sent the client numerous bills and called them repeatedly with no results, and recommend you write the accounts off or sell them to a collection agency.

If you continually correct or delete invoices, or issue credits or refunds for overpayments, you have a very confusing space in your business—creating a fertile environment for fraud. As a separate issue, it makes you look unprofessional and disorganized to your clients, as well. Get your system streamlined and secure!

Objective #2: Ensure no one can delete an invoice, duplicate an invoice number, issue a credit or write off an unpaid account without your knowledge and consent.

Many small business accounting systems allow you to set up system administrator controls to prevent these issues.

If you do not feel you can competently research and implement the control systems in your accounting software, then examine and consider your options. You can call and talk to the technical support team, take an online class to learn the system, or hire a consultant to get expert advice. They will tell you what controls your system offers and how to use them. It is likely your system does all sorts of things you never knew it did. Until now, you might not have even understood the need for them!

Some of those controls are already in place and will, at the touch of a button, issue reports for your review, or limit what functions others can perform without approval from the administrator, which should be you.

You should also find out if your system will allow you to run an audit trail, which is simply a report on all activity within the system. Find out what controls your system includes, and learn how to use them to protect your company.

Remember, if someone can delete an invoice, they can conceal the theft of payments made against it. Your books will balance, and you will not detect the fraud. Controlling the ability of your accountant to change or delete invoices is critical.

> **Controlling the ability of your accountant to change or delete invoices is critical.**

Objective #3: Tie all received money to an AR account.

If you do not have a record of issuing an invoice, and you receive a payment—check it out promptly!

I once received a payment for services I could not identify. No one in the office had any idea what was going on, there was no corresponding invoice, and I was on the warpath. *Why? Isn't getting money a good thing?* Yes, but if someone is sending me unexpected money that I didn't issue an invoice for, then someone in my organization is performing billable work without going through the regular channels—a HUGE FraudPoint!

> **Immediately investigate anything that isn't processed in the expected fashion.**

As it turns out, it was simply an internal error in which we invoiced the wrong client—who had not yet contacted us about the error—and the real client, who knew how much he owed us, just paid his bill without waiting to receive an invoice.

Immediately investigate anything that isn't processed in the expected fashion. Exceptions may mean fraud is being committed by an employee who has found a way to provide billable items to your clients, and is planning to intercept the payment. If this employee partners with your accountant to falsify or fail to issue invoices, you can suffer major losses.

It is not uncommon for crooked accountants to print an invoice on a duplicate version of your accounting program, list a post office box—which they control—as the "Remit to:" address and then alter incoming checks so they can be deposited into the fraudster's account. Receiving a payment for a missing invoice may be a red flag for this kind of fraud. Be aware of the green, yellow and red flags initially introduced in Chapter 5, *Red Flags*.

Objective #4: Take control of all incoming checks and bank deposits.
The exact process for doing this is detailed below. Just remember that ensuring all of your cash goes where you intend for it to go is one of your most important AR objectives.

Now that you know how to monitor your invoicing, let's move on to how to process and protect the money you receive for those invoices.

Keep in mind, every invoice sent out—which shows on your books as a receivable—should generate an incoming payment. As in the other modules, you need to set up both prevention and detection controls for your Accounts Receivable module.

You began the basic process of setting up prevention controls when you started getting your own mail. You implemented certain detection controls when you started reviewing your bank accounts regularly. Now, you are going to add onto those basic steps for more extensive security.

STEP 1
Set up an AR tab in your Business Bible, print out an AR report—which should show all open invoices--and file the report accordingly.

Your AR report should include:

- *Client Name*
- *Invoice Number*
- *Due Date of Invoice*

This assists in planning cash flow, since you can see the payment due date and anticipate what payments should be coming in and when.

- *Aging—you can omit aging and rely on the due date of the invoice, if you prefer.*
  This will be blank if the invoice is under 30 days old, or will show several days past due if it's older. If a bill sent on January 15 is considered due on February 15, this column will be blank on February 10, but will have 5 in it on February 20. Although it may seem redundant, this makes it easier to quickly scan the information on the report and find past due invoices. Use this to reflect your own billing deadlines.

- *Amount of invoice*
  I like to have invoices listed individually under a client's name, as a single client may have multiple invoices due on different dates. This way I can see the total amount they owe, as well as when each payment is due.

- *Notes*
  Gather information about the specific project, if you often do multiple projects for the same clients. You may also invoice for progress payments on large projects. Be clear about each invoice. Example: Progress Payment #2, or Landmark Shopping Center, or even They will pay 50% in 30 days and the balance by June 1.

My report also includes a Total AR figure at the very end of the report. If the total of the Accounts Receivable is higher than the total Accounts Payable, I'm a happy business owner!

3:09 PM 05/17/18				**Open Invoices** As of May 17, 2018					
	Type	Date	Num	P. O. #	Terms	Due Date	Class	Aging	Open Balance
ABC Pipe									
State Highway Project					Net 30				
	Invoice	04/11/2018	1212			04/11/2018	Trucking	36	3240.00
	Invoice	04/19/2018	1234			04/19/2018	Trucking	28	3420.00
	Invoice	05/08/2018	3456			05/08/2018	Trucking	9	2700.00
	Invoice	05/16/2018	6313			05/16/2018	Trucking	1	3600.00
Total KAN005-81									12960.00
Total ABC Pipe									12960.00
Smith Concrete									
14556 Mission Drive									
	Invoice	05/08/2018	6767		Net 0	05/08/2018	Trucking	9	1035.00
Total 14556 Mission									1035.00
Total Smith Concrete									1035.00

This is an example of an Accounts Receivable report, which my accounting program calls Open Invoices. It is a list of all the money owed to your business and when it is due.

STEP 2

Have your endorsement stamp ready when you open your mail. *For all checks, you will immediately endorse incoming payments. (This was introduced previously when we discussed handling your own mail.)*

Use a self-inking customized stamp, which can be found online from any office supply store, and which says "For Deposit Only," followed by your company name.

The minute you open an envelope with a payment in it, turn the check over and stamp it in the endorsement area. Once endorsed, the check cannot be deposited into a non-company account or presented for cash. DO NOT include your bank account number on the stamp, so you can deposit it into any company bank account.

STEP 3

Mark items on your AR report with the date you received the payment.

You can simply hand draw a line through both the invoice number and the amount of each invoice, then note the date at the side. At any time, you can see who paid, what they paid and when they paid it.

If anyone comes into your office to pay their account in person, make sure your staff brings either the actual payment—cash or check—or proof of a credit card payment, to you for documentation at least once per day. After you have personally viewed it, check it off on your report. Remember, all final processing for deposit must be completed by you personally.

	Type	Date	Num	P. O. #	Terms	Due Date	Class	Aging	Open Balance
3:09 PM **05/17/18**					**Open Invoices** As of May 17, 2018				
ABC Pipe									
State Highway Project					Net 30				
	Invoice	04/11/2018	1212			04/11/2016	Trucking	36	3340.00 ⁷/₁₃
	Invoice	04/19/2018	1234			04/19/2018	Trucking	28	3420.00 ⁹/₁₃
	Invoice	05/08/2018	3456			05/08/2018	Trucking	9	2700.00
	Invoice	05/16/2018	6313			05/16/2018	Trucking	1	3600.00
Total KAN005-81									12960.00
Total ABC Pipe									12960.00
Smith Concrete									
14556 Mission Drive									
	Invoice	05/08/2018	6767		Net 0	05/08/2018	Trucking	9	1035.00
Total 14556 Mission									1035.00
Total Smith Concrete									1035.00

This is an example of how I mark up a report.

STEP 4

Store the payments in your Business Bible—which is stored in your locked safe—until your deposit day.

If you haven't gotten around to setting up a safe for your accounting materials yet, deposit checks daily rather than leaving them around the office. You must give your full attention to the money coming into your business.

Most of us don't take the time to pay bills every time one comes in the mail. Going to the grocery store daily would be inconvenient, and managing your business deposits is no different. You may make your deposits as seldom or frequently as you choose, if you are willing to take the time to follow the process. Installing a safe as quickly as possible will give you flexibility.

Carelessly rushing through deposits, instead of giving them your full attention once a week, may open the door to fraud. Personally, I use a clear plastic page protector sheet at the very front of my Business

Bible, where I place all incoming checks as soon as they are endorsed and marked as paid on the AR report.

I recommend you consider how often you need to make deposits, then set a regular time to do it. You should deposit them at least once a week. You may opt to deposit more frequently due to a high volume of payments, an exceptionally large check, the need for immediate cash, or if you receive payment from someone who is unreliable—and you want to be sure the check clears.

Make a point of setting aside the time to carefully follow the rest of the steps each time you make a deposit.

STEP 5

Deposit Day! Set aside a few minutes to work, uninterrupted, and get the checks out of your Business Bible.

1. Review each check, to be sure it was endorsed.

2. Check your AR report, and make sure each paid invoice is checked off.

3. Count the number of checks you will deposit, and write it on a sticky note.

4. Add up the total dollar amount of the checks, and write it on the same sticky note.

5. Place the sticky note on the front of the page protector where you stored the checks.

6. Prepare your deposit. You have options for this step.

   • If you already endorsed the checks, marked the AR report, and documented both the number of checks and the amount of the deposit, you can safely give them and the completed bank deposit slip to your accountant to take to the bank.

Remember, you will need to provide the payment information to the accountant so she can post the payments in your accounting system.

- You can provide the deposit information to your accountant so she can update your system, but make the physical deposit yourself.

- Most banks offer electronic deposit options. The process may be more cumbersome and expensive for business accounts than the options available for personal accounts. Determine if this is an option for you. The advantage of an electronic deposit is that it's done at your convenience (which could be within minutes of receiving a check) via either a mobile app and secured linkage with the bank, or with a separate scanner placed in your office.

No matter what else is going on, you must still follow the steps for this module. Make sure all checks are correctly deposited into your account, and nothing was lost due to fraud or error.

7. The following day during your bank account review, verify the funds were accurately credited to your account. Because you endorsed the checks before releasing them, no one else should be able to access the funds. Since you made a record of paid accounts, the number of checks deposited, and the amount of the deposit, any discrepancies that do occur should be simple to track down and fix.

8. After confirmation, remove the sticky note with the deposit information on it from your Business Bible, and throw it away.

STEP 6

Ask your accountant to run an updated Accounts Receivable report, or run one yourself.

Compare the old and new reports, side by side. Any receivables that weren't marked as paid on the old report should remain on the new report. Unless you have an extraordinary number of receivables, this should take less than five minutes.

You will see new receivables reflecting invoicing done since the last report, but only paid and closed transactions should be missing from the new report. (If you have a high number of daily invoices and deposits, you may want to do this more often than once a week.) Although receivables have probably been added to the new report, which reflects items invoiced since the last report, nothing should be missing unless you have recorded a corresponding payment. If something is missing, find out why. Use source documents to confirm the payment was received, and have a serious talk with your staff about the process.

Failure to comply in the future will be grounds for dismissal. Any item removed from the Accounts Receivable report without your personal knowledge and consent, whether due to a received payment or a write off, must be investigated.

As you monitor your Accounts Receivable report, you will need to have a consistent policy about handling past due invoices, ensuring that no one in your office makes an adjustment or writes off an invoice without your direct approval. Although you may choose to follow up on late payments yourself, you may want to have your staff make the initial contact. Personally, I don't become directly involved unless it is an exceptionally large invoice, or it is over 60 days in arrears.

Here's a must: You need to determine the point at which you will personally follow up on a past due invoice:

- Anything over 30 days?

- Over $1,000?

- From new clients?

- For certain products or services?

Remember, any opportunity to steal an incoming payment and delete the corresponding invoice from your system is a huge FraudPoint! Your best defense is to follow these steps carefully and watch for anything unusual or unexplained.

As you monitor your AR processes on a regular basis, be on the lookout for:

- Invoices to clients you don't recognize.

- Seriously past due accounts—especially from clients who normally pay on time.

- Duplicate invoice numbers or amounts.

- Or anything else that just doesn't look right to you.

Certainly, ask your accountant about things you don't understand, but never hesitate to personally confirm the information you are given. The more clearly your staff understands that you will nearly always follow up on questionable items, the more likely they are to be honest and truthful with you.

If you receive payments by credit card, be sure to regularly verify that each transaction on your merchant account is tied to a receivable. It is more difficult to divert credit card payments than those made by check or cash, but thieves can be creative. Nothing should be removed from your Accounts Receivable report unless you have confirmed a payment has been received.

If you don't have a deposit record for a client whose account shows as paid, and the accountant says they paid by credit card, check your merchant account for confirmation. If you don't have time right then, make a note on your AR register to check it when you have time. Ask questions often—your employees will know fraudulent activity will be caught.

Summing Up

Standard accounting recommendations for prevention of AR fraud include elaborate instructions about segregation of duties between multiple accounting employees and departments.

Although a lot of fraud can be derailed by delegating company financial duties in this way, it is completely impractical for most small businesses. Having separate people collect mail, process incoming cash, handle invoicing, process credit card payments, reconcile bank accounts, and deal with past due invoices may make your business more secure, but only a fairly large business can justify a half a dozen people in their accounting department.

Fortunately, now you don't have to worry about that. Just follow the FPS Accounts Receivable module carefully, and you should always know where your money is!

CHAPTER 17

Accounts Payable

**Without a good prevention and detection system in place,
you can lose thousands of dollars a year—and never even notice.**

Many years ago, I found a recurring charge for $34.99 on my company phone bill; one I did not recognize. I finally discovered it was a charge for a website, set up on my behalf without my knowledge or authorization. Fraud experts refer to this activity as "cramming," where an outside party crams unauthorized charges onto an otherwise legitimate bill. This is especially common with telephone bills.

The company charged me the false fee every month for nearly three years, and buried it at the back of a 48-page phone bill—under a vague and confusing description. By threatening to complain to the FCC, I received a complete refund of my money—which was over nine-hundred dollars! Employees can set up similar automatic charges on your accounts for a variety of personal goods and services. They can easily conceal these charges on lengthy credit card bills, invoices, or bank statements. Without a good prevention and detection system in place, you can lose thousands of dollars a year—and never even notice.

Accounts Payable (AP), a.k.a. "Paying the Bills," while less fun than Accounts Receivable, is a critical part of your business. It requires close monitoring because it is vulnerable to multiple types of fraud. Developing an efficient and secure system to manage what bills you pay, in addition to how and when to pay them, is critical to your business on many different levels. If you pay your bills late or haphazardly, you will get a reputation for being a "Late Pay." This designation can lead to:

- Unwillingness to extend you credit

- Lowered credit ratings and FICO scores

- Higher interest rates on loans

- Limited ability to purchase business equipment and materials

- Expensive late charges on your accounts

- Higher rates for basic services like insurance and credit cards

Managing your AP in a careless or disorganized way opens the door to a variety of financial woes, in addition to some of the simplest and most expensive fraud schemes out there.

Because of the interconnectedness of financial systems within your company, problems within one area will often spill over into others.

For instance, carefully managed AP processes help you prevent and detect:

- Theft of check stock

- Unauthorized bank transactions

- Credit card fraud

- Bribery or kickbacks

- Non-payment of taxes

Organized AP processes help prevent errors, such as making duplicate payments or underpaying vendors due to lost invoices. Whether deliberate or accidental, paying invoices more than once is an expensive waste of money, and it puts you in the position of relying on the organization and honesty of another company to correct the overpayment.

Many fraud schemes start as the result of an innocent error the owner doesn't discover, but which a fraudster will recognize as an opportunity to steal without being caught. If you process and pay invoices without careful oversight, make frequent processing mistakes, or turn everything over to your accountant to handle without your supervision, you are leaving an attractive window of fraud opportunities open for unscrupulous employees.

The success of the FPS Accounts Payable module depends on the successful implementation of the previous systems. If you haven't started managing your company mail, you have lost control of your AP before you even start. Why? Because you don't have any idea where the invoices came from, and your accountant can pay them—whether legitimate or not—with the push of a button. Just as the FPS Accounts Receivable module depends on accurate internal invoicing for proper functionality, so the FPS Accounts Payable module depends on the screening of incoming mail and verification of invoices in advance of their entering the AP phase.

If you think that sounds like a little bit of work, it is. If you think it is beneath you, the business owner, to open the mail, review the invoices and personally sign all the checks—it is not! Chapter 12, *Mail* discussed the importance of looking over your mail before passing it on. As you implement the AP system, you will build on how you handle the mail, and how that mail becomes part of your company's financial processes.

Although you occasionally see tricky, complicated schemes in AP fraud, the clear majority are disturbingly simple. Remember:

Low Tech = Big Check!

Why is your Accounts Payable so crucial? Simply this—AP is fertile ground for things like:

- Billing schemes
- Paying shell companies

- Concealing personal purchases

- Fraudulent expense reimbursements

- Check tampering

Many of these schemes are easy to automate. Once set up, the thief can effortlessly get money from your business repeatedly, opening the victim company (that's you) to a constant drain of cash. Over time, any one of these—let alone multiple schemes—can bankrupt you.

Because you pay bills often, a successful fraud scheme might become so routine you do not see the evidence right in front of you.

The ease of setting up a profitable, efficient, and ongoing AP fraud system is frightening. Even with this system in place, you must stay on your toes.

Although employees other than an accountant can employ these strategies, particularly fraudulent personal purchases and reimbursements, an honest accountant may catch the perpetrator and notify you of fraud. A dishonest accountant can either run the scheme himself, or demand a "cut of the action" from the crook to overlook evidence of the crime.

Let's take a moment and examine some of these schemes in more detail:

1. **Personal Purchases** *Employee uses company resources, such as a company credit card, to buy personal items.*
   A person can "legitimize" non-authorized purchase receipts by placing them in the middle of a pile of legitimate purchases. Once it becomes clear you never review these items, the thief may give up all effort to conceal the unauthorized purchases, making it even easier to catch—if you simply look. For instance, an accountant authorized to purchase office supplies can buy personal things like shoes or vitamin pills—right along with the company purchases.

Employee may buy excessive amounts of legitimate items and take the surplus home. Ink cartridges are a frequently stolen item. You order them often, they are expensive, and you probably have no idea how quickly you use them. They are small, portable, and easy to steal. Unless you review the invoices or receipts, confirm the supply closet stock, and know how many you should normally use, this is simple to pull off. Even if you are reviewing receipts for obviously fraudulent items, the over-purchasing of common items—such as ink cartridges, postage stamps or copy paper—may be easily overlooked.

Don't be too trusting here. People turn in personal receipts masked as business purchases for things like dry cleaning, flowers or gifts, electronics, travel expenses, meals, automotive repairs, fuel, and so on. The list is large, and includes many items that may be legitimately used by your business. They just aren't *always* ...

I use subscription services, such as Amazon Subscribe and Save, to gain control over regular expenditures. Many supply companies now offer similar automated programs, and may even give you a discount for regular purchases. You can arrange to have commonly used items, such as copy paper, ink cartridges, toilet paper, and so forth, automatically delivered to your business on a regular schedule. If you personally oversee stock and submit orders, a thief may be a lot more careful about asking you to purchase unnecessary items.

2. Fraudulent Reimbursements or Expense Reports *Employees typically commit this fraud when they request reimbursement for out-of-pocket expenses or document charges to a company account.*

Some common fraudulent purchases are business trip hotel rooms or an expensive lunch with a client, for which the employee fills out an expense report. These schemes often involve money spent away from the office, so they can be problematic to verify.

3. **Personal Vacations** *An employee may arrange a trip and present it as a business meeting or seminar.*

In fact, it is a personal trip the company has been tricked into paying for. Picking up literature to prove you were at a seminar can be quite simple, even if you didn't stay for the presentations. It works for meals; knowing who someone ate lunch with can be difficult to discern. A fraudster often turns in numerous receipts for business lunches, trips, or expensive gifts. It is later discovered many expenditures were completely personal—and often included a lover!

4. **False Vendors or Shell Companies**

Thieves often make regular payments to nonexistent vendors, then divert the money to personal accounts. They may also slip invoices from their personal vendors onto your AP, which you unknowingly pay along with your real bills.

They might create false invoices from real companies with whom they have a connection, even though you don't owe them money. Your accountant might make regular payments to her brother's plumbing company, her husband's computer repair service, or her best friend's housekeeping business, and then split the take with them.

Another huge market is fraudulent consulting services. Companies pay staggering amounts of money each year to consultants, even though they may never receive any services— or the consultant does not even exist! If your accountant told you that she wanted to hire a consultant for $100 per month to keep the office up-to-date on new payroll tax requirements and procedures, you may never know if any services were received.

Additionally, they may add invoices for personal creditors to your AP list, so you unknowingly pay their bills when you pay the company bills. A bill from a plumber or lawn service company may not catch your attention, if your company regularly uses those types of services.

5. **Check Tampering** *Even with the advent of highly secure check stock, check forgery and alterations remain common and expensive areas for fraud.*

A careful thief removes writing on a printed check with a piece of scotch tape, and writes in whatever they want. If a dishonest employee tries it, an honest accountant is likely to catch it when reconciling the bank account; but what if the accountant does it? Since checks are frequently used and widely accepted, they are a very attractive target for creative thieves.

The frightening thing about many AP scams is they only need to be set up once to generate regular payments for years. To avoid making late payments, I often set up automatic payments on accounts that I pay regularly, such as credit cards or car payments. This can be a real time-saver and protect you from late fees if you are careful about monitoring them; but if you are not, a thief can use this technique to steal a lot of money for a very long time.

The objectives for the FPS Accounts Payable module include:

Objective 1

Everything listed on your AP report is a genuine payable.

The best time to review and approve invoices is before they make it into your system, not after. Generating a payment is easy after invoice entry, so some of your most important oversight occurs before invoices are submitted to accounting.

Objective 2

Understand how your company receives requests for payment from vendors.

Are your incoming invoices mailed, emailed, or hand delivered? Since you need to review all invoices before posting, you want to consider the best system to ensure you see them first. Requiring invoices be sent to a post office box is one secure method. Having them emailed to an address that no one in your office can access is another.

Make sure employees know you might request verification at any time.

Objective 3

Establish as much transparency in your purchasing and reimbursement transactions as possible. Review reimbursement requests on a regular basis, and question anything you don't understand. Consider some sort of preapproval process if you see frivolous purchases. Make sure employees know you might request verification of such transactions or confirmation you received the goods or services in question at any time.

> *Let me interject a word of caution: Do not make your employees feel interrogated. Let them know you appreciate clear and orderly reports. Be sure they have a good understanding of your expectations. Controlling expenses leaves more money for things like raises, bonuses, and benefits. They must know your caution is not intended as an accusation of dishonesty!*

Question anything you want, but only make an accusation if you have a good reason. I often question credit card expenditures, even if I don't really need information. I want everyone to know I'm looking. If you are friendly and reasonable when asking questions, you may want to investigate anyone who becomes defensive or offended about answering your inquiries, as they may be hiding something. Sometimes thieves discourage you from looking at your own company expenses by guilt-tripping you for asking; don't fall for it!

Objective 4

Clearly become the person in charge of ensuring all company obligations are fully honored—no company resources are spent for illegitimate purchases. Be actively and personally involved in this process. Take this responsibility seriously; no one else in your organization will do it as well as you. Why? Because it is your money!

I read an account of a mother whose son lost a contact lens while playing basketball in the driveway, back when contacts were extremely expensive. After he told her what had happened, she went out to look for it herself. He told her not to bother; he'd looked for the past hour with no luck. Even if it were still there, he had undoubtedly stepped on it. He was terribly sorry, but it was gone.

The mother insisted and found it in under a minute.

Her son, amazed, asked how on earth she had found it so quickly when he had failed after an hour. She replied: He was looking for a tiny piece of clear glass, and she was looking for a hundred-dollar bill!

Your employees may be careful, but you are the only person looking for hundred-dollar bills when reviewing financial data. This system gives you the tools you need to find them. So let's get started!

STEP ONE

1. Intercept invoices at their point of entry. (Be sure your employees know all invoices come to you first.)

2. Initial and date stamp them upon receipt.

3. Carefully review them and get all questions answered before accounting enters them into the AP system.

4. Review them again when processing payments.

Send out payments only after your review process is complete and any questions are answered.

Questions to ask yourself when reviewing:

1. *Do you recognize the vendor?*
   Your accounting program may allow you to restrict the ability of your staff to add vendors, which will go a long way toward eliminating the danger of false companies being listed as authorized vendors. For many companies, this is a good idea.

2. *Does the vendor list a street address or just a post office box?* Fake companies often operate out of a post office box. Check new vendors occasionally and make sure none have the same address. Also check to see if any new vendor has the same address as anyone on your payroll. These are both huge red flags, and very common components of AP fraud!

3. *Does the vendor list a phone number?* If not, look the company up online and confirm its authenticity.

4. *Does the invoice clearly delineate charges?* You should have quantities, dates of delivery, unit prices, and a clear description of all charges. If it's a consulting invoice, make sure you are receiving legitimate, clearly defined services.

5. *Does the invoice include an unusually large quantity of any items?* If you are a cabinet maker and your monthly order of wood goes up 50%, so should your sales. If they are out of sync, find out why. Remember how simple it can be to order extra product and take it for personal use.

6. *Does the unit cost seem right?* If there has been an increase, you may need to verify the reason.

7. *Do you want someone in your organization to confirm the invoice before making the payment?* My estimator and project manager review materials quantities and compare them to the estimate to be sure our customers are receiving the correct quantity of material. This also ensures extra materials are stockpiled appropriately. As an added bonus, this review improves our estimating.

8. *Are you buying this item a lot more often than normal?* Again, pilfering extra stuff is often easy. If nothing in your office routine has changed, but you are buying ink cartridges every couple of weeks instead of as part of a large monthly office supply purchase, find out why.

9. *Is a regular monthly bill consistent with previous ones?* Monthly phone bills are often huge, complex, filled with acronyms for various taxes and fees and at least 15 pages long, which make them susceptible to cramming, as covered earlier. Go through a couple of them with a fine-tooth comb to be sure you understand everything, and there were no services or charges you didn't authorize. You can call a phone company representative and request information on every service, fee, and tax on the bill. Then, once you know the current bills are correct, average three months of bills to form a baseline. If the amount of the

monthly bill doesn't vary by more than $20, I just approve it without review.

This works with many regular invoices, and will save you a lot of time and money. Do a periodic review, perhaps yearly and then be done with it. Dishonest employees can do many things to run up your bills, such as buy-

It is always possible to cheat, but make it harder and riskier.

ing phones for family members, adding people onto your company insurance plan, or purchasing subscription services or membership plans. Having a good idea of how much your normal bill is will help you to detect anomalies quickly.

In short, is there anything on an invoice you would like to question, verify, or reject? Do it now, and don't enter it in your system for payment until you are satisfied with the answers!

In my construction company, I receive tens of thousands of dollars in bills for materials each month, and I can't always personally confirm they are accurate. I check all the items listed above, especially the delivery address, to be sure materials aren't delivered to unauthorized locations. It is still possible to cheat, but I made it harder and riskier.

STEP TWO

Give the invoices that you have reviewed and approved to account-ing. For invoices you need others to verify, give a copy of the bill to the appropriate person for approval, and hold onto the original. You can have your accountant enter the invoice in your system if you like, but the notes that show on the AP report should be marked PENDING.

Never give out an original to anyone without retaining a copy. After the appropriate project manager reviews and approves the invoices, they are given to my accountant and she either removes the "Pending" note, or enters the approved invoice. I follow up and ensure we get the invoice approved before the due date. We also double check the accuracy of our AP by running a job cost report at the end of each project to be sure the quantities are in line with the project estimate.

STEP THREE

Commit to dispersing funds on a certain day of the week or month, and give the process your full attention. This makes it much easier to prevent or detect AP fraud schemes, and it makes you a more careful steward of your company funds in general. If you have ever called a company to request payment, and found they only cut checks on Thursdays, you know they have a structured AP system.

On your predetermined day, either print or request the following items:

- **AP Report**

  All current obligations, including monthly loan payments, generally due in the next 30 days.

- **AR Report**

  Complete details, including aging, on all money owed to your company.

- **Check Registers**

  I use two registers, since I have an operating account and a separate payroll account.

- **A Credit Card Balances Spreadsheet**

  All credit card balances, available credit, payment due dates, and interest rates. I use this sheet when reviewing my credit cards, to be sure no one is charging things without my knowledge. No logon or password information is on this sheet; it is for planning and budgeting only.

Credit Card Balances

Card	ID #	Interest Rate	Statement Date	Credit Limit	Outstanding Balance	Available
American Express - Platinum	#12345	9.90%	6th	10000.00	4166.19	5833.81
American Express- Hilton	#3456	15.00%	15th	5000.00	-	5000.00
Capital One Spark Visa	#1234	22.00%	25th	12000.00	8758.79	3241.21
Chase Marriott Rewards	#0987	16.24%	1st	25000.00	8437.22	16562.78
Citibank Aadvantage MC	#5678	18.24%	5th	12000.00	-	12000.00
Discover	#9874	7.00%	19th	5000.00	-	5000.00
US Bank Visa Club Carlson	1812	5.00%	30th	7000.00	79.00	6921.00
Total Credit Available on Credit Cards				94870.00	21441.20	77594.99

- **Estimated Payroll**

  If your final payroll obligations are not complete by the time you do your AP, at least get an estimate for planning purposes, so you will know how much money you will have available for other expenses.

- **Notes**

  Anything you need to know before approving AP, keeping in mind that you will not be processing checks again until the following week. Plan ahead!

  For example:

  - A vendor requested early payment.
  - You received a defective product and are withholding payment.
  - A tax payment is coming due before the next AP processing day.
  - An invoice was lost in the mail and your account is now past due.

STEP FOUR

On the AP Worksheet, list the money in your bank accounts, including payments you will receive within the next few days.

Use the information you have gathered to start filling out the AP Worksheet, a tool to help manage cash flow. This worksheet helps you plan your income and expenses, and shows current assets and liabilities. It is NOT as detailed as your financial statements are, and it doesn't serve as a formal accounting document. You don't need to balance to the penny; it is simply a financial snapshot to assist with cash flow planning and disbursement.

FPS ~ Accounts Payable Worksheet

ASSETS:	
Bank Balance: Operating	+ $23,437.43
Bank Balance: Payroll	+ $12,848.92
Bank Balance: Saving (Not shown in balance total)	$ (34,482.91)
Incoming deposits (Expected by Friday)	+ $ 7,890.00
LOC draw	+ $ 0.00
LOC available (Not shown in balance total)	$ (25,000.00)
SUBTOTAL	**$44,176.35**
LIABILITIES:	
Payroll – # of checks 8 ; #432 to #439	+ $10,072.00
Credit card payments (on current balances)	+ $ 0
AP – # of checks 1; # 1425 to # 1425	+ $ 1,481.85
AP – X-fer # 1	+ $ 408.70
AP – Credit Card Pass Through, # 1	+ $ 692.59
AP – Online Payment, # 0	+ $ 0
AP – Card Hold, # 0	+ $ 0
LOC payment	+ $ 0
Savings transfer -	+ $ 1,000.00
LOC balance (Not shown in balance total)	$ (0)
Misc	+ $ 0
SUBTOTAL	**- $ 13,655.14**
TOTAL (Subtract Liabilities from Assets)	**$ 30,521.21**

I do not float checks, but may occasionally cut checks for critical items if they need to be mailed later in the week, or if I know I have a payment coming in and the bill cannot wait until the next AP cycle. All unmailed checks are kept locked in the safe.

This worksheet gives me a very clear idea of how much liquid cash I have on hand. If you have long-term investment accounts you can list them, but I choose to only show cash or liquid investments on this form. I maintain a separate account used for holding any cash I do not want to leave in my checking account, but which has not yet been designated for long-term investment. There are no checks for it. I list on my AP Worksheet any money held in this account, as it is part of my cash reserve and is available for emergencies or cash shortfalls. I then list my credit card balances, if any, and any balance owed on my Line of Credit (LOC), since I consider those to be short-term liabilities.

You may want to change items on this worksheet to reflect the way you receive payments and use credit. Do what works for you!

The Difference Between a Short-Term and Long-Term Liability

You owe a short-term liability during the next twelve months, and a long-term liability for a period longer than a year. On this worksheet, you will show only currently due payments. You may owe a long-term liability of two hundred thousand dollars for your office building, which will show on your balance sheet; the short-term liability consists of payments due in the upcoming 12 months, and will show on your financial statements; but you will only show the current $1,000 installment on your AP Report.

Sometimes I will make a note of a large expense coming due soon, such as an annual insurance payment. I will begin to set money away for it, even though I won't be paying it in the current week.

Remember, this is a planning tool, not a financial statement. Anything that helps you better plan how you allocate money is okay; there are no hard and fast rules.

STEP FIVE

Once I have determined how much money I have available, I start breaking out how I intend to allocate the money. Using the AP Worksheet, I note payroll expenses, including taxes, first.

My currently-due APs are the next things listed, so I move on to approving and adding up what I intend to pay.

As you can see from the example, my AP report, aka the Unpaid Bill Detail, the report shows the name of the vendor, including a symbol, such as an asterisk, for those who accept credit cards for payment and a backslash for those who do not, a reference or invoice number, the project the expense is associated with, a due date and the amount of the invoice. Each vendor is listed by name, and each invoice owed is listed separately.

I no longer depend on someone else to tell me how I spent my money!

When printing your report, be sure to leave plenty of room for your payment instructions. I leave extra space on the right side of the report for these notes. Mark these reports with a pen so no one can alter them,

	Type	Date	Num	Due Date	Aging	Open Balance
Unpaid Bill Detail						
Ins Co of America						
	Bill	05/14/2018	123456	06/14/2018		1,481.85
Total Ins Co of America						1,481.85
ABC Concrete *						
	Bill	05/05/2018	1234	06/04/2018		702.87
	Bill	05/05/2018	4321	06/04/2018		539.00
Total ABC Concrete *						1,241.87
Dave's Asphalt Construction, INC						
	Bill	04/11/2018	1882	05/11/2018	6	2,682.56
Total Dave's Asphalt Construction, INC						2,682.56
Casey's Truck & Equipment**						
	Bill	05/11/2018	01379664	06/10/2018		223.06
	Bill	05/14/2018	0168587	06/13/2018		469.53
	Bill	05/14/2018	01380079	06/13/2018		2,340.10
Total Casey's Truck & Equipment**						3,032.69
Ed's Repair* %						
	Bill	05/01/2018	23485	05/01/2018	16	408.70
Total Ed's Repair* %						408.70

Unmarked AP report

and remember to *never* use an erasable pen when marking reports or filling out checks.

Mark Your AP Report:

1. Which invoices do you want to pay? I circle the individual invoices chosen for payment. If I owe several invoices to a single vendor, I circle each one I want paid, then write down the total amount on the right-hand side.

2. Add them up, look at your available resources on the AP Worksheet and ask:

   • Am I short on cash?

   • Should I delay paying something until a later date? If you find you cannot pay all the invoices you circled, just place an X over the ones you will pay later.

   • If I have extra money, do I want to pay some bills early or transfer money to an interest-bearing or holding account for use at a later time?

For Invoices to Be Paid by Check:

1. Write a check mark next to the amount of the payment, which should be on the right hand side of your report.

2. Number the payments sequentially, so you know how many checks you need. For example, I write #1 next to the checkmark by the first invoice and circle it.

3. Continue the numbering sequence throughout the invoices.

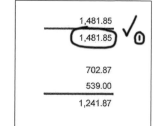

Invoice to be paid by check.

Credit Card Payments:

When you enter a vendor into your AP system, you will place a symbol next to their name which will show when you print your AP Report, and will indicate their credit card policy. Not only can using a credit card to pay bills give you a great deal more fraud protection than a check does, many card companies will pay you cash back or rewards points for using them, which can be very profitable. Just be careful to use your cards as a payment strategy, not to finance long-term debt.

Invoice to be paid by check.

- Use a single asterisk to indicate Visa and MasterCard are accepted.

- A double asterisk means they accept American Express.

- A percent sign means they accept cards but charge a fee.

- Write a backslash after their name if they do not accept credit cards.

- Leave it blank if you don't know yet.

Note: In most accounting systems, the way you entered the vendor's name at the time you set them up in your system will be the way their name appears on your AP report, as well as how it will be printed on the check. Markings must be discreet, so there won't be any problem when they deposit your check. If you write: "ABC Enterprises – Visa" it will appear that

BB : FPS ~ Credit Cards

FPS ~ Credit Card Payments – date

Card #		Available Credit:				Pass-thru/ Hold	
	Vendor and Notes	Payment Amount	Date Paid	QB √	Bank √	Notes	
1)		$					
2)		$					
3)		$					
4)		$					
5)		$					
Total Paid:		$					

Card #		Available Credit:				Pass-thru/ Hold	
	Vendor and Notes	Payment Amount	Date Paid	QB √	Bank √	Notes	
1)		$					
2)		$					
3)		$					
4)		$					
5)		$					
Total Paid:		$					

Card #		Available Credit:				Pass-thru/ Hold	
	Vendor and Notes	Payment Amount	Date Paid	QB √	Bank √	Notes	
1)		$					
2)		$					
3)		$					
4)		$					
5)		$					
Total Paid:		$					

Card #		Available Credit:				Pass-thru/ Hold	
	Vendor and Notes	Payment Amount	Date Paid	QB √	Bank √	Notes	
1)		$					
2)		$					
3)		$					
4)		$					
5)		$					
Total Paid:		$					

Balance Payments

	Card Name and Last #4	Payment Amount	Date Paid	QB √	Bank √	Notes
1)		$				
2)		$				
3)		$				
4)		$				
5)		$				
Total Paid:		$				

way on your AP report and printed checks, which may confuse their bank.
I have never had any complaints from a vendor or a bank about a symbol
following the name of the Payee on a check.

- Circle the invoice amounts, just as you did for check payments,
  but on the right side next to the amount you want to pay, write
  C#, and then fill in the last four digits of the credit card you
  wish to use. If you have only a single company credit card,
  listing the card number will not be necessary.

Once you have selected which invoices are to be paid with which card,
you will want to condense that information for ease in payment and tracking. The FPS Credit Card Payment form makes it simple to see which bills
you want paid with each card, how much the credit limit for that card is,
and if you want the charges paid off as soon as they post to the card.

- If you use multiple cards, list the charges authorized for each
  card.

- Decide if you want the credit card account to be paid as soon as
  the charge posts to the account, or held until funds are available.

  ✓ Mark charges as "PASS THRU" if you want them paid as
    soon as they post to your account.

  ✓ Mark them as "HOLD" if you want them held for payment
    at a later time.

  ✓ Total up the different charges on your form, retain the
    original, and attach a copy to the AP Report when you give
    it back to your accountant for processing. She will note the
    date she made payment to the vendor, and under QB, will
    make a check mark, showing that the payment was recorded
    in QuickBooks. You will mark the Bank space when you see
    the total payment to the credit card company clear the bank.

Some vendors offer early-pay discounts or other incentives. If they also accept a credit card without charging a fee, it is a double win for you! Many cards still offer an interest free grace period of around 30 days, if you pay your balance in full within that time. Make a point to understand how your vendors and your cards offer discounts and charge fees, so you can use them to your best advantage.

Electronic Funds Transfer

You may have accounts which you pay by electronic funds transfer (EFT). One example is making your car or other loan payments to your bank by approving a transfer of funds from your checking account to a loan account. Since the money will be transferred out of your checking account, you must mark it as a payable.

- Circle the payment amount of any automatic withdrawals or EFT payments, just as you did for checks and credit cards.

- Write an "X" to the right side next to the circled payment amount, followed by an underlined sequential number.
  By marking all the different payment methods this way, you can scan down your report and see the exact form of payment to be used for each approved payable, whether it is paid by check, credit card, or transfer. It is essential to the accuracy and ease of your follow-up processes.

AP Report : aka Unpaid Bills Detail
As of May 17, 2018

√=1, C #1425

	Type	Date	Num	Due Date	Aging	Open Balance
Ins Co of America						
	Bill	05/14/2018	123456	06/14/2018		1,481.85
Total Ins Co of America						1,481.85 √ ⓪
ABC Concrete *						
	Bill	05/05/2018	1234	06/04/2018		702.87
	Bill	05/05/2018	4321	06/04/2018		539.00
Total ABC Concrete *						1,241.87
Dave's Asphalt Construction, INC						
	Bill	04/11/2018	1882	05/11/2018		2,682.56
Total Dave's Asphalt Construction, INC						2,682.56
Casey's Truck & Equipment*						
	Bill	05/11/2018	01379664	06/10/2018		223.06
	Bill	05/14/2018	0168587	06/13/2018		469.53
	Bill	05/14/2018	01380079	06/13/2018		2,340.10
Total Casey's Truck & Equipment**						3,032.69
Ed's Repair* %						
	Bill	05/01/2018	23485	05/01/2018		408.70
Total Ed's Repair* %						408.70 X-1

*692³¹ #1234

Complete the Accounts Payable Worksheet

List:

- Amounts paid by each method, Check, Credit Card, and Transfer.
- The number of checks used, and the beginning and ending numbers.
- How much money you have left.

This is for my planning purposes only so I do not give it to the accountant, but I do place it in my Business Bible in the AP section. I usually keep the completed forms for three to four weeks, allowing time for all noted transactions to clear the bank. Then I shred them.

I no longer depend on someone else to tell me how I spent my money!

Place the following items in a designated folder, and give them to the accountant:

- **Completed AP Report, aka Unpaid Bill Detail**

   All payment information is clearly marked, including the number of checks provided, with the beginning and ending check numbers noted in the upper right-hand corner.

- **Blank Checks**

  The numbers are entered into the check log when removed from the safe. You will only give out the exact number of checks needed. Never give out an extra one "just in case." All check stock is numbered, tracked, and issued directly by you on an as needed basis!

- **Completed Credit Card Payments Form**

  Retain the original and give the accountant a copy. She will return it to you with the other AP items, along with her notes indicating the status of your designated payments. Since contacting vendors by phone to pay accounts by credit card payments takes a little longer than issuing a check, this step may not be complete when the AP packet is returned to you. The notes section allows your accountant to indicate whether the payments have been completed or not.

Within 24 hours, the Accountant Returns the Following:

✓ The original, hand marked AP form.

✓ Printed checks, with the backup for each invoice and stamped envelopes attached.

✓ A current checking account register, with all AP checks shown.

✓ The Credit Card Payments Form, with actual payment dates and amounts noted, as well as payment confirmation in the accounting system.

  Reminder: When you make a payment by credit card, your accountant will need to go into your accounting program and mark the account as paid by credit card, which transfers that liability to a credit card account and keeps your books in balance.

✓ If the payment is marked on the Credit Card Payments Form as a Pass-Thru, a corresponding payment to the credit card will also be listed on your check register. A Pass-Thru simply means you have money available to pay a bill, but choose to do so by credit card instead of EFT or check, usually to gain a reward benefit of some kind.

A payment listed as a Hold means that you do not have money to pay a bill immediately, and that payment liability will be transferred on your books to the credit card account.

✓ Back-up documentation for the bills to be paid by credit card or EFT. You will want to review this back-up in the same way you do for bills being paid by check.

The Final AP Step: Making and Verifying Payments

The first thing I do is clear the top of my desk, so I have work room. Then I use the following process:

- I place the AP Report on my far left side.

  I can refer to the transaction I am preparing to process. Placing the piles so you can move from one pile to the next in an orderly way, without shuffling papers all over the top of your desk, will make a huge difference in how efficiently and accurately you move through this process. Left-handed people may want to put papers on the opposite side. Organization and sequential order are key, so everything is at your fingertips.

- I place the check register to the right of the AP Report, so I can verify the transaction was entered correctly.

- I place the Credit Card Payments form underneath the register. This allows me to confirm all payments, however they were directed to be made.

- I place the stack of back-up documents, with checks and envelopes attached, directly in front of me, so that I can efficiently review, sign, and prepare them for mailing. Back-up for invoices being paid by credit card will also be in this stack.

- I leave an open space to the right of the checks I'm signing so that I have an area to place the backup after review, as well as space above my work area where I can put the envelopes that are ready to mail.

After I'm organized, I follow these steps:

- I look at the upper right corner of the AP Report and confirm the beginning check number on the register corresponds with the number of the first check removed from the safe.

- I glance down the check numbers on the register to ensure there are no gaps in the sequence, and that the last check number shown on the AP report is also the last check listed on the register.

This will confirm all checks removed from the safe have been accounted for. You will immediately know if any checks are missing. Remember, if your accountant asks for another check because one was damaged during printing, that check must be returned to you to destroy and record in the check log in your safe.

No one but you is authorized to destroy a check!

- Verify the name of the first vendor on the AP Report matches the payee on the check register or credit card payment form.

- Determine if the amount of money on the check register or credit card payment form matches the amount you approved to pay the vendor, as shown on the AP Report.

- Draw a line through the check number on the register to document you compared the AP Report to the check register.

- An EFT will be listed in the register and marked off the same way as a check. If the payment was made by credit card, check off that payment on the Credit Card Payments Form.
  This shows the transaction was approved, and the name of the vendor and the amount of the payment match the check register or Credit Card Payment Form. I then mark through the name of the vendor on the Accounts Payable Report, which shows that a payment was initiated for that vendor.

Once you are sure the approved AP Report matches the check register, move on to confirm the check register matches the physical checks. Take the first check and its backup from the pile and examine it. Compare the register to the physical check:

1. The number on the register matches the number of the check.
2. The name on the check register matches the payee on the check.
3. The amount of money on the register matches the amount on the check.
4. For a credit card payment, review the back-up and confirm it matches the approved amount on the credit card form.

Next compare the information on the check with the backup:

1. The name on the check matches the name on the invoice.
2. The amount of money shown on the check matches the invoice.
3. If needed, have a member of your staff review the invoice, although this should have been done prior to entering the invoice into your system.
4. The mailing address on the check matches the "Remit to" address on the invoice. *Fraudsters often change a vendor address to a personal address, then intercept the check and alter it for personal use—don't skip this step!*

5. It all generally looks and feels right. If it does, then sign the check and initial the back-up to show you personally reviewed it. I also write the check number or last four digits of the credit card on the front of the back-up when I initial it. Your signature on the check—which is done only after you have confirmed all information is correct and just as you intended—is an indication that you have thoroughly and carefully done all you can to guarantee the right person is being paid the right amount of money for services you actually received, and you have sent the payment in such a way that vendors have the best possible chance of receiving the money owed them. As the business owner, this is your personal responsibility—*don't ever shirk it!*

Never discount the importance of trusting your gut instinct. If you have a question about a payment, or just feel uncomfortable about anything you see during the payment process, investigate. You can mark the backup with a sticky note and then place in a FIFI file for follow-up, if necessary.

Additionally, you can choose whether to make EFT or Credit Card payments yourself, if you are uncomfortable allowing anyone else to have access to this information. I choose to have the accountant do it as I direct, and then personally follow-up on the transactions. This method is easier for me, but you may choose differently.

6. Sign the check, put it in an envelope, and place it in a pile to take to the post office. I personally mail the checks. You can have someone else mail the checks if you choose, since you will verify they all clear the bank properly, but I nearly always mail them myself. Once the backup has been approved and the check has been signed, staple the check stub to the back-up, and give to your accountant for filing.

7. Place the verified check register, Credit Card Payments Form, and AP Report in your Business Bible, for use during the daily banking and credit card reviews. I retain the AP Report for a month or so, which allows me to answer any questions about what was paid and when.

The importance of controlling the way money leaves your business, and confirming it reaches its intended target, cannot be overemphasized.

I know the Accounts Payable system may initially sound like a lengthy, complicated, time-consuming process—but it is not! If you are feeling confused or overwhelmed at this point, relax. It only takes me about 60 seconds to process a typical check, and under two minutes for one with a lot of backup to review.

It is the most important financial process of my entire week, and I give it my full attention! Although the first week or two you do this it may seem a little cumbersome, after that you will find your own rhythm and breeze through it. Your company will be much safer, due to the few minutes each week you commit to this important process.

This completes the active processing of AP; you will complete this module as you follow up during your daily banking and credit card review to confirm all the transactions are completed properly. We have already discussed the importance of monitoring your daily banking, so you should be familiar with looking at your daily transactions.

Now we are going to make that basic review a little more accurate.

Take the check register you marked up at the time you processed the AP, and which had all the check numbers marked through when you signed the checks, and put it in your Business Bible in the Banking section. Every day when you review your bank accounts, you will mark your register in the following way:

- After a check clears the bank, draw a line through the dollar amount on the right hand side of the register. On the bank website, occasionally click on the check number—which should be a hotlink—to bring up a copy of the front and back of the check. Visually review the check. Make sure nothing looks altered, and the payee on the check matches your register. If you have only a few checks clearing, you may want to look at all of them in this way. If you have a number of checks that day, you may decide to just look at a few. Either way, make a habit of looking at least a sample of what is clearing each day. Remember, the bank is *giving away your money* based on these checks, so make it a practice to review at least some of them.

- If something appears on your online bank account, but not your check register—such as an automatic credit card payment or a check issued after processing your weekly AP—write down the details at the bottom of the check register. Write a circle to the left of it to indicate that it appeared in the bank, but not in your register. After verifying it is a legitimate transaction, mark through the circle and provide the information to your accountant to enter in your system.

- If an AP check is issued in an emergency by someone other than you, or if you issued one outside of your weekly process, your register will list checks you may not have reviewed and marked. If you've marked your register by drawing a line through each check number as you signed it, you will know which checks you have not personally reviewed. When those checks clear the bank, mark through the dollar amount. Then hit the hotlink to bring up a copy of the check for your review. Verify the payee, date, amount and signature, then mark through the check number. Always do this with any transaction you did not personally oversee!

Basically, you are doing the approval process backwards. You have more protection if you review all the checks and sign them yourself prior to issuing them, but that is not always possible in a business. This way, you can notify the bank and act immediately if something you didn't authorize occurs.

After all the transactions on a register sheet have cleared and been marked off, you can shred it or retain it for a time. I draw a star at the bottom of a fully cleared register sheet, and hold onto it until the bank statement comes. That way, if I have any questions, I can compare the statement to the register.

When I do my daily account check, I always note the date and bank balance at the bottom of the register. By doing this, I track how often I check the account and how much money I have on a given date.

A voided and shredded check should be noted on the check log, and shown as "VOID" on the check register. You should never see this check number again. If you do, find out why! Anytime you see a check number clear the bank that is too far back in sequence, at all ahead of sequence, or which doesn't seem like it is consistent with your check numbers—follow up on it immediately! Don't ask your accountant to do it. You can ask if he or she has an explanation, but you must verify the information yourself at the source.

File Your AP Report

As noted above, make sure you save the marked AP Report in the AP section of your Business Bible.

I retain mine for about four weeks before giving them to my accountant, who keeps them in a notebook for future reference. If someone calls about the status of a payment or I want to verify no duplicate payments are being made, I have the record at my fingertips.

You have now closed the loop on how money moves through your company, and protected your internal FraudPoints.

You have:

- Verified the money coming into your business through Accounts Receivable;
- Confirmed the validity and accuracy of invoices on your Accounts Payable;
- Reviewed each invoice before payment;
- Completed each check, EFT, or credit card payment correctly; and
- Verified that the payments posted to the intended bank or credit card account.

In the years since discovering the embezzlement, my company has more than tripled in size. Recently, I drove into my company parking lot in the middle of the day and was staggered by the number of cars parked there. For some reason, it really struck me how every one of them were depending on me to protect the company from mismanagement or disaster. There was a great deal riding on my ability to protect the financial security of the company.

It was a humbling moment, and one that sunk deeply into my heart. Knowing I am doing my very best to protect the people who depend on my company for their day-to-day support is what keeps me motivated to use my system every time I pay bills. The security is worth every moment it takes; I hope it will be for you, too.

Summing Up

Managing your AP is the crux of the entire Fraud Points System. I cannot overemphasize the importance of controlling the way money leaves your business, and confirming it reaches its intended target properly! This gives you comprehensive control over your business finances. I took charge instead of just placing faith, and could confirm my accounting staff was following my directions. I know I will never again be the naive victim of a devious and unethical employee, and it feels good.

CHAPTER 18

Payroll

Of all the things your company does for its employees—Christmas and Holiday parties, paid leave, providing health insurance coverage, or giving rewards for effective safety practices—nothing is as important as meeting timely, correct payroll obligations.

In addition to maintaining a happy, functioning workforce, avoiding the legal problems you can face over sloppy payroll procedures is key. Furthermore, no matter what people's opinions are about politics, religion, or marriage, they are all firmly committed to the idea their paychecks must clear the bank. Whether mistakes are deliberate, accidental, or the result of financial fraud, the complications and expenses caused by payroll inaccuracies can be devastating.

Besides the obvious issue of losing good employees over paycheck problems, many external organizations take a legal interest in your payroll, including:

- Your state's Division of Labor Standards

- The U.S. Department of Labor

- Labor Unions

- Trade Organizations

- A Variety of Taxation Entities—all of which can make your life very unpleasant

- The nice attorney who will be happy to sue you on behalf of your wronged employees

In short, not paying your employees or your payroll taxes properly can shut you down—and even land you in jail. If your payroll is inaccurate, whether due to sloppiness or fraud, your employment taxes are likely flawed, as well. Tax issues are a major threat to your business.

Often, company officers do not want to be bothered with accounting or tax matters. It is not uncommon for a director or chairman to instruct an employee to take care of paying payroll taxes. If that employee fails to pay payroll taxes, the officer should be worried. Delegation of authority does not relieve a person of responsibility to collect and pay taxes to the IRS. Courts have consistently held that the authority that permits control carries with it a nondelegable duty to ensure that withholding taxes are duly collected and paid over to the government. Purcell, 1 F.3d 932 9th Cir. 1993.

You can access more information by visiting the Journal of Accountancy online at JournalOfAccountancy.com.

Conveniently, most of the processes you will implement to avoid payroll fraud will enhance the accuracy of your payroll obligations. While preparing to write this chapter, I reviewed some old research about payroll fraud, as well as reading current news on the topic. I must tell you, it scared the daylights out of me all over again!

Payroll fraud continues to increase relentlessly. The schemes are quickly expanding both in scope and size, primarily due to the outsourcing of so many payroll functions. Additionally, the IRS is taking a much more aggressive stance on unpaid payroll taxes, whether the underpayment was deliberate or not.

It is a triple-whammy of fraud risk!

Owners commit some of the simplest types of payroll fraud. If you pay employees in cash, hire undocumented workers, underpay employees for hours worked, claim hourly employees are contract workers, refuse to pay overtime, or falsify any aspect of your payroll or related tax reporting systems, you are in big trouble! Never take the risk of doing anything questionable on your payroll. Not only will you get caught—which is very likely—it will wreck you financially. You will be prosecuted and subject to both legal and financial penalties.

Never ignore being out of compliance! Fix it as soon as possible.

Consult with a reputable accounting or payroll service company if you have questions about following the letter of the law.

If you find you have been violating a law, talk with an attorney who specializes in tax or payroll matters to correct the issue. Never ignore being out of compliance! Fix it as soon as possible.

Next, look at how unscrupulous employees or payroll processors may take advantage of your payroll system. Payroll involves entering employee data and hours worked, then issuing payroll and paying taxes, so there are several FraudPoints to monitor.

Examples include:

- *Paying Ghost (Nonexistent) Employees*
  You wouldn't think this could possibly happen, but it does all the time.

- *Multiple Paychecks Under Variations of Someone's Name*
  The use of a maiden name or substituting initials for a first name can make it appear checks are going to different people, when in reality the same person is collecting all of them.

- *Continuing to Pay Former Employees and Appropriating the Checks* The accountant "forgets" to delete someone from the payroll system, and continues to generate checks, which are then stolen.

- *Giving Unauthorized Raises, Vacation Pay, or Bonus Pay* In one ingenious case, a sneaky accountant gave himself a big bonus on a regular basis. The payroll reporting system didn't include bonus pay as part of the payroll totals. Prior to giving the weekly reports to the owner for review, the accountant destroyed the separate page of the report which dealt with bonuses. The owner was none the wiser for a very long and expensive time.

- *Diverting Severance or Vacation Pay for Terminated Employees* The payroll system sets these funds aside, and the former employee may not be aware they are entitled this payment. However, a sneaky accountant can still process a check to pay them, and then appropriate it.

- *Overstated Working Hours or Time Sheet Fraud* An absent employee gets a friend to clock in for him, or works with the accountant who receives a kickback for altering the records.

- *Manually Overriding Electronic Time Sheets to Overstate Hours* Again, this will often involve a kickback scheme between an employee and an accountant—or another employee—unless the accountant is doing it for herself.

- *Shenanigans Committed by a Payroll Service Provider* This issue, which has exploded in recent years, will be covered later in this chapter.

- *Diverting Payroll Taxes for Personal Use* This will be touched on in this chapter, but taxes have their own chapter. Just remember, nonpayment of payroll taxes can cost you everything you own and land you in jail—*even if you weren't the one stealing the money!*

- *Simple, Old-Fashioned Check Forgery* Payroll involves a lot of money going out on a regular basis. Thieves can easily funnel both checks and automatic deposits, so be mindful of both. You must be just as careful in tracking the check stock for your payroll as you are for your accounts payable!

Make no mistake—payroll fraud is real, common, and expensive!

Additionally, due to tax ramifications, it poses more personal risk to the business owner than virtually any other type of fraud. The IRS does not care who stole the money. The business owner is on the hook for it and the government can seize personal assets—such as your home—to pay off the debt.

Whether mistakes are deliberate, accidental, or the result of financial fraud, the complications and expenses caused by payroll inaccuracies can be devastating.

A corporate veil will not protect you from this kind of seizure. Trust Fund taxes withheld from an employee's pay and entrusted to the employer's care are subject to different laws.

According to the Association of Certified Fraud Examiners (ACFE), payroll fraud is the leading cause of accounting fraud and employee theft.

1. It occurs in 27% of all businesses.

2. It happens nearly twice as often in businesses with less than 100 employees.

3. The average length of a payroll fraud scheme is nearly three years.

In my case, the fraud involving my payroll system included:

- *Check forgery*

- *Adding family members to the insurance policy without paying for them.*

- *Leaving former employees on the insurance policy* We never discovered if there were kickbacks, or if it was simply done to hurt the company.

- *Asking to have a payroll check replaced, because she said she washed it.* I have no idea why this happened, as she was already forging checks and could have written herself one. Both the original and replacement checks cleared the bank. Never replace a check without personally placing a STOP PAYMENT on the original.

Many companies are using payroll services to combat the inherent risks.

It gives you some protection from tax errors, but carries other unique risk factors. In most cases, if the payroll service makes an error in calculating or paying your taxes, they are responsible for all penalties and interest, although you still must pay any taxes due. You must include that in your contract with them, as the IRS will come after your company—and often you personally—for the funds, including fines or interest.

Additionally, if that payroll provider is unable to pay, you are still on the hook for all monies owed. Be certain that any company you hire is bonded and insured. Many states do not require these companies to be bonded, which means if they steal your tax money you may have no way to recover what you paid them. Calculation and management of taxes today is extremely complex. Hiring a professional is wise, if you know how to manage the associated fraud risks.

Since your company may issue payroll by using checks, direct deposit, or by allowing a payroll provider to issue payments, the best way to control your payroll will be determined by you.

Your new skills in thinking like a thief will come in handy as you construct a system to serve your company, no matter how you decide to issue payroll. Maintain an open mind and a willingness to change systems, if needed. Do not simply throw up your hands and give everything to a payroll service provider. Without proper oversight, you face many of the same fraud risks as you do when processing payroll internally.

Objectives:

- Pay only real employees

- Pay those employees accurately

- Verify all taxes are paid correctly

- Make sure all paychecks and tax payments will clear the bank

Steps to achieve these objectives:

1. Implement secure systems for tracking employee hours. Employees who document their own hours with little supervision or verification may quickly perceive an opportunity to overpay themselves.

2. Keep an accurate employee master list, so you always know how many paychecks should be issued, and who is to receive them.

3. Control who can alter your employee master list. Keep it updated so you can compare it to your payroll, if you have any questions. This information is very sensitive and must be secure. This register should include:

   - Legal name, which must match what is printed on checks

   - Employee's address

- Social Security Number
- Number of Dependents
- Hourly Wage or Salary
- Authorized Deductions, Insurance Premiums, Retirement Contributions and Child Support
- Date and Amount of Last Raise
- Date of Hire

4. Maintain control of your payroll check stock. This bears repeating. Lock it up, log it when removed, and monitor it regularly.

5. Use the IRS website to verify payroll taxes are paid accurately and on time. We will cover this in more detail in the chapter on taxes.

6. Follow the same basic system for check processing and bank account monitoring as you do for Accounts Payable.

This FPS module contains guidelines and suggestions to help you determine the best way to protect your company. The exact implementation depends on whether you process payroll inhouse, use checks or direct deposit, or outsource it to a payroll service provider.

As You Prepare to Process Payroll, Ask Yourself:

- **Do you recognize the name of everyone receiving a check?**
  Do a quick visual scan to compare the names on the payroll register with the employee master list. The more employees you have, the higher your risk of ghost employees.

- **Are payroll hours consistent with your norm?**
  Look at the number of hours logged. If someone worked a high number of hours, were the additional hours authorized? Are you sure everyone worked the hours they reported?

- **Does the total amount dedicated to payroll fall within your normal range?**

  If your number of employees is the same, and nothing special is going on that requires additional time, the dollar amount of your payroll should be similar from pay period to pay period.

- **Are there any changes to the taxes you are paying?**

  Verify the average amount of taxes you pay and watch for variations. Tax payments and retirement account contributions are often the targets of fraudsters, as they both involve a lot of money going out on a regular basis. Owners are unlikely to review any source information, such as original statements or online accounts, to ensure the required payments are being made.

My CPA told me of an incident in the large accounting firm where she used to work. A new accountant dutifully deducted 401k contributions from employee checks and placed them in an internal holding account. She didn't realize it was her responsibility to initiate the payment to the investment company who handled the funds.

Make no mistake— payroll fraud is real, common, and expensive!

When the error was discovered over a year later, fixing it was a nightmare! The company had to calculate exactly how much interest each person would have earned and the share price they would have paid each time a transfer should have been made. A little attention to detail can save you big problems down the road.

Internal Payroll Processing Module for Checks

1. *Review a preliminary payroll report.*

   It is much easier to ask questions and make needed adjustments *before* payroll is run. Check the names and pay rates against your master list. I review the names and hours weekly, but I only check the payroll master list details sporadically, due to time constraints.

2. *Determine the number of payroll checks needed.*

After logging the required checks, remove them from the safe and give them to accounting, along with an approved payroll register. This is similar to the process you use for AP.

3. *The accountant will return a payroll packet to you, including:*

- Your approved payroll register
- A current check register
- A receipt for your scheduled tax payment
- Printed payroll checks, ready for your signature
- Envelopes for the checks

4. *Check your tax payments.*

Because my embezzlement caused huge tax problems, I am very sensitive—my kids say paranoid—about tax payments. I do a quick check on my federal taxes by dividing the amount of federal withholding by the payroll total, to get a rough percentage. Mine is normally 22%. If the percentage is consistent, and the tax payment coupon matches the amount on the report, it passes the small test. I verify the tax payments are made by checking both my online checking account and the IRS website.

5. *Review the check register.*

Make sure the checks you removed from the safe are accounted for. Check the beginning and ending numbers, and then scan the sequence to be sure none are missing.

6. *Review the names on the preliminary report and the check register.*

To prevent payroll ghosts, your preliminary report should be identical to the names on the check register. Since the preliminary report is what I reviewed and approved, that is what I compare to the check register so I know no changes were made when the checks were processed.

7. *Compare the rest of the information on your check register to your preliminary register.*
   Be sure that no changes were made. Confirm the check numbers and amounts by running your finger down the columns and making sure they match.

8. *Set the preliminary report aside.*
   Now that you have confirmed your reports match the check register, you are ready to verify that the printed checks exactly reflect what was approved.

9. *Set the check register on your left side, and place the blank payroll checks in front of you.* Compare the first check with the register:
   - Does the check number match?
   - Is the name correct?
   - Does the amount of the check agree with the check register?

10. *Cross through the check number on the check register, sign the check and put it in an envelope.*

11. *After you complete the process with all checks, file the check register in your Business Bible under "Payroll Account."*
    Leave it there until everything has cleared the bank. I highly recommend maintaining a separate payroll account at your bank.

12. *File the tax payment coupon in the "Taxes" section of your Business Bible.*
    Remove it after verifying the payment cleared the bank and was properly recorded by the IRS.

13. *File the Payroll Report in your Business Bible—you can either place it in the back of the Payroll Account section, or set up a tab for Payroll Reports.*

You have all the information at your fingertips, if anyone asks a question. I shred mine when processing the following week's payroll.

14. *Return all payroll check stubs to accounting.*

15. *Distribute payroll checks.*

Periodically surprise everyone by either walking through your business to hand out checks, or have everyone come to your office to get their—and *only their*—paycheck. If you have left over checks, you could have a ghost!

16. *Verify your online payroll account.*

I issue checks on Friday, so they typically clear the bank in a batch on Tuesday. I check the online payroll account on Tuesdays, to verify the bulk of incoming checks. I look again on Thursdays to confirm the balance before processing payroll again.

I did my payroll system this way for several years after my embezzlement. Last year, when my daughter joined the company as CFO, she wanted to handle payroll herself. Because she earned an MBA and worked in bank management for several years, she was well qualified to do this. In fact, her company nickname is "The Dream Crusher," since she is always telling the rest of us why we can't spend any money!

After a lot of debate, we decided she would process and sign payroll, but a current check register and payroll report would be provided for my review. There were errors on paychecks, due to an accounting program update during her first few weeks. Although the errors themselves were not her fault, she failed to do several FraudPoint steps to confirm everything was accurate prior to printing the checks. She thought they were a waste of time. If you put information in correctly, the program will process it correctly, right?

Not necessarily!

The amount of time involved in cleaning up system errors, which would have been much simpler to resolve in advance, was significant. Now she checks those items before she signs the checks, and I review the paperwork once payroll is processed. Since I have not actually laid eyes on the checks themselves, I do my bank verification a little differently.

As with any other check I have not signed, I circle the check number on my check register. When I do my daily banking review, I mark off the amount on the check register to show it cleared the bank, but only after opening the hot link to review the front and back of the check. Blood may be thicker than water, but green—as in money—can still rule the world. Always verify.

Payroll Processing Services

Over the last few years, many businesses have decided to outsource their payroll, tax, and benefit payment processes. It frees up a great deal of time for their office staff, it shifts the responsibility for complex tax calculations onto a specialist, and it gives the owner peace of mind.

In a perfect world, that is true. But there is a downside. Sometimes the wrong tax identification number is entered. One consulting business had three businesses under its master umbrella, including a nonprofit, each with its own tax ID. It had outsourced its payroll to an outside payroll processing source. Inadvertently, the tax numbers had been switched on the nonprofit with the for-profit company. That got the IRS' attention.

After a deluge of notices, and financial demands from the IRS, it was noticed that the wrong tax number had been used. Corrections were finally made, and all settled down. The countless hours spent dealing with the IRS, going through files, and trying to figure out what had happened would have been easily averted if the FraudPoints System had been in place.

Fraud in the payroll processing arena is common, expensive, and totally unexpected. Unless you continually compare source information directly from the taxing entity to the reports generated by your payroll system, you really have no idea if your obligations are being met. Additionally, as mentioned above, many areas do not have any bonding requirements for these companies. If they steal your money and go bankrupt, you may be in a very difficult situation.

If your tax obligations or employee retirement funds have been stolen and spent, you may have no way to recover any money. Additionally, the law will still require you to pay all taxes, penalties, and interest, as well as missing retirement funds, even though you have already paid the payroll service company for them.

Here are a few ways payroll service providers have cheated their clients, and how you can help prevent it:

- **They don't make your payroll tax deposits.**
  A printed receipt from the payroll service means nothing. Only a recorded payment on the IRS EFTPS website is official. You must verify this personally. Even a screenshot of your tax account can be altered with free software available on the open market. Always look for yourself!

- **They underpay your taxes.**
  For instance, they may report to the IRS your payroll for the week was $10,000, and pay the taxes on that amount, when your payroll was $30,000—a much higher tax liability. They collect the correct amount of money from you, provide you with a receipt showing correct reporting and payment, but only pay the lesser amount to the IRS. Remember, you are still liable to pay the correct amount to the IRS, plus all applicable interest and penalties, even though you already paid the processing company correctly.

- **They set up a pyramid scheme for stealing tax money.**

  They pay everyone's tax payments later and later with money they receive from new clients. If you allow the company to have Power of Attorney, you won't even receive any tax notices; they will all be sent to the payroll company which will not inform you about the problem. Although I focused on federal taxes, your state taxes, sales taxes, and local taxes can all be impacted by fraud. My accountant made a terrible mess of my sales taxes, costing me over $125K, and three years fighting with the Department of Revenue.

- **You can be overcharged on a regular basis**

  If you give them the right to withdraw money directly from your bank account, verify they take the correct amount each week.

  Never accept printed reports from the payroll service in place of verifying the information on your own.

The two most frightening things:

1. The IRS can use a very big net to hold anyone with check-signing authority and tax oversight accountable for underpayments.

2. The 941 Payroll Tax is basically the only tax that allows the IRS to pierce the corporate veil of your company, which is the legal separation protecting your personal assets from being taken to satisfy company debt.

The majority of payroll service companies perform a valuable service, and serve as a tremendous resource for the businesses that use them. They are generally honest and reliable. Many are bonded and insured. They can save your company hundreds of hours each year in payroll and tax processing. They can offer a protective shield for your company if an error in tax payments is made. *But, you must use them wisely.*

Take the time to review the payroll reports and confirm everything is correct. Never accept printed reports from the payroll service in place of verifying the information on your own.

Specifically:

- *Review each name on your payroll report.*
  Owners are often advised to personally pass out checks so no ghost employees are paid. Since many people are now paid by direct deposit, you may have to find a different system. One possibility is handing out printed copies of each person's pay stub.

- *Confirm all taxes are paid on time and in full.*
  The IRS website will be your best friend for confirming all your various federal taxes are paid, and that required returns are filed. Never be afraid to follow up on the information your service provides to you. You are liable for underpayments and errors, and you must be the person to confirm everything is properly done.

- *Regularly check employee retirement or other savings accounts.*
  Be sure they are funded correctly.

- *Consider setting up an online alert for the name of your service provider.*
  Then you will be notified of problems reported by other customers, or legal issues they experience.

- *Always review the items on your invoice from the provider.*
  Be sure you understand all fees and charges. Don't be afraid to do the math, question items you don't understand or demand answers for any irregularities. This is your money and your responsibility—the security of your business is on the line.

Questions to Ask Yourself:

1. Do you need to change a process to protect a FraudPoint?

2. Should you hire or fire a payroll service provider?

3. Are you sure you are meeting all your legal obligations?

Take the list of objectives, write down your concerns, examine your current payroll processes, and if necessary, make an appointment with an accounting professional who is not a part of your business. Let them guide you through the process of setting up your own unique payroll module. You'll be glad you did!

Summing Up

Payroll is one of the Achilles heels of a business. If taxes aren't paid in the correct amounts and on time, it's you that the IRS will come after—not the bookkeeper, the accountant, or the payroll service you engage. The FPS-Payroll will help you handle your payroll obligations as safely and accurately as possible.

CHAPTER 19

Credit Cards

**Unless you are a Tibetan monk living on a
remote mountain top, you are probably familiar
with credit cards, use them daily,
and may view them as a necessary evil.**

iving without a credit card is a real challenge in today's world. As a
business owner, a company credit card is often the easiest way to allow
trusted employees to make company purchases. In my opinion, used
wisely, credit cards are the best things since sliced bread!

Potential Benefits

- Up to 30 days of interest-free financing on most cards.
- You don't issue a check every time your business makes a
  purchase.
- Many categorize purchases for accounting and tax preparation.
- Discounts for things like car rentals, travel expenses, and special
  event tickets.
- Getting cash back or paying your bill with accumulated points.
- Warranties for major purchases, which may double the manu-
  facturer's warranty.

- One phone call removes the payment for defective products or services.

- Secure airline tickets and hotel rooms at virtually no charge, using points.

- And last, but certainly not least: They offer incredible fraud protection!

Note: not all credit cards offer all these benefits; some have more; some less. Investigate them carefully, and watch for changes in the cardholder agreement.

Ways to Get the Most from Your Credit Card

One office supply company I use allows me to make purchases on a store account and gives me a discount for paying my account in under 30 days. They include a nice promotional item every time I order, *and I can pay my account with a credit card.* I use my Chase Business Ink card, which pays me five points per dollar for office supply purchases, and gives me 30 days with no interest.

In summary, here's what happens: I order office supplies and get a discount for paying my bill in under 30 days, plus I receive a gift from the office supply company. Then I earn five credit card reward points for every dollar spent, and I get another 30 days' interest free from the credit card company, effectively "double-dipping" benefits. It's a sweet deal!

For you to maximize what your cards can do, start here:

1. To determine the exact benefits of your existing cards, go on-line and carefully read the account details. Make a list of every benefit you would like to use—*don't leave money on the table!*

2. Call a representative with any questions.

3. If you want to obtain a new card, go online and research the best card for your needs. For instance, search: "Best Credit Card for Travel Rewards" or "Best Card for Cash Back."

4. Subscribe to blogs written by people who research and recommend a variety of cards.

5. Look up "Travel Hacking."

6. Check out websites, and subscribe to applicable sites.
   They can provide a multitude of free information, although some also have books you can purchase. Most make their money when you apply for a card on their site, so use the link they provide if you liked their information. Their research costs you nothing—they get a fee from the credit card company.

Although there are many benefits offered by credit card issuers, there are also dangers. Do your research before deciding if a card is the right fit for your business. Read consumer reviews, and don't just rely on what the credit card website tells you.

Remember:

If you make only the minimum payments each month, the card company will make a mint off you. They are highly motivated to loan you more money than you can quickly repay.

1. You never want to carry a balance for any length of time.

2. You must absolutely pay on time! Your interest rates will skyrocket.

3. Second only to the IRS, credit card companies are the most ruthless debt collectors on the planet! They will make your life a living hell if you don't pay them. I cannot emphasize this strongly enough.

If you are not able to manage a checking account or a debit card properly, you shouldn't even consider using a credit card. Additionally, business cards usually carry higher credit limits. You can dig yourself into a very deep hole if you are not careful.

When using a checking account or a debit card, there is a limit to the amount you can spend. If you overdraw your account, the bank will refuse to honor any additional charges. You can't just go to another bank and open an account without putting money into it.

If you max out one credit card, then make bare-minimum payments and get another card—you *can* do the same thing all over again. Although you can get yourself into trouble with a bank account, it is much more limited than a credit card account. Your bank won't let you spend $20,000 unless you have it in the bank, but a credit card company will let you spend that money—and more—if they think you can pay it back later, *along with plenty of interest fees and late charges, of course.*

In fact, if you only make minimum payments, the card company will make a mint off you in the long run. They are highly motivated to loan you more money than you can quickly repay.

For instance, let's say you opened several high-limit cards when earning a lot of money. Unless you stop paying your bills, or you max out **Never use credit cards** all of your accounts, your credit card carrier does **as long-term financing!** not know you suffered financial reverses or lost a major client. You can go right ahead and spend that money, even though you know you can not easily pay it back.

If you use credit cards to earn benefits, you win! If you use them for long-term financing, you lose—big time!

Credit Card Management Strategies

There are two basic ways you can use credit cards in your business: Authorized everyday expenditures, and incorporating them into your Accounts Payable system.

Each option requires different FraudPoints.

Objectives for Both Employee Use and Bill Payments

1. Be aware of the benefits, limitations, protections, requirements, and penalties of each card. Read the cardholder agreement and benefit literature. Know which cards offer extended warranty protection, discounts with certain companies, and free international transactions.

2. Set up an internal control system. Regularly monitor all charges. Watch for unauthorized or unusual transactions.

3. Make a strategic plan to earn benefits. Learn which cards offer the best benefits in desired areas.

   - Do not discover you could have had an additional two-year warranty on an appliance—after it breaks.

   - The same card that pays five reward points for every dollar spent at office supply stores also offers that benefit when I pay my bills for landline, mobile phones, or internet services. I earn nearly ten thousand points each month, just for buying copy paper and paying those bills by credit card instead of writing a check. The card costs me nothing if I pay it within the 30-day window. How awesome is that?

4. Set up a secure place to store your cards, preferably in the safe with your check stock, which will keep them safe from sticky fingers and prying eyes. Inventory them regularly to be sure none are missing.

5. Establish clear guidelines for how cards can be used by employees and accounting staff, then monitor the accounts carefully.

FPS Credit Cards Module: Basic Procedures

1. Set up a credit card section in your Business Bible: Volume Three. Alternately, you can designate a separate binder just for credit cards. I have a large number of them, so I have a dedicated notebook for mine, with the cards divided by the issuing bank.

2. Insert all cards into a transparent sheet, designed to hold credit cards. These are available online or at any office supply store.

3. Place your cards inside the sheet, then photocopy the front and back.

4. Put this sheet into a standard sheet protector, and place it behind the card sheet. Now, when you remove a credit card you can see exactly which card was removed. You also have all the information necessary to report the card stolen or lost.

5. When you remove a card, take a sticky note and write the name of the borrower and the date you extracted the card, then place it over the empty card slot.

6. When you replace a card, remove the sticky note and throw it away. My staff all know this procedure. It is their responsibility to watch me replace the card and remove the sticky note, otherwise the card is still officially checked out to them.

7. Make a spreadsheet that includes the name and last four digits of each card, the website URL, the password and a section for notes. Mine is titled: "Credit Card Daily Review."

8. Place it in a clear sheet protector and file it in your Business Bible, right behind the credit cards. Do not *ever* leave this where anyone can see it, even for a moment. Someone with a cell phone in their pocket and 10 seconds alone can take a photo of this secret information any sleuth would be proud of.

FPS ~ Daily Credit Card Review

Monday

Card	Last 4#	Logon	Password	URL	Current Points/Notes
1.Am Ex Delta	1234	Obermiller1	Baby 2	www.online.americanespress.com	
2.Bank of America	3456	Obermiller2	Baby 3	www.bankofamerica.com	
3.Chase Ink	6789	Obermiller3	Baby4	www.chase.com	

Tuesday

Card	Last 4#	Logon	Password	URL	Current Points/Notes
1.Barclay Haw	1234	Obermiller1	Baby 5	www.barclaycardus.com	
2.CapOne Spark	3456	Obermiller2	Baby 6	www.capitalone.com	

Wednesday

Card	Last 4#	Logon	Password	URL	Current Points/Notes
2.Citi American Air	1234	Obermiller1	Baby7	www.citibank.com	
9.Chase Sapphire	3456	Obermiller2	Baby8	www.chase.com	

Thursday

Card	Last 4#	Logon	Password	URL	Current Points/Notes
1.Chase United	1234	Obermiller1	Baby9	www.chase.com	
2.Chase IHG	3456	Obermiller2	Baby10	www.chase.com	

Friday

Travel Account	Logon	Password	URL	Current Points/Notes
AADVANTAGE	Travel	Germany!	http://aa.com	
CLUB CARLSON	Hotel	TakeATrip	https://www.clubcarlson.com	
DELTA	Cheryl	FlyAway	http://delta.com	
MARRIOTT	Roy	Suite	http://marriott.com	

9. Set up a weekly schedule to check the online account for each card. Keep a record of authorized charges to avoid fraud. I log onto an account, look for recent charges and payments, and then investigate anything unusual or unauthorized. If I find something that needs to be corrected, I contact the card company and then place a screenshot of the information in my FIFI files so I remember to follow up.

10. Review hard copies of credit card statements you receive in the mail before passing them on to accounting, even though you should have already checked them online several times. Your best chance of having fraud removed from your account relies on discovering it quickly. Ultimately, it is your job—not the credit card company's—to find fraudulent charges. Also, before you pass an approved statement off to accounting for payment, remember to examine every page. Remove and shred any convenience checks, which are printed checks that allow you—or anyone who has access to them—to pay bills or obtain cash against your credit account.

11. This step is optional: Even if I do not plan to carry a balance on a card, I set all of mine up to make an automatic minimum payment from my bank account.

    You can make additional payments, or pay the account off at any time, but it saves me from expensive late charges for accidental late payments. If you are worried about someone accessing your checking account, set up a separate bank account in which you keep only a very small amount of money, and use it for automatic payments. If the card company makes an error, they only get a small amount of cash.

    I have never had a problem with a company taking an unexpected payment, but I have had occasional problems with late payments because I simply forgot, I was traveling, or had timely payments lost in the mail.

12. Shred any unused credit card applications. Never throw them in the trash. Someone can grab a pre-approved offer and take out a card in your name—a common practice in identity theft.

13. After activating a new card, file it in your Business Bible, make a new front and back copy of the credit card sheet, and notify your accountant to add it to Accounts Payable—both as a payment method and as a vendor. One additional step I take is to place the paperwork received with a new card into the AP section of my Business Bible, with notes about spending requirements to receive any special bonus offers. I keep a sheet protector in the front of this section specifically for this purpose. That way, when I pay my bills I know how much I need to spend by a certain date in order to get the promised bonus. Those points are worth money—don't miss out!

Additional Steps for Cards Issued to Employees

1. Use a written and signed agreement; you can find examples online, but they should include:

   - Who is authorized to use the card.
   - What the card can be used for.
   - Daily spending limits or other purchasing restrictions.
   - How you expect purchases to be documented.
   - Recommendations from your lawyer about what language to include.

2. Keep front and back copies of the card, as well as a sticky note on the card slot, identifying the employee who checked it out and the date it was removed.

3. Obtain a designated card for employees who use one on a regular basis.

4. Use an expense report system that requires employees to record each use.

5. Require the employee to keep all receipts, and have your accountant reconcile each receipt against the credit card statement, in the same way you clear checks to reconcile your checking account.

6. Verify:

   - Every charge on the card matches a receipt
   - Every receipt is noted on the expense report
   - The expense report makes sense

7. I often question credit card charges, even if I don't have any questions. Why? Because I want them to know I am looking!

8. By using the SKU shown on most receipts, you can research an item purchased on the company website or over the phone.

The SKU is the code for the specific item. Never be apologetic about politely checking on any expenditure, if you have questions about it.

Some of these steps seem silly, such as documenting approved use of the credit card and the authorized users. Sadly, they are not. For example, let's say you catch an employee's wife buying gas with your card. When questioned by the police, he may lie and say other people are doing the same thing because you gave them permission, as a way to provide a covert raise without raising your employment taxes. If you don't have a written agreement to the contrary, you could have a difficult time proving your case. I once caught an employee loaning a company truck to his ex-wife to drive to another town and watch their son play basketball. His explanation? *I never said he couldn't do it.* Be clear about your guidelines!

Benefits of Using Credit Cards for Accounts Payable

I use credit cards as an integral part of my AP system for several reasons:

- They prevent financing and past due charges from my vendors. In my business, I routinely purchase thousands of dollars in materials from suppliers. I won't receive payment for the project using these materials for 30 to 90 days. By taking advantage of a 30-day interest-free credit window from the vendor, then paying that account with a credit card for another 30 days of interest-free credit from the card company, I can eliminate many finance charges altogether. Additionally, some vendors offer a discount for paying in less than 30 days, and still accept payment by credit card. I get a discount *and* free short-term financing.

- They allow me to conserve cash for payroll, loan payments, or vendors who do not accept credit cards.

- They offer me protection against disreputable vendors who sell defective products and refuse to honor warranties.

  Several years ago my husband and I bought a used Mercedes from a dealer in another part of the state. The purchase included a 1,000-mile warranty. At exactly 800 miles, the transmission failed. The dealership owner refused to honor the warranty unless we brought the car to a specific repair shop nearly four hours away. After several discussions about this, I felt we were getting nowhere. Then, I reminded him that I had put $20,000 of the purchase price on my American Express card and gave him one hour to approve the repair at a certified repair shop close to me. Otherwise, I would call the card company and contest the charge. Approval took only 45 minutes.

- I earn my very favorite thing in the world—credit card reward points! Honestly, I don't stop at a convenience store and spend a dollar on a soft drink in cash. Everything that can go on a card, goes on a card! Most of us have been indoctrinated to believe credit cards shouldn't be used to pay for daily expenses, but when was the last time you got a reward for paying your electric bill by check? The average business owner can earn the equivalent of a second tax-free income by using credit cards wisely.

- They give me outstanding fraud protection. When you write a check, fraudsters possess the information needed to steal money from your checking account. They can even print business checks that draw on your bank account. When someone uses a check or a debit card to get money from your bank account, they get REAL money.

  If a fraudulent check or debit card transaction drains your bank account, you may get your money back at some point, but it can take a while. If you don't have a good relationship with your bank, such that they will extend you credit on your account, your real checks may bounce. When someone hacks your credit card, they get POTENTIAL money. Most card companies will immediately remove a contested charge from your account, while it is investigated and before a final resolution is reached.

- In short, credit cards offer free financing, fraud protection, and awesome rewards. Get on the gravy train and grab some, but be wise about how you use them. Educate yourself!

Steps to Use Credit Cards for Accounts Payable

Set up a spreadsheet titled "Credit Card Balances." Keep it separate from the highly confidential sheet in your Business Bible, which is already filed in your "Credit Card Section."

Credit Card Balances						
Card	ID #	Interest Rate	Statement Date	Credit Limit	Outstanding Balance	Available
American Express - Platinum	#12345	9.90%	6th	10000.00	4166.19	5833.81
American Express- Hilton	#3456	15.00%	15th	5000.00	-	5000.00
Capital One Spark Visa	#1234	22.00%	25th	12000.00	8758.79	3241.21
Chase Marriott Rewards	#0987	16.24%	1st	25000.00	8437.22	16562.78
Citibank Aadvantage MC	#5678	18.24%	5th	12000.00	-	12000.00
Discover	#9874	7.00%	19th	5000.00	-	5000.00
US Bank Visa Club Carlson	1812	5.00%	30th	7000.00	79.00	6921.00
Total Credit Available on Credit Cards				**94870.00**	**21441.20**	**77594.99**

The spreadsheet includes:

- Bank, brand, and last four digits of the card
- The statement closing date
- The interest rate
- The card limit
- Any outstanding balances
- Available credit
- Notes

Do not include passwords or other information someone could use to hack your account; it is used to plan which cards to use when paying bills or making purchases.

1. The "Credit Card Balances" sheet should be updated weekly, preferably the day you approve Accounts Payable. You will either do it yourself, or share your username and password with an employee. I select someone other than my accountant to update this sheet. I feel safe about it because I check each card weekly and would quickly detect any fraud. Everyone in the office knows my system. If they make an unauthorized charge, they *will* get caught.

2. As per your AP system, when approving payables and marking the Accounts Payable report, you will write a C# next to every invoice you choose to pay with a credit card.

3. Look at your "Credit Card Balances" sheet to determine which cards to use. Consider:

   - The credit limit and the available credit for each card.

   - The interest rate, especially for any charges you might not pay within 30 days. (The goal is to never carry a balance, but if I know a client will pay me in 60 days, I may decide to pay a month of interest to manage my cash flow, but I want that interest charge to be as small as possible.)

   - What rewards do you want? You might choose a 3% cash back on gasoline to pay your fuel account. If you are planning a vacation, you may opt for a hotel rewards card. If you buy an electronic item, use a card that provides an extended warranty. Become familiar with the benefits of each card and take advantage of them.

- Make sure your vendor accepts the card you want to use. Most take MasterCard and Visa, but not as many take American Express or Discover. Use a simple code to identify which cards each will accept, as described in the AP module.

4. Go back through your Accounts Payable report, and write the last four digits of the chosen card wherever you wrote C#, to indicate a bill would be paid by credit card.

5. Finally, on a separate sheet, write down the name of each card you are using. Underneath that, list the names of the vendors and payment amounts. I use a "Credit Card Payments" form, which is explained in the AP module within the previous chapter on page 220. Or, you can you can simply make a hand-written list if you only use a few cards. Your accountant can clearly see all the payments being charged to each card, and it gives you a list to reference during your weekly credit card review.

6. Put a copy of the "Credit Card Payments" sheet in the packet with the rest of the Accounts Payable paperwork and give it to your accountant for processing. Have your accountant return the sheet to you after completing payments. Use it during your periodic credit card checks to confirm authorized charges.

7. If you intend to pay off the card as soon as the charges post, mark it on the form as a "Pass Through." Otherwise mark it as a "Hold."

If you manage your cards wisely, using self-control and strategic planning, they will quickly become an incredibly valuable tool that helps make the most of your money.

Now get out there and start charging!

Summing Up

If you follow this module, your credit cards can become a second profit center, since they give you the ability to earn additional revenue by simply managing how money moves through your business. You decide if you want them to be a source of cash-back for the business, a means to purchase items with reward points, or a way to take a nearly-free vacation as a reward for all your hard work.

CHAPTER 20

Taxes

**Because taxes are complicated,
preparing them is—to most of us—tedious and boring,
yet noncompliance is expensive and risky.**

once watched a nature program where a shark attack expert appeared as the guest. He offered some helpful hints for dealing with aggressive sharks, like gouging their eyes or pounding on their snouts, but the host clearly wasn't buying it. He asked the expert, "I know you have to be prepared to do something in a situation like this, but is anything really going to help?"

The expert smiled and replied, "Well, it can. But if you ever look back in the water and see a large shark advancing on you with its mouth open, jaws extended, and back hunched up—there's just no getting around the fact you are fixin' to have a bad day!"

Now, with that being said, are you prepared to deal with IRS agents, if you discover your taxes haven't been paid?

My Accountant's Drawers

Many years ago, I dealt with a revenue officer concerning business tax payment issues. My internal check register contained an error that would have significantly overdrawn my checking account, had the required tax payments been made.

Unbeknownst to me, and likely because my young bookkeeper didn't want to be in trouble for error in the account balance, she took my signed tax-payment checks and hid several in her desk drawer instead of mailing them. (This bookkeeper had no connection with the accountant who embezzled from me). I didn't discover the truth until the past due tax notices came. When I explained the situation to the revenue officer, he asked why I hadn't noticed the checks did not clear the bank. I explained my bookkeeper balanced the checking account, so I was not aware of the problem. I signed the checks, they were deducted from the balance on my register, which still showed as positive because she failed to correct the error. So, as far as I knew, everything was okay.

I did not realize this man's position wasn't an anomaly, but instead the generally unspoken, unofficial position of the IRS.

He became quite belligerent over the fact I didn't do the monthly checking account reconciliation myself. I explained I didn't have time, but I hired a seemingly competent person to do the task. He became even more unpleasant and told me I should have caught the error. "Furthermore," he went on, "you need to keep in mind, the single most important thing any business owner does is to ensure all taxes are paid in full and on time."

(I do want to emphasize the initial problem with the bank balance was simply the result of accidentally entering a deposit twice. There was no fraud involved; just an employee who didn't want to be in trouble for making a careless mistake that was causing a big problem. Having said that, the FraudPoints Systems for Accounts Payable, Daily Banking, and Taxes would have quickly caught the math error, as well as the uncleared tax payments, and this situation would have been avoided.)

I was incredulous! I could hardly believe the arrogance of this revenue officer, who clearly had no idea how many important things I dealt with daily. Didn't he realize running my business and making money were the most important things I did? Doing the paperwork required for the taxes and paying them was quite a burden. I was relieved to pass the task along to a bookkeeper, who I felt was competent, so I didn't even have to think about it. What I did do was make sure the checks to pay them were signed, and then trusted everything else would go as it was supposed to without additional follow-up. Big mistake!

Being terribly naive at the time, I did not realize this man's position wasn't an anomaly, but was instead the generally unspoken, unofficial position of the IRS.

Since then, I have come to realize non-payment of taxes, regardless of who makes the error, is a deadly threat against your business. It is worthy of your personal attention, so ensure

> **Nonpayment of taxes, regardless of who makes the error, is a deadly threat against your business.**

that you properly address it. Remember, your personal assets are on the line for noncompliance issues, whether they are due to theft or just simple errors.

If you have always delegated tax filings and payments to someone else, you probably do not know where to begin. Within *FraudPoints!*, I do not provide legal tax information. Nor do I tell you which taxes to pay, teach you how to calculate your payments, or instruct you on filing returns. I only offer advice on seeking tax professionals to manage your obligations, and monitoring that your payments are being made and are clearing the bank.

Because taxes are complicated, preparing them is—to most of us—tedious and boring, yet noncompliance is expensive and risky.

> **The IRS requires several less-known filing deadlines for businesses throughout the year. Do you know them?**

There is a strong temptation to hand them off to someone else, and walk away from the whole thing–*but don't do it!* Remember, the government will come after you for the money, including punitive nonpayment penalties, even if your tax preparer is convicted of criminal acts regarding the reporting and payment of your taxes. I know it isn't fair, but it has been well established in court. They are your taxes, so the buck stops on your desk. Luckily, just like accounting, you do not have to prepare and file the taxes to manage them.

First, you need to carefully review your unique tax and filing requirements with your tax professional. Besides your Federal obligations, there are many others based on your state of incorporation, where you operate, jurisdiction, and the type and size of your business. Make sure you clearly understand how specific taxes and filings apply to you, as well as the basics of how to calculate them and when payment is due. Doing this proactively is much simpler than dealing with the trouble and expense of doing it wrong and fixing it later.

In my opinion, although any tax debt is serious, 941 payroll taxes are the top priority for strict compliance. These are often referred to as "trust fund taxes." They consist of monies you withhold from employee paychecks, which are then combined and paid with your employer contributions. FICA taxes, which include social security deductions, are one example.

The IRS takes the nonpayment of trust fund taxes very seriously. Because trust fund taxes consist of money withheld from your employees' pay, money only temporarily entrusted to your care, the nonpayment penalties are huge.

The nearly unlimited ability of the IRS to aggressively pursue a business owner to collect delinquent taxes must be seen to be believed.

The ability of the IRS to aggressively pursue a business owner to collect these taxes must be seen to be believed. The IRS will blow straight through your corporate veil and go after your personal assets to collect. It's the sort of thing unsuspecting business owners lose their homes over.

Talk to a competent tax consultant to ensure you are always in full compliance. If your total payroll dollars or numbers of employees change, your required tax payment schedule may also change. For instance, a company with a low payroll and only a few employees might pay their employment taxes monthly or even quarterly, while a larger company probably pays electronically on a weekly basis. If you swap from issuing payroll checks twice a month to weekly, or even change payday to a different day of the week, it may change your tax payment deadlines.

Stay on top of these changes! Ask your tax consultant if you are approaching a threshold that will trigger a reporting change. Discuss the implications of any potential changes in advance.

Although I primarily focus on payroll, your business will be subject to a variety of taxes. They can be confusing, and the nonpayment penalties are typically very expensive, even for honest mistakes. Additionally, a change in your corporate status, such as changing from an LLC to a C Corp, may change your filing requirements. I would rather pay a tax consultant for services than pay fines to the government, so I always use expert tax help.

FPS ~ Tax Payments & Filings

Entity & Type	Due Date	Who Will File	Pay by:	Complete	Notes
IRS – 941 3rd Quarter	10/31	CPA	EFT		
MO Employment – 1st quarter	4/30	Internal	Check		

Tax Module Objectives

- Gain a clear and accurate understanding of your tax obligations

- Determine when all tax filings and payments are due

- Learn how to confirm tax payments have been made and received

- Establish a good working relationship with a tax professional

STEP 1

Make a comprehensive list of deadlines for all tax filings and payments, and regularly review upcoming obligations. Remind yourself of upcoming due dates in time to prepare for them. Some filings require up-to-date financial information on specific sales or purchases, copies of documents you may need to locate, or large payments you should include in your budget.

You cannot comply with requirements in a timely way if you only discover them the night before they are due. I recommend reviewing upcoming requirements at the beginning of each month and setting up clear internal deadlines, so you have plenty of time to prepare.

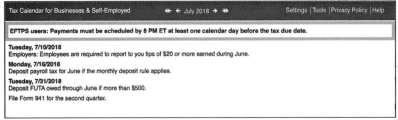

Example of the tax calendar listings from the EFTPS website.

Everyone knows they must file personal income taxes by April 15. The IRS requires several less-known filing deadlines for businesses throughout the year. Missing these deadlines can cost you a lot of trouble and money. Create a method to recall your due dates, whether you opt for a spreadsheet of filing dates or enter them on your calendar. Filings might be weekly, monthly, quarterly, or yearly.

Determine who will prepare and file different returns. For many years, I handled most of the tax filings myself. Then my CPA reviewed everything and filed the annual returns. Keep in mind, your CPA deals with multiple businesses with the same deadlines. Be sure you get required information to them early enough for timely filing.

The key is awareness of your deadlines. Store the information in an organized fashion, so you can refer to it and verify your business meets all its responsibilities. Hiring someone else to fill out your tax returns does not in any way diminish your responsibility for filing them. Additionally, a tax preparer has the legal right to depend on the accuracy of the information you provide. A preparer cannot file accurate returns without correct information. His or her liability for filing errors does not protect you if the information you gave was wrong. Take charge!

STEP 2

Verify that the taxing entity received your payments. Whether due to an error, theft, or mail issue, you are the one holding the bag if your organization does not meet tax requirements. If you pay by check, confirm the endorsement and make sure it clears the bank. If you make electronic payments, check your statements, as well. Your taxing entities may issue a receipt or offer online payment confirmation. Research their system and follow up on it.

With federal taxes, you can use the Electronic Federal Tax Payment System (EFTPS) website, *www.eftps.gov*, to verify all payments and filings, including the dates and amounts. If there is a problem, you will see it there. This is especially important if you use a payroll service provider. They can issue you fake confirmations that seem to demonstrate they properly filed your returns and payments, even if that is not the case.

The government considers the EFTPS to be accurate and valid. If the website doesn't match your records, you need to resolve the problem personally and immediately. I verify tax payments weekly through my bank account, and go to the EFTPS website monthly to print a copy of the current month's payments.

If you discover you missed a deadline, take care of it quickly. Depending on the severity of the error, you may want to engage a tax attorney to represent you. Ignoring missed tax payments or returns is big trouble. Sometimes even minor issues can cause a lot of trouble later, so follow through on any problem you notice.

For convenience, you can include other mandatory report submissions or license renewal on your list of deadlines, even if they are not directly tax related. If you miss a payment deadline, the government will find you, and they will fine you. A required filing without a tax payment may not generate a notification, but it will pop up later and cause you a lot of trouble.

Some years ago, I received annual corporate registration paperwork to complete for my state, a simple one-page form requiring a $45 payment. I filled out the paperwork and gave it to my bookkeeper instead of mailing it myself, since I needed her to fill in a single piece of financial information. After giving it to her, I completely forgot about it.

Many months later, after that bookkeeper left my company, I applied for a small equipment loan. Initially, the bank approved the application, but I then received a call from the bank president, informing me the loan was on hold. My corporation did not have legal standing in the State of Missouri. During a routine document review, the bank requested my Certificate of Good Standing, a document that verifies a company is current on all tax payments and filings. The bank said my corporation had been legally dissolved earlier that year, as I had not filed the required annual paperwork.

I told him that was absurd. I had given everything to the bookkeeper for submission to the state, and had paid all the required taxes since that time. I was correct, but unbeknownst to me, the bookkeeper had stuffed the incomplete form into a desk drawer and failed to complete it and mail it in. There was no gentle reminder, no past due notice, and no notification of any kind that the critical report never arrived. The great State of Missouri simply dissolved my corporation. This caused huge problems, both with my bank and the state government.

The bank was not happy when they discovered they were doing business with a legal entity that didn't exist. They threatened to call in all my loans and close my accounts. The State refused to cooperate and ultimately charged me hundreds of dollars in fines to reinstate my business; a process which took several months. It was an expensive and time-consuming mess!

Although my corporate filing wasn't a tax, it was still a report the State required if I wanted to continue doing business as a legal entity. If you lose your corporate authority, there are horrible tax implications. Be careful about this sort of thing, and watch your deadlines carefully.

If you miss a payment deadline, the government will find you, and they will fine you.

Finally, keep in mind, stealing tax payments is an easy way for an embezzler to take a lot of money. Because taxes require the transfer of large sums of money out of your company, these funds are an attractive and lucrative target. Most business owners don't pay enough attention to these payments. If you accept only a printed receipt from your accountant's computer or your payroll service's email to verify that they fulfilled your tax obligations, you stand on dangerous ground.

Summing Up

The bottom line is awareness concerning the legal requirements of your business. Track the deadlines and verify everything possible. With more and more reporting and verification options available online, there is really no excuse not to take charge of this tedious —but critical—part of your business. Use your tax professionals as valuable resources, but follow up on what they do. An unpaid vendor can cause you a lot of trouble, but an unpaid taxing entity can shut you down. Never forget that!

CHAPTER 21

Your Daily 20-Minute Routine

**You will never regret the time you spend
safeguarding your business,
so do it consistently and do it well!**

How do I pull all of this together? you may ask. By now, you should be:

- Getting Your Own Mail
- Controlling the Use of Your Checks and Credit Cards
- Regularly Checking Your Accounts Online
- Carefully Approving and Issuing Accounts Payable
- Tracking the Accounts Receivable Deposits
- Monitoring Payroll
- Verifying Your Tax Payments
- Becoming Aware of All the Financial Systems in Your Company

If you started these things one at a time as you read this book, you may need just a little help continuing to move your processes along smoothly. You may need to refine your procedures to be more efficient if they take you more than an average of 20 to 30 minutes per day.

If you haven't already started your own FraudPoints System, now is the time to go back and:

1. Review the Summing Up at the end of each chapter.

2. Assemble your Business Bible, one piece at a time.

3. Implement each step for a week or two.

4. And move on to the following modules.

While there is no way to precisely measure how often people follow written advice, studies show many repeatedly buy self-help books—often on the same topics—yet only a small percentage incorporate what they read into their lives. When I experienced my embezzlement, I had no idea how I could have prevented it. Now I do; and having read this book, so do you!

I can't imagine going through all of it, had I known how to prevent it but failed to do so. What if I could have stopped it, but just didn't get around to it? Use this book to make yourself a more effective and confident business owner. If you do, peace of mind will be your reward.

OK, Let's Get Started

So, as they say in wrestling, "*Are you ready to rumble?*"

Set aside a specific time you are going to act on your various controls. For instance, perhaps you will check your bank accounts first thing each morning, get the mail at lunchtime, record deposits before leaving the office, and handle Accounts Payable on Thursdays. It doesn't matter when you do these things, so long as you have a plan and follow it consistently. No one is perfect, but if you are hitting your goal at least 90% of the time, you will have a pretty good idea of what is going on in your business.

I know most people use an electronic calendar to track and plan their activities. I determined a Monday through Friday written calendar

Monday	Appointments/Errands:
9:00 – 10:30 Morning Routine	
☐ Review calendar & Action File	
☐ Check in with Staff	
☐ FraudPoints review	
○ Process mail	
○ Check online bank accounts	Calls/Emails:
○ Check online credit card accounts	
☐ Clear email	
☐ Phone calls	
10:30 – 12:00 – Limited Availability	
☐ Schedule marketing for the week	
☐ Action File items	
☐ Itemized Tasks →	Tasks:
☐ Water office plants	
12:00 – 1:00 Lunch & Errands	
1:00 – 1:30	
☐ Check in with Staff	
☐ Unexpected tasks and calls	
1:30 – 4:00 Limited Availability	
☐ Scheduled business tasks →	
☐ Book related tasks →	
4:00 – 4:30	
☐ Review next day	
☐ Prepare Action File for next day	
☐ Touch base with staff	
☐ Leave by 4:30	

Example of my daily planner sheet

template, with plenty of space to write in needed information, and used in conjunction with an electronic calendar to store longer-term commitments, works best for me.

These templates are placed inside of sheet protectors and I insert them at the front of my Business Bible. I use dry-erase fine point pens to check off planned items and to make notes. At the end of each week, I wipe it all clean and start over.

If I send someone to the bank on Wednesday with a deposit, I make a note on the Thursday page with the amount of the transaction. When I do my Thursday bank review, I remember to confirm it was properly credited to my account. By using this system, I can quickly make sure I follow up on banking, plan my controls around other commitments, or note items that require follow-up—such as a questionable charge on a credit card.

Please remember: You will occasionally forget a planned control. That's OK! In fact, don't try to be so perfect you throw up your hands and quit the first time you make an error. Life interferes, business is messy, and no one is perfect! If you set such a high bar that your FraudPoints become a horrible chore, you won't be able to keep it up. Be as consistent and thorough as you can, knowing that imperfect controls are far better than none.

Because I keep these page protectors in the front of my Business Bible, which is securely stored in my office safe, I place items in it that would not be wise to leave in my FIFI files in the desk drawer. For instance, if I have a check I need to hold for a day, a highly confidential piece of information requiring action on another day, or anything I need to safely keep at my fingertips, I store it here.

Please remember: You will occasionally forget a planned control.

The sheet protector pages act like big envelopes; I can take the items that need follow up and slide them inside the same page as the matching daily schedule. In fact, I use the first sheet protector in my book to store incoming checks, as we generally only deposit checks one day a week. I never lose track of these items, and I keep them in a totally protected place.

Be sure you deal with your staff in a positive way, so they know you are monitoring these parts of your company to protect everyone, and not to spy on them. You must be open with them about the basics, even though you keep some of the details confidential. Don't tell them exactly what you will confirm or when. Sadly, there are people who would use that information to determine where your business is the most vulnerable. Be wise during all disclosures. Think like a thief. Set up processes that protect your company, and never apologize for honoring your responsibilities as the owner.

If you don't understand how to do something, go back and review the appropriate section of this book. If you require assistance in instituting controls over a specific part of your business, talk to an outside CPA for advice. Customize your controls so they work for your unique business needs, as well as your personal style and schedule. As long you are meeting your FraudPoints objectives, feel free to customize the processes as needed. Have a little fun with it! After all, watching your money should be interesting.

Take charge and remember a lot of people depend on your soundly managing your business. You were brave enough to undertake the monumental task of running a business; now be bold enough to protect it from those who would do it harm. You will never regret the time you spend safeguarding your business, so do it consistently and do it well!

**Think like a thief,
set up processes that protect your company,
and never apologize for honoring
your responsibilities as the owner.**

CHAPTER 22

Stop, Thief!

**I would have been afforded more protection
under the law had I murdered my accountant,
than I had as the victim of her crimes.**

Since my embezzlement, I have extensively read about financial fraud, court processes, handling by law enforcement of various crimes, and the aftermath for crime victims.

I reached some unpleasant conclusions concerning how victims of embezzlement are treated in comparison to victims of other crimes.

While most crimes invariably leave behind negative consequences for the victims, the victim of a financial crime may be held legally liable for the consequences of the crime—which often inflicts even more damage to their personal and business finances—and at the same time have to negotiate a minefield of legal and tax compliance issues. These parallel issues may well eat up whatever resources the embezzler didn't steal.

I am unaware of any other crime that allows government officials to so effectively and aggressively persecute and punish victims.

Although more devastating crimes surely exist—such as violent assault or murder—I concluded very few crimes result in allowing, and even encouraging, government officials to treat the victims like criminals.

As if surviving an embezzlement isn't challenging enough, the bigger challenge often lies in surviving the aftermath. For me, that was the most frustrating thing of all.

Some of the very people in charge of enforcing the law, who I thought would be on my side, used their power to punish me. I believe they attempted to appear efficacious by quickly collecting maximum tax revenues without regard for unduly damaging my company or me personally. A more reasonable approach would have still resulted in the required tax payments. They had no respect for the fact that the entire situation was the result of a federal crime.. They put no effort toward resolving tax issues in such a way as to help preserve my business and protect my employees' jobs.

I am not aware of any other crime that allows government officials to so effectively and aggressively persecute and punish the victims. As part of setting up a payment agreement with the IRS, I had to fill out forms that required me to give an itemized list of every asset I owned. I do not know if I can adequately express how it felt to be on the brink of bankruptcy as the result of a crime, and then have to give a list providing the value of my living room furniture and wedding rings to the IRS, as security against the resulting tax debt.

Owners who discover embezzlement must deal very carefully with the thief, lest they be charged with a crime themselves. Many justifiably angry business owners, after discovering a theft, have searched the purses, backpacks, or automobiles of suspected thieves. Despite the correctness of their assumptions, even when they found the thief in physical possession of stolen property, they were subject to prosecution for violating employment laws or employee rights to privacy. Even searching a company-owned desk or locker, unless you have clear permission to do so, may be a violation of "expectation of privacy" laws.

My attorney told me of one case where an employee made it clear to her employers and coworkers that a certain drawer in her desk was off-limits, as she kept her medication there and HIPPA protected her privacy. Later, when the embezzlement was discovered and the police searched the desk, they found this drawer was where evidence of the fraud was being kept. Know your rights!

This caution for employee rights also applies to outraged owners who make hysterical phone calls or angry personal visits to an employee's

Parallel issues may well destroy whatever resources the embezzler didn't steal.

home upon uncovering a theft. The thief may easily take the business owner to court, accusing owner of threatening behavior.

Talk to your business attorney about handling employee theft, and notify your employees about related company policies. Explicit processes for potential events can protect everyone, should you discover a theft. Do not become angry or yell at a suspected employee. Never restrain a person physically, even to prevent him from leaving until the police arrive.

I cannot stress enough how important it is to know your rights *before-hand,* rather than discovering you committed a crime by your response to a theft.

It is common for thieves to bring false charges against their employers to cast doubt

Be sure you don't give legal ammunition to those who would do you harm.

upon their own guilt. The best defense for criminals may still be a good offense, especially if they are clearly guilty! I spoke with several victimized business owners who declined to prosecute provable fraud because the thief threatened to bring completely unfounded sexual harassment charges in retaliation. They felt the PR damage to their company over such an accusation would outweigh the benefits of fraud prosecution, especially since they felt restitution was unlikely.

You can, however, on the advice of your attorney, handle some things creatively. Several actions I took after consulting with my attorney were:

- On payday, I called and asked him if I had to still issue her a paycheck for her final week. He said I did, so I printed one.

However, we have an internal policy that all employees must have written permission on file for us to either mail their paycheck, or give it to another person. When Tammie's husband called and asked us to mail her check, we happily told him that, since we had no such form on file for her, she would have to personally come to the office and pick it up herself. She never showed up.

- When I received a phone call from someone who said they were a prospective employer and asked for Tammie's references, I refused to provide any information but date of hire and last date of work. Many employers have been sued for giving out bad references, even when they were richly deserved. I had fired employees in the past who then placed multiple calls to the office, posing as potential employers, trying to trap us into saying something negative which they could then sue us for, so this wasn't entirely unexpected.

  I felt a real sense of moral responsibility to protect other businesses from hiring a thief, so I called my lawyer for advice. He said if it happened again to simply say, "I'm not allowed to disclose any information; please call my lawyer for a statement." He felt that would convey the idea there was a big problem, without getting me into trouble. Since no one else called for a reference, sadly, I never got to use that line.

- Although prior to a conviction your embezzler is legally presumed innocent, after conviction or confession, they are proven guilty and you have more latitude about what you can say and do. After my accountant pled guilty in court, I went back to my office, issued her an IRS form 1099 for nearly half a million dollars in unreported income, and then turned her in for tax fraud. Was it revenge? Perhaps; it did feel a little like it.

However, as a business owner you are legally required to report income people receive from your business, so I was actually just complying with the law. (Pardon me while I adjust my halo….)

The point here is to review everything you want to do with your attorney *before* taking any action. I was incredulous that I actually had a responsibility to issue her a paycheck after terminating her for theft, but my attorney also advised that I had the right to make collecting it a little uncomfortable for her. Your embezzler has rights, but so do you! The key is to keep your emotions in check and rely on your legal counsel to keep you out of trouble.

Be sure you don't give ammunition to those who would do you harm.

1. Ensure your employee manual is clear about your rights and your employees' rights.

2. Clearly define privacy expectations with your employees.

3. Explain how you would conduct a search and inform them of the consequences if you discover they committed theft.

4. Be clear about expectation of privacy rights and where your ability to search their personal property or workspace begins and ends.

5. Specifically define what constitutes theft.

A huge hazard I wish our elected officials would address surrounds the way taxing and regulatory entities treat businesses impacted by fraud. Tax problems are a common result of an embezzlement.

My experience with taxing authorities, both state and federal, was abysmal.

Each jurisdiction has their own requirements for a variety of taxes and filings. Although some revenue officers and officials will treat you fairly, others will not. They seem to possess a great deal of power, yet are subject to very little accountability. Impacted businesses must hire expensive accountants, tax consultants, business attorneys, or other professionals in self-defense during the time when they can least afford them.

I would love to see state and federal governments protect businesses who were in compliance before their embezzlement, and who are only noncompliant as the result of a criminal act. Most of the officials I spoke with agree with the idea, but none pursued the matter.

Although every situation is unique, here is a list of basic steps:

Call Your Attorney

His or her familiarity with your business structure, fraud controls, and your employee manual, will assist in providing you with instructions and cautions. Fraud will likely leave you with legal problems of one kind or another, so get legal advice immediately. Be proactive.

Call Your Local Police

Share the details of the situation and request their advisement on the matter.

My local police department in Harrisonville, Missouri—who could not possibly have been more supportive and helpful—immediately sent over a detective who asked for my financial records, as well as information from my bank. The department conducted much of the initial accounting investigation, which not only saved me considerable money, but was also instrumental in convincing the FBI to take my case. Not all police departments follow the same procedures. Quickly find out how they operate, and who you need to hire for assistance.

Call Your Bank

Set up a relationship with a personal representative when you open your bank account, so you have a specific person to call for assistance.

Tell her the exact details about what you have discovered, and ask for help in securing your accounts and investigating the extent of the fraud. You may even want someone to come to your office and help you sort things out. Since the bank may be legally liable to some degree, they should be anxious to help you lock things down. A word of caution: Since the bank might be required to reimburse you for some of the losses, be sure to bring your attorney into the conversation early to advise you of your rights. Their obligation to refund your money will be subject to certain time limits, as well as the circumstances of the fraud.

According to the National Check Fraud Center found online at *CkFraud.org*:

> Current Uniform Commenerical Code (UCC) filings outline specific check fraud responsibilities for banks and corporations. Court decisions have already established guidelines for legal responsibilities, and failure to meet these guidelines can cause a bank or company to experience financial loss.
>
> UCC Revisions now define responsibilities for check issuers and paying banks under the term ordinary care. Under Sections 3-403(a) and 4-401(a), a bank can charge items against a customer's account only if they are "properly payable" and the check is signed by an authorized individual. However, if a signature is forged, the corporate account may be liable if one of the following exceptions applies:
>
> - *According to UCC Section 3-103(7), ordinary care requires account holders to follow "reasonable commercial standards" prevailing in the area for their industry or business. Under 3-406, if they fail to exercise ordinary care, they may be restricted from seeking restitution from the payee bank if their own failures contributed to a forged check signature or*

an alteration (for example, raising a check amount from $50 to $5000).

- *Section 4-406 also requires customers to reconcile their bank statements within a reasonable time to detect unauthorized checks. This typically means reconciling statements as soon as they are received.*

- *The concept of comparative fault —Sections 3-406(b) and 4-406(e)—can shift liability to the check issuer. If both the bank and corporate account holder have failed to exercise ordinary care, a loss can be allocated based upon the extent that each party's failure contributed to the loss. Since banks are not required to physically examine every check, companies may be held liable for all or a substantial portion of any given loss—even if the bank did not verify the signature on a fraudulent check.*

- *Liability for counterfeits that are virtually identical to originals will be examined on a case-by-case basis. The process used when issuing the check will be reviewed to determine if the company exercised ordinary care or contributed to the loss.*

Call Your Credit Card Companies

If you even suspect someone compromised a card, replace it.

Go over your past statements carefully, looking for unauthorized charges. Again, the card company may have to reimburse you for fraudulent charges, even if someone incurred the charge years ago. Discuss it with them and speak with your attorney. If your accountant accessed any of your card accounts, you should consider getting new cards, even if you don't see any fraud on them. Better safe than sorry.

A word of caution: A card which you issued to an employee for company purchases, but which they abused, is probably not reimbursable by the credit card company as fraud. It is possible you may have some coverage under your company insurance, but that depends on exactly how your policy is written. It is important that you monitor all cards regularly, and that your employees know you will catch unauthorized expenses!

Change Logons and Passwords for All Accounts

Your accountant, now unemployed and hard up for money, might use a previously un-impacted account.

Change all the security questions and answers. Be sure you choose questions and answers unique to you, and which your accountant is unlikely to know. Questions like your oldest child's name, or what your favorite pizza is, may be well known by someone you have worked with for years. Take charge of these accounts, set up all the online access and security yourself, and then give out the information only as needed.

Inventory Your Check Stock

Look for missing or duplicate numbers, which could indicate stolen or extra checks. Although banks are often required to refund money for forged checks within a certain time period, they can refuse to do so if they believe the loss is due to your negligence. You provide the bank with the justification to decline a future loss claim if you do not void or stop payment on missing or unauthorized checks. At this point, it is your responsibility to stop the previous employee from utilizing them. In several cases I researched, the embezzler continued to pass forged checks, even after being charged with fraud.

Carefully Watch Your Mail

Most accountants have all the information needed to obtain credit cards in your name; watch incoming card statements to be sure they haven't already done so. Additionally, monitor your incoming invoices very carefully, and watch for invoices or payments that seem unusual in any way. Err on the side of caution and investigate anything that makes you stop and look a second time. Trust your gut instincts.

Obtain Copies of Your Credit Report

Request them from all three major reporting bureaus. Consider subscribing to a reporting service which will alert you to activity under your business or personal accounts.

You might have other problems you haven't discovered yet. Review your credit report and be sure you do not have any unauthorized credit accounts or loans.

If you use inhouse credit accounts with suppliers, check for unauthorized charges. You may want to set up a list of authorized users, or set up a PO system for purchases. Make sure those suppliers know the situation, so that they can alert you if any unauthorized person tries to use your account.

Hire an Accounting Expert to Examine Your Computer

Find someone highly skilled with your accounting program to examine all activity; an expert will know where to look for irregularities. If the employee installed more than one copy, look on all versions. Work with the expert to explore anything suspicious.

Physically Search AR and AP Files (both paper and computer)

Carefully examine your payables.

- Compare paper copies with computer records.

- Look for past due or unusual invoices.

- Would the invoiced item be a normal purchase for your company?

- Can you tie materials purchased to specific jobs or activities?

- Does everything on the invoice look legitimate?

- Investigate any unfolded invoices. Nearly all invoices will have been folded prior to being placed in an envelope and mailed. An unfolded bill can be a tip off that it was printed on your computer and submitted for payment to a fraudulent vendor.

Do the same thing with receivables.

- Do you recognize the customers?

- Do you have a lot of past due accounts, especially for new clients or established ones that usually pay timely?

- Do you see unexplained credits, refunds, or write-offs being given?

- Look for jobs that incurred expenses, but do not have a corresponding invoice to the client. (I found around $40,000 in unbilled services, and never discovered why it happened.)

Contact Your Vendors

- Immediately inform them of the fraud.

- Review your account together.

Look for unauthorized charges, past due balances, and refunds or returns.

If you find balances you were unaware of, explain your situation and try to work out payment arrangements. A surprising number of people were willing to work with me because fraud impacted them at some point.

I kept in continual contact with multiple vendors over the 18 months it took me to pay my outstanding bills—and I did pay every dime! During that time, if I knew I would be sending a payment even a day late, I called and let them know. My business survived because not a single vendor took me to court for payment, which they had every right to do. I owe a great deal of my current success to my fellow businesspeople who were willing to work with me in this regard.

Keep an Eye on Clients

Years ago my husband and I owned a small gym. After firing an assistant manager, I took over his shift for several weeks. I had three separate people come in to work out, who didn't sign in upon entry. When I asked them to please do so, they told me my former employee had told them if they paid cash for a one-year membership, they got a 50% discount. He then instructed them not to sign in when they came to work out.

Honestly, these clients had to know something fishy was going on when they paid cash, had no written contract, and were told not to sign in. But, some people will take a clearly dishonest deal if it works to their advantage. Watch for unusual arrangements with clients, and check them out immediately.

Check Your Vendor Lists

1. Do you recognize all of the companies?

2. Watch for names that sound connected to one of your employees. For instance, they have a similar last name, shared initials, or a matching address.

3. Check vendors who list a post office box instead of a street address.

4. Check for unusual activity. For example, if you have high expenditures or multiple transactions with an HVAC company, but you don't recall having the heating or cooling fixed, check into it. If you paid a lawn service $5,000 in small checks over a 6-week period, find out why.

5. Carefully review any consulting agreements, along with all associated billings and payments, as embezzlers commonly use these companies as a way of committing or hiding fraud.

6. Look at the type of vendors. If you are paying bills to a marina, but don't own a boat, you may have a problem.

Evaluate the Damage

Determining if you can stay in business can be the most demanding part of this whole process. If so, develop a realistic plan.

- Assess your immediate financial health.

- Determine the resources available to you for cash flow or credit.

- Talk openly with your bank about your challenges, needs, and prospects.

- Ascertain your standing with necessary suppliers.

- Formulate a working plan to maintain revenue.

- Consider how you can reduce expenses, including payroll, if necessary.

- Talk with your attorney and financial advisors about settling your debts, if you are unable to pay them in full.

Vent your frustrations and fears to people who will support you as you grapple with the fallout.

You could find, as I did, your fraud earned you a bad reputation for paying your accounts late. You might discover your credit accounts are maxed out. You will have to divide your time between dealing with the embezzlement outfall and ongoing business demands, but you can do it.

Now, after all the necessary steps listed above—take good care of yourself!

What If It Can't Be Saved?

Sadly, some businesses do not survive a major fraud. Don't bury yourself in unnecessary debt to extend the life of a fatally damaged business. Recognize that the death—murder—of a business can feel like the loss of a loved one. People go through many stages of loss, including anger and grief.

Take care of yourself. Talk to close friends who will give you emotional support. Counsel with a therapist or clergyman. Beware of serious depression. Don't be afraid to ask for help. Withdraw from unnecessary or demanding responsibilities for a time. Set whatever personal boundaries are needed to give you time to heal. Rest. Ponder what you have gained from this hard experience. Avoid bitterness. Pray or meditate.

Find a positive way to deal with your stress. Try to step back and gain some perspective. It may feel like the end of the world, but it is not. It's OK to be sad for a while. Things will get better. Don't be too rough with yourself, but recognize when it's time to get up and move on. Take what you've learned, and go make the world a better place.

Summing Up

Suffering a major financial fraud is a horribly traumatic experience, no matter what the eventual outcome is. It will affect your diet, your sleep, and many other aspects of your physical and psychological health. Be sure to eat well, take vitamins, exercise, and take some time to relax. Don't neglect your family or your spiritual life. My clean-up process took nearly three years; it is a marathon, not a sprint. Vent your frustrations and fears to people who will support you as you grapple with the fallout.

Try to maintain a positive outlook. Look for something good in every day. Remember that this too shall pass, and you don't want to ruin your physical or mental health in the process of getting through it. Look for opportunities to serve others, which will help them, as well as taking your mind off your own troubles. Diana Richardson, a businesswoman from a neighboring town who had experienced a similar crime in her company, called me often to check up on me and give me moral support. She even offered to attend the court hearings with me. I am forever grateful for her kindness.

You can do this!

CHAPTER 23

Final Thoughts

**I didn't want to help people cope with disaster—
I wanted to help them prevent it!**

As of now, the winter of 2018-2019, nine years have passed since I discovered the embezzlement that changed my life forever.

I survived debt, tax persecution, guilt, embarrassment, stress, and heartache. I look back on those early months as a bleak period in my life. In my home state of Missouri, January, the month I discovered my embezzlement, is a dreary, cold month. This imagery coincides with a lot of my memories from that time.

I don't remember a lot of details clearly from those first few months, and I see many of my recollections through a fog. Sometimes my husband will talk to me about significant things that happened during that time, and I'm amazed to discover I have no memory of them.

Two-and-a-half years after the detection of my embezzlement, a friend I had not seen in some time came to visit. My appearance and general demeanor appalled her. Although I hadn't stopped showering and combing my hair, she said I looked exhausted, worn, and depleted. I felt—and apparently looked—as though I had barely survived a long illness. I was worn out, depressed and functioning at about 50% capacity.

Honestly, I did not take complete stock of the toll these crimes took on me until after the crisis ended. By this time, my business had not only recovered, it had thrived. My marriage was strong, my general health was good, and I had gained a lot of perspective. Still, it was difficult to overcome the toll which the stress and pain had taken on me.

Early on, I started writing a book to deal with my pain and confusion. It expressed the difficulty of overcoming unfairness and crisis in life. Although it was cathartic and helped me work through some of my feelings, I never felt passionate about it. Additionally, it seemed the bookstores were already full of books by people sharing similar experiences of overcoming difficulties. I didn't feel I could add anything uniquely worthwhile to the good information already available.

I survived debt, tax persecution, guilt, embarrassment, stress, and heartache.

I considered giving up any book writing idea when a friend and fellow businessperson, Jeffrey Combs, said, "No one needs a book like that; there are already thousands of them. What people need is knowledge on how to prevent devastating circumstances like yours in the first place. Now, *that* is a book I want on my book shelf!"

The whole direction of my thinking and writing changed. I decided the place for that sort of emotional examination and purging was my personal journal. I also decided that focusing on so much sadness and negativity was pretty depressing. I survived my embezzlement by taking action, not by sitting around feeling sorry for myself, and a major part of that commitment to action was directed toward making sure my company would never be victimized again. I contemplated how powerful action is in the face of crisis, and realized that the passion I had for rebuilding and protecting my company was worth sharing with others.

I thought about how much practical knowledge I gained from my own experiences. I pondered my many hours of research on prevention and detection of financial fraud. I considered the hundreds of heartbreaking accounts I'd read of everyday business people victimized by fraud.

I knew then I didn't want to help people cope with disaster—I wanted to help them prevent it!

My writing changed. I began to outline the methods I developed to protect my own business. I had not found any books applicable to non-accountant business owners. I saw a need and I filled it. I found my voice and my passion for the topic through this process.

I struggled with insecurity. Who, after all, wanted to hear from me— someone with only two years of community college ... My only real claim to fame was having enough naiveté to make me an easy target for obvious and long-term financial fraud. How could I possibly present myself as an expert on accounting fraud when I wasn't even an accountant?

Then, although filled with insecurity, I started speaking on the topic.

I spoke to several different community and business organizations. I discovered something amazing; I did have credibility! People wanted to learn from my experiences! Very few businesspeople I encountered were accountants. Like me, they struggled with effectively managing this critical area of their businesses.

My survival gave hope to many of the people who came to listen to me precisely because they were experiencing similar struggles. In fact, almost every time I spoke, someone came up to me afterward to share their own experiences and difficulties—often in tears.

Nearly everyone had either directly experienced fraud, or had a personal connection to someone who had. Some of their stories were heartbreaking. Countless numbers shared that their main hope revolved around keeping their homes as they liquidated all their business assets to stay afloat. It didn't appear to be a likely outcome for many that I spoke with.

I hope you find value in *FraudPoints!* I did my best to be honest about my successes and my failures; what I did well and what I did not. And the pain of looking back and knowing I could have prevented the whole thing. I wish I had only known how ... the "how" of what I've shared with you.

My goal was to give you the wakeup call along with the tools that will help you look at your business through new eyes: the eyes of a thief.

Use your new knowledge, and your empowerment, to outsmart them.

Writing a book is, in many ways, like birthing a child. You struggle, you cry, you bring something forth, and you look to the future.

When I imagine *FraudPoints!* impacting other small business owners down the road, I see myself, long retired, sitting with a business person who says, "I really enjoyed your book, and I have followed your advice for years. It has helped me to be a better business person, but I've never caught a single embezzler."

And I will smile and say, "Excellent! I wonder how many of them we scared off!"

Wishing you all my best with your business and your life,
Cheryl Obermiller, The Pothole Queen
Founder and Owner of Obermiller Construction and Trucking, Inc.

About the Author

Cheryl Obermiller is an expert in small business fraud. As the owner of Obermiller Construction, she built a business from the ground up to become a successful multi-million dollar company that employs dozens of men and women. And she did it after undergoing a betrayal and embezzlement from a trusted employee; dealing with an out-of-control aggressive IRS representative; spearheading the prosecution that sent the embezzler to prison; and did it while raising eight children.

She is author of *FraudPoints! The Small Business Owners' Guide to Outwitting Embezzlers, Thieves, and Scallywags.* As a frequent speaker and media guest, she reveals the discovery of the embezzlement of her company over an eight-year period, and how small businesses (under 100 employees) can discover through her unique FraudPoints System if fraud is in play; how to deal with it; and how to successfully prevent it from happening.

Cheryl is an animated storyteller and no-nonsense businesswoman who delivers practical solutions. Her Keynotes, Workshops and Trainings will engage audiences of all ages; her delightful sense of humor will leave them elated that they spent an hour or a day improving their business skills with her knowledge and expertise.

To book her for your company, association or a consultation, contact Cheryl Obermiller at:

www.CherylObermiller.com | Cheryl@FraudPoints.com

How to Work with Cheryl Obermiller

As an animated storyteller and no-nonsense businesswoman, Cheryl Obermiller delivers practical solutions to real world business problems.

As a frequent speaker and media guest, she reveals the discovery of an eight-year-long embezzlement of her company. She explains how small businesses (under 100 employees) can use her unique FraudPoints System to discover if fraud is in play, how to deal with it, and, if so, how to successfully prevent it from happening again. Her book, *FraudPoints! The Small Business Owner's Guide to Outwitting Embezzlers, Thieves, and Scallywags,* plus lessons learned from twenty-six years of everyday business experiences, are the basis of her presentations.

Her Keynotes include:

- FraudPoints, Protect You and Your Business from Financial Catastrophe

- Stop Thief! What to Do If You Suspect or Discover Fraud

- The Best Accountant in the World May Be Setting You Up for Financial Fraud

- The Emotional Pitfalls of Setting Up Financial Controls

- Preserving Your Family While Administering an Estate

- The Fraud Triangle vs The Honesty Triangle

- The Business Owner's Bill of Rights, and Your Rights and Responsibilities as a Business Owner

Her Workshops and Intensives include:

- How to Travel the World Nearly Free by Paying Your Business Bills on Credit Cards

- The Three Best Ways to Protect Your Business from Financial Fraud

- The Importance of Setting Up Financial Controls for Your Fundraisers, Teams, Estates, and Non-Profits

- Red Flags, Yellow Flags, and Green Flags; Understanding Signs of Fraud, Risk, and Security in Your Business

To book her for your company, association or a consultation, contact Cheryl Obermiller at:

www.CherylObermiller.com | Cheryl@FraudPoints.com

 facebook.com/fraudpoints/

 linkedin.com/in/cheryl-obermiller

 twitter.com/FraudPoints

Index